RISING HILLS AND SINKING VALLEYS

A Descendant Of Joseph & Emma Shares Her Story

© 2012 Kimberly J. Smith

All rights reserved. No part of this book may be reproduced in any form whatsoever, whether by graphic, visual, filming, microfilming, tape recording or any other means, without the written permission of the publisher, Latter Day Legends, except in the case of brief passages embodied in critical reviews and articles where the title, editors and ISBN accompany such review or article.

All rights reserved under International and Pan-American Copyright Conventions.

Latter Day Legends, an imprint of Digital Legend Press & Publishing
Salt Lake City, UT

To see the complete library, visit www.digitalegend.com
For info write to: info@digitalegend.com or call toll free: 877-222-1960

ISBN: 978-1-937735-41-8

Printed in the United States of America First Printing: November 2012 (V1)

Cover design and book interior layout by Alisha Bishop.

Rising Hills and Sinking Valleys

A Descendant Of Joseph & Emma Shares Her Story

Kimberly J. Smith

Latter Day Legends

Salt Lake City, Utah

To my children Bryan and Leahna,

their children, and beyond…..Never forget.

Contents

Lineage i
Acknowledgements iii
Introduction vi
Chapter One 1
    A Woman of Faith
    A Bond of Genuine Love
    Loyal Heart, Damaged Trust
    Tried but True
    Peering Through the Haze
    Righteous Desires

Chapter Two 29
    Alexander Hale Smith
    A Man of Adventure
    Crossroads
    Onward and Forward
    A Bitter View
    A Sail on the Horizon

Chapter Three 67
    Discovery and Loss
    A New Life

My Mother, Mary Sue Roberts Smith 86

Chapter Four 89
    Storytelling
    Over Hill and Holler
    The Noland Clan
    Over the Mountain
    A People of Faith
    Leaning on the Lord

Chapter Five 106
    A Whole New World
    Endless Trails

Chapter Six 122
    Trials in Missouri
    The Lonely heart of a Wounded Child
    The Power of Prayer

Chapter Seven 138
    Unspoken Connections
    On the Move....Again

Chapter Eight 150
    Solitude
    Music: Therapy for the Soul

Chapter Nine 160
    Bear Tracks
    The Struggle of Where to Fit In
    On the Run
    A Trip to the West
    "I Was Born in the Year of Our Lord...."

Chapter Ten...176
    New Life, New Direction
    Genealogy: The Door to My Past
    A Winding Road by the Rivers Edge

Chapter Eleven..196
    A Voice From the Dust
    A Precious Spot on a Lonely Hill
    Mannequins, Jail, and Blood on the Floor

Chapter Twelve 214
    Every Little Thing
    Dodging A Bullet

Chapter Thirteen..228
    A Healing of Hearts
    Back to School
    Nostalgia's Embracing Arms
    The Discussions
    Waters of Life
    A Moment of Truth

Chapter Fourteen 252
    The Great Salt Lake:
    Making Peace With the Lion

Chapter Fifteen..272
    Out of the Box
    Dark Places in a Bright New World
    Archives
    A Worthy Pen Never Rests
    A Voice of Warning
    A New Temple

Chapter Sixteen...296
    A Knowledge of Faith and Trust
    Through the Lens
    Missionary In Training

Chapter Seventeen...314
    A Home On a Hill
    Furthering the Work
    Called To Serve

Chapter Eighteen 330
    Departures
    Coping
    Refuge Across a Frozen Mississippi
    A Season of Time Perfects the Song

Chapter Nineteen..346
    Pageant
    Mission Accomplished
    Time to Sing

Chapter Twenty..360
    Following Promptings

Chapter Twenty-One..372
    Leaving On a Jet Plane
    The Wonder of the Land Down Under

Chapter Twenty-Two..384
    Progression

Epilogue...398

Notes...404

LINEAGE

Joseph Smith, Jr.--------------------Emma Hale

Alexander H. Smith-------------Elizabeth Kendall

Arthur M. Smith------------------Minnie C. Smith

Joseph F. Smith------------------Mary Sue Roberts

Kimberly Jo Smith--------------Gregory D. Davis

Bryan D. Davis, Leahna S. Davis

Acknowledgements

It would take a volume in and of itself to appropriately thank all who have had a hand in getting this book finished. There are many who housed us during our travels, those who offered affordable rent while Bryan attended BYU, individuals who have funded our work and countless selfless friends and strangers who helped in ways they were not even aware of. There were times when we thought the road we were on would come to a sudden end only to be blessed at every turn due to the kindness of others. If you have helped us, you know who you are, and our gratitude holds no end.

There are few individuals, however, that I must mention for their input in my life and toward this book have been priceless. Many times I needed information that I had no access to and my dear friends Christy Best and Sharalyn Duffin Howcroft who work in Church Archives never failed to answer any questions I had. They are also two of just a handful of people who know just how silly I can be. Yes, the girls in Church Archives can testify that Joseph Smith did have a sense of humor and was indeed a prankster and that it runs in the family, for both Christy and Sharalyn have been at the receiving end of one or more of my pranks!

No one could understand the things I was processing while writing this book more than my dear cousin and friend, Garcia Jones. She was an invaluable help to me and I will

Hills & Valleys

never forget all of the times I have stayed with her and Ivor, her loving husband. They have both enriched our family.

I could not leave this page without thanking my parents, Joseph and Sue Smith. They have both afforded me a heritage rich in the history of man, filled with patriotism to this nation and a stalwart faith in the Lord. Both lineages have come with a desire to build upon and sustain the Kingdom of God. Though our lives while growing up were immersed in instability and chaos, I chose to pull from those experiences elements that would contribute positively to my future and let the darker elements dissolve in silence. So I have found gratefulness for the childhood I had and for the parents who raised me, both of whom are genuinely good and loving souls.

I am ever grateful for the uniting bond that I share with my siblings, Candy and Tim. It has and always will be a most singular and precious relationship in my life. And to my children, Bryan and Leah, whom I love above all else in this world, you know my heart and spirit. The experiences we have shared throughout life and on the road have proven that one can be both mother and friend to their children. I am ever grateful for all that have.

Everything I am inside is pink and blue. Pastels without, soft clouds above, blue sky everywhere with an occasional rain but from renewal, not anger. My mind has no boundaries. Its floor is poetry, the wallpaper music. The windows are always open to allow the humor to drift in and out. The furniture is made of air, I am forever floating. At times ill words or deeds of others creates foulness, but I am ever glad of the jolly bubble that rests within me to push out

Acknowledgements

the offensive intrusion. I am content to swing upon this happy moment, casting laughter to and fro, receiving it back tenfold. I have made joy my threshold and will always follow the light which leads me there. Yesterday, today and tomorrow I am and will always be. Because of longevity where the spirit is concerned I choose to be happy even though the world may be drowning in darkness. I have set joy as my threshold and light as a beacon, therefore I ever walk forward and smile.

—Kimberly Jo Smith

Introduction

It is snowing as I begin to write. The last week of April in Nauvoo should be well away from the winter scene holding the hands of spring, but there it is before my eyes; clouds of snow swirling down at a slant. I can peer through the white mass and within my imagination glimpse a full spring in bloom. The winter blast is out of character for the season, but these days so much is out of character in the world. In fact, society has striven at an accelerated pace to change the character of goodness to a point that it has become unrecognizable. What was once sound moral fiber is unraveling and it is happening right before our eyes.

We were told of this time long ago, and here it is before us; the impromptu seasonal weather changes, drought, moral decline, deviation from our Father in Heaven, worldwide catastrophic events. In its true prophetic warning from passages written ages ago, what was once good is now called bad, and what was called bad is now labeled as good.

Matthew 24:8 tells us that these things are just labor pains. It is a time of warning to those who are preparing for the coming times; times which progressively grow worse and approach the time of deliverance, which will be at the second coming of the Savior. So should we live in fear of all of these signs? Goodness, no. Fear is not a characteristic of the Lord. We only fear when we do not know Him or His ways. It is wise to be observant and prepared, but more importantly to live life every day to its fullest. There are those who spend their whole lives focused on end times to such an excess that they forget to live and have healthy relationships with those around them, especially their family. Wilford Woodruff, fourth president of The Church of Jesus Christ of Latter-day Saints, was approached by several brethren who wanted his input on the timing of the second coming of the Savior. His answer was one of the wisest I have heard yet.

"I would live as if it were to be tomorrow, but I am still planting cherry trees."[1] Here President Woodruff expresses the importance of living our daily lives in a functional, interactive, loving and stable manner, building our spiritual environment in preparation for meeting the Savior, yet actively engaged in our temporal surroundings.

One of the things I believe that we should all be involved in concerning spiritual and temporal happiness is the healing of our families from issues of the past and present. It is necessary to be a healthy and united family in order to not only withstand the times that are coming but to be worthy to stand in the presence of our Father in Heaven and His Son Jesus Christ. It is the responsibility of the generations alive today to work their way back and extensively look at the journey of their family to see where the paths have been altered. We must discover how they became overtaken by briars and thistles, causing so many to deviate and go astray, becoming embittered toward siblings, cousins, parents and children. It is an activity which has built thick walls that have cut asunder the relationships of many who would be friends and family.

Introduction

This is my family story, the Smith family story. It is an account of how I overcame the traditions that had been passed down through four generations causing extensive bitterness, contention and division, all of which are tools that the adversary uses to destroy family unity. It is amazing to me how many years the family of man has allowed Satan to have such power over them, when they could have been a family united by love.

If there has been any time that the need was great to bring our families together it is now. Without that bond, there will be many who will scatter in chaos as the times grow even darker. The change comes through forgiving ourselves and one another, loving ourselves and one another and letting go of the issues that we have been holding onto for generations. We cannot hold on to those issues and the Savior at the same time so it is vital to let the issues go and embrace Christ. As we do so we will be filled with the light of His pure love and our wounds will heal. If we will just take that step, He will hold us up and show us how to get through all of our pains and sorrows. We will become whole. Elder D. Todd Christopherson, a member of the Quorum of the Twelve Apostles of The Church of Jesus Christ of Latter-day Saints said of the Savior:

"We can turn to Him as we seek unity and peace within because He understands. He understands the struggle, and He also understands how to win the struggle."[2]

I have always felt Christ in my life, even as a child. As I encountered many difficulties while growing up it was not uncommon for me to just begin to talk to Him and seek comfort. When I felt that there was no other friend to be had, I knew that He was there and would never leave me alone. Having the comfort of that bond has saved me in many ways from going down paths that would have threatened to endanger my spirit. At times when I did fall by the wayside, His hand was always extended to help pull me up. The values I have gained through knowing of His love have made it possible for me to process the darkness that has surrounded members of both my father and mother's family, allowing me to sift through the bitterness to find truth.

It has been a long journey filled with unexpected surprises, pain, fear, and hesitations but I have always walked forward because I knew I was supposed to. I knew that in all things I would be guided by the Holy Ghost if I had faith and would never be led astray. Even though at times there was no indication as to where I was going or what lay ahead, I have never been disappointed and my reward has been a fullness of joy.

This journey is ongoing. I am still learning and discovering, as we should all be. Knowledge never decreases unless we allow it to. It is so interesting for me to look back upon the pages of what has brought me here, to examine this book that is my life. It puts into perspective the awareness that our Father in Heaven plans things carefully and that we are free to choose our own direction as we feel prompted. How we choose defines our lives at that moment and determines whether or not we will increase or decrease in spiritual growth. As I look back I have seen the sorrow of electing to go my own way, the wisdom of choosing what is right and the fulfillment of following the promptings of the still, small voice.

Introduction

The story of my part of the Smith family is one of trial, pain, sorrow, bitterness and division but underneath the frozen tundra lies a goodness of humor, joy and pure love that runs through all of the cousins today. It was merely hindered for a season, the cloak of winter causing hearts and minds to draw within themselves toward dark corners where there was little light and warmth. As for me, I do not like being cold, so I and many others have decided to come out into the sun. We have decided that the light is better and the spirit full. This is my story.

Hills & Valleys

Teaching Eternity-One Eternal Round
Joseph and Emma share a moment of peace
under the willow tree in Nauvoo
Used by permission of artist, Kerri Guthrie

Portion of a letter written by Emma to her husband Joseph while he was in Liberty Jail:

Quincy March 7, 1839

Dear Husband,

Having an opportunity to send by a friend I make an attempt to write, but I shall not attempt to write my feelings altogether, for the situation in which you are, the walls, bars, and bolts, rolling rivers, running streams, rising hills, sinking vallies, and spreading prairies that separate us, and the cruel injustice that first cast you into prison and still holds you there, with many other considerations, places my feelings far beyond description. Was it not for conscious innocence, and the direct interposition of divine mercy, I am very sure I never should have been able to have endured the scenes of suffering that I have passed through, since what is called the Militia, came in to Far West, under the ever to be remembered Governor's notable order; an order fraught with as much wickedness as ignorance and as much ignorance as was ever contained in an article of that length; but I still live and am yet willing to suffer more if it is the will of kind Heaven, that I should for your sake.[4]

Chapter One

"Let us learn from the past to profit by the present,
And from the present to live better in the future."

—William Wordsworth

I am not a remarkable person by any means. Like any human individual I have gone through trial, sadness, joy and laughter. Like many, I have remarkable ancestors who have passed down through their own experience and example key elements that have taught me the value of knowing the Savior and the importance of the Atonement in the healing process. These examples became essential as I meandered through life, running into what seemed like insurmountable obstacles. Family division, contention, physical and emotional abuse were all avenues that I would encounter as I grew. To gain an understanding of how I overcame such obstacles one must go back to the beginning, four generations back to a time when The Church of Jesus Christ of Latter-day Saints suffered a great loss, while a widow and her children adjusted to life by a roaring river, facing an uncertain future

My great-great-grandfather, Joseph Smith Jr., who organized The Church of Jesus Christ of Latter-day Saints in 1830, has been spoken of worldwide in great measures of love and hate for generations. It was the accelerated measure of hate at the hands of mobs which took the life of both Joseph and his brother Hyrum in 1844. Since that time, the Latter-day

Hills & Valleys

Saints have been filled with a renewed faith and gratitude for the sacrifice of the Prophet and Patriarch, and for the strife endured by the many pioneers who gave their own lives as they pushed forward in building up the kingdom of God. For some, however, the time has been marked by unresolved issues which never seem to be answered with enough satisfaction to enable the questioning mind to let go and be at peace. The most common of these questions is why did Joseph's wife Emma remain in Nauvoo when the rest of the Latter-day Saints made the trek west?

I have spent much of my fourteen years as a member of The Church of Jesus Christ of Latter- day Saints endeavoring to learn all I can about the history of my great-great-grandparents Joseph and Emma Smith. Situations evolved in the latter portion of those years which allowed me to move to Nauvoo, Illinois, calling it my home. Never in any time of that study did I learn so much or feel so acutely the beautiful spirit of the place which would be the last home Joseph and Emma built together. Those were precious days as I ventured as a babe into a new realm of discovery. Embracing one's own history is a sweet and wondrous feast. My heart was both broken and healed as each page of my ancestors' lives unfolded before me.

A Woman of Faith

In order to convey an understanding of why Emma made the choices she did following Joseph's death, one must examine events of her early life which she was called to pass through. In that process there is a discovery of the character traits which define Emma as a true daughter of God.

Chapter One

Compassion, sympathy, stalwart faith, a love of service, endurance and empathy can all be found within the heart of the woman who stood by her husband as he attended to his calling. Emma's strong character and faith would be the premise which would enable her to endure the many trials and losses that occurred during her marriage to Joseph. As I came to know Grandmother Emma and the trials she suffered, I began to understand why she remained in Nauvoo.

Emma's devotion to Christ and inclination to do what is right emerges as a pattern of her character from a young age. She was a woman who had been obedient to God since childhood. Emma's father, Isaac Hale, had not allowed prayer in the home, until one day he happened upon his six-year-old daughter praying for God to soften his heart.[1] Clearly Emma's character embraced the desire to live a life that is geared toward Christ-like attributes. The genuine concern that she felt for her father's spiritual welfare exemplifies Emma's ability to care deeply about others, an attribute she would exhibit throughout her entire life, giving of herself tirelessly and completely. Emmaline B. Wells, who was the fifth Relief Society President and a women's rights activist, wrote in her account of Emma:

"Sister Emma was benevolent and hospitable; she drew around her a large circle of friends, who were like good comrades. She was motherly in nature to young people, always had a houseful to entertain or be entertained. She was very high-spirited and the brethren and sisters paid her great respect. Emma was a great solace to her husband in all his persecutions and the severe ordeals through which he passed; she was always ready to encourage and comfort him, devoted to his interests, and was constantly by him whenever it was possible. She was queen in her home, so to speak, and beloved by the people, who were many of them indebted to her for favors and kindness."[2]

In her own patriarchal blessing which was given December 9, 1834, it was made clear that Emma was a faithful servant unto the Lord and that she was blessed with many responsibilities because of her faithfulness.

"Emma ... thou art blessed of the Lord, for thy faithfulness and truth, thou shalt be blessed with thy husband, and rejoice in the glory which shall come upon him. Thy soul has been afflicted because of the wickedness of men in seeking the destruction of thy companion, and thy whole soul has been drawn out in prayer for his deliverance; rejoice, for the Lord thy God has heard thy supplication. Thou hast grieved for the hardness of the hearts of thy father's house, and thou hast longed for their salvation. The Lord will have respect to thy cries, and by his judgments he will cause some of them to see their folly and repent of their sins; but it will be by affliction that they will be saved. Thou shalt see many days, yea, the Lord will spare thee till thou art satisfied, for thou shalt see thy Redeemer. Thy heart shall rejoice in the great work of the Lord, and no one shall take thy rejoicing from thee. Thou shalt ever remember the great condescension of thy God in permitting thee to accompany my son [Joseph] when the angel delivered the record of the Nephites to his care. ... Thou shalt be blessed with understanding, and have power to instruct thy sex, teach thy family righteousness, and thy little ones the way of life, and the holy angels shall watch over thee and thou shalt be saved in the kingdom of God, even so, Amen."[3]

A Bond of Genuine Love

The love and affection that Joseph and Emma shared is evident in their correspondence with one another when they were separated for long periods of time. While Joseph was in Liberty Jail, Emma wrote to him pouring out her sorrow for the many trials they had witnessed, yet at the same time expressing her will to endure even more hardship for her husband's sake.

"I shall not attempt to write my feelings altogether, for the situation in which you are, the walls, bars, and bolts, rolling rivers, running streams, rising hills, sinking vallies and spreading prairies that separate us, and the cruel injustice that first cast you into prison and still holds you there. ... Was it not for conscious innocence and the direct interposition of divine mercy, I am very sure I never should have been able to have endured the scenes of suffering that I have passed through ... but I still live and am yet willing to suffer more if it is the will of kind Heaven, that I should for your sake ... and if God does not record our sufferings and avenge our wrongs on them that are guilty, I shall be sadly mistaken. ... You may be astonished at my bad writing and incoherent manner, but you will pardon all when you reflect how hard it would be for you to write, when your hands were stiffened with hard work, and your heart convulsed with intense anxiety ... but I hope there is better days to come to us yet. ... I am ever yours affectionately. Emma Smith."[4]

In many of Joseph's letters to Emma he referred to her as, "My dear, affectionate Emma," emphasizing a deep love for his wife. In one correspondence written in 1842 while he was in hiding, Joseph expressed how much concern and care he had for his wife and children.

"If I go to the Pine country, you shall go along with me, and the children; and if you and the children go not with me, I don't go. I do not wish to exile myself for the sake of my own life. ... It is for your sakes, therefore, that I would do such a thing. ... I am not willing to trust you in the hands of those who cannot feel the same interest for you that I feel."[5]

Loyal Heart, Damaged Trust

Emma's devotion to Joseph and his calling as a Prophet of God was one of loyalty and sincerity. Evidence proves that she loved her husband and stood by him through countless trials, joys, and sorrows they experienced during the period of the Restoration. But through their hardships, a change began to take place in Emma. Although her moral values, service and compassion remained the same, her trust in others had been severely altered. Since the time they had lived in Kirtland, Ohio, many who had been close friends turned against them, even betrayed them. The one person she trusted the most died in the Carthage Jail on June 27, 1844. From that point on it seemed that she could only trust herself and God.

The Kirtland Bank failure of 1837 impacted the Latter-day Saints in Ohio on many levels. Individuals who had been seeking to open new banks during this period had been turned down by the legislature in Ohio. Therefore Joseph created The Kirtland Safety Society, an anti-banking establishment that was a joint stock company and would be operated as a bank even though they had no charter. Other individuals who had been denied charters were doing the same in Ohio and as things progressed, some members of the Church invested their lands and holdings in speculation, being lifted up excessively in pride. But the progression was short lived. Enemies of the Latter-day Saints spread word that their printed notes were of no worth and other banks refused to accept them. When The Panic of 1837 hit throughout much of the United States, there were many banks that suffered the effects due to the scarcity of money. The Kirtland Safety Society was forced to close causing many who had exhausted all of their funds in speculation to lose everything.[6] Some felt that since Joseph was a prophet he should have foreseen the failure, when in fact they had been cautioned previously by the Lord to avoid being lifted up in pride or it would prove their downfall.

"And if ye seek the riches which it is the will of the Father to give unto you, ye shall be the richest of all people, for ye shall have the riches of eternity; and it must needs be that the riches of the earth are mine to give; but beware of pride, lest ye become as the Nephites of old"[7]

At one point in 1837, elders of the Church met in the Kirtland Temple to proclaim Joseph a fallen prophet. Heated discussions among the discontented became so volatile that Joseph was forced to flee Kirtland to preserve his life.[8] Good friends, such as Parley P. Pratt, would find themselves overcome by the spirit of apostasy, betraying the Prophet's trust.[9] At length Pratt would be welcomed back into loving friendship by Joseph and the Saints. However, many others who had turned against Joseph would allow their hearts to remain darkened. Is it any wonder why Emma, who would have been the one to witness most intimately the pain and sorrow her husband and children suffered at the hands of others, was so wary of trusting people, even friends? Even the government was a source of discontent instead of support during the years that the Saints suffered persecution. On June 27th, 1844, Thomas Ford, Governor of Illinois, went to Nauvoo to assure the citizens that Joseph and Hyrum, who were in the Carthage Jail on charge of treason, would be protected and receive a fair trial. In his absence, the governor placed Joseph's bitterest enemies at the jail for protection.

"Contrary to his promise, Governor Ford left that morning for Nauvoo without Joseph and Hyrum, taking instead Captain Dunn's Dragoons from McDonough County, the only troops that had demonstrated neutrality in the affair. En route, he sent an order to all other troops at Carthage and Warsaw to disband, except for a company of the Carthage Greys to guard the jail. The Greys were Joseph's most hostile enemies and could not be depended upon to protect him."[10]

Emma seems to have been confident that her husband would return to her; after all, he had always been delivered of his enemies before. When Joseph said his last goodbye to her, Emma's response was, "You're coming back!"[11] One can only imagine the ultimate betrayal which was felt in learning that as she entertained the governor and his men while they were in Nauvoo to appease the unsettled members of the Church, her husband was being murdered.

The days following the martyrdom of Joseph and Hyrum Smith were filled with immeasurable sorrow amongst all of the Latter-day Saints. For the family members the grief was inconsolable and the depth of Emma's sorrow was sorely witnessed by those around her.

"Emma, after fainting at the sight of the bodies of her husband and dear brother in law and friend, Hyrum. Came back into the room and steadied herself. Walking over to her husband's side, kneeling down she clasped him around his face and sank upon his body. Suddenly grief found vent and sighs and groans and words of lamentation filled the room. Her children, four in number, gathered around their weeping mother and the dead body and grief that words cannot embody seemed to overwhelm the room."[12]

John P. Greene, who came to the Mansion House on June 28, 1844, could hear the unrestrained woeful cries of Emma coming from within. Rushing inside, John went over to her, clasped her hands and said, "Oh, Sister Emma God bless you." And he began to pray, asking that she might find peace. She cried aloud saying, "Why O God am I thus afflicted? Why am I a widow? Thou knowest I have always trusted in thy law!" Brother Green assured her that such affliction would be to her a crown of life. She answered quickly;

"My husband was my crown, for him and for my children I have suffered the loss of all things; and why, O God am I thus deserted, and my bosom torn with this tenfold anguish?"[13]

The pain was acutely felt as I read Emma's reaction to Brother Green. All that my heart, mind, and spirit could comprehend of the emotion was that it felt like a heart breaking in two. The desperation of every syllable was filled with unbearable pain. Here was a woman who had given her all to her husband and to the work of building up the kingdom. She lost parents, children and other family along the way. She faced forced migration, persecution, humiliation, degradation, and intimidation with strength and fortitude. She moved tirelessly forward in an attempt to stay one step ahead of death. Emma's devotion and loyalty to the restoration work was deeply embedded. She gave all to her husband, a man she was bonded to eternally and loved immeasurably. Having walked so far, in tireless endurance, is it any wonder that her heart was sorely broken upon hearing of her husband's and brother-in-law's deaths?

With sorrow at her gate and a world of judgment at her feet, Emma faced the prospects of starting over again. Though a flurry of opinions both positive and negative swarmed around her, she began this point of her life in survival mode. The woman who had sacrificed so much for so many, now turned to the priorities which lay before her.

"I Have No Friend But God, and Nowhere to Go But Home."

—Emma Smith

Though Emma's choice to stay in Nauvoo was primarily based on personal reasons, she would learn as early as six weeks after Joseph's death that it would not be easy. It was a great sorrow to the family that Joseph had not left a will of any kind. Without a will to designate what was his personally, it left the family in a quandary because both the Church and Joseph were heavily in debt, and the creditors were soon upon the heels of the Church and the family. The United States government was one of those creditors.

In 1840, several prominent members of the Church signed a note in order to purchase a steamboat from the government from Robert E. Lee. The future president of the Confederacy had been in charge of selling government surplus which had been used for improvements on the Mississippi River between 1837-1840. The intent of the purchase was to establish a trade business using the steamboat to bring goods from St. Louis and other areas to Nauvoo in order to adequately accommodate the rapidly increasing population growth. But inexperienced navigators ran the boat aground on its first outing, causing damage that the Church did not have the funds to repair. The following years would bring disputations and lawsuits concerning who was actually responsible for the debt, for several individuals had signed the note but denied responsibility since damage to the boat was due to negligence of others.[14] These debates were still in process when Joseph and Hyrum were killed and were a major source of turmoil within the Church and Smith family. Since Joseph died intestate, his properties went to Emma as a widow's right, yet claiming rights to those properties were contingent upon the decision of the courts concerning the demands of the creditors. It was quite a tangled web as some of the properties were in Joseph's name as Trustee in Trust for the Church so it crossed over into even deeper legalities.

Three weeks after Joseph's death, Emma went to Carthage to seek appointment as administratrix of the estate. Considering all she had been through, it is easy to imagine why she took such a bold step. Foremost on her mind would have been securing at least some property so that they might survive as a family. The appointment, however, would be revoked within a short time for she was unable to pay what was needed to secure the bond, after which the courts assigned Joseph Coolidge to handle the financial affairs of the estate.[15]

Many Latter-day Saints went west feeling as if Emma was in fine shape for she was allowed to keep several properties. In actuality the family was left quite destitute. Although Emma received a dower payment of $1,809.41 from the estate settlement, much of that was used to pay the taxes on some of the homes which were set to be auctioned off. There were other debts that when all was said and done became her responsibility. She paid those debts even though it took most of her life to do it.[16] Throughout the next few generations, details concerning the dire situation Emma and the children were left in became mired in innuendo. It was told in my generation that Brigham Young was responsible for their impoverished condition. When I did my own research I learned that Brigham had no power over who was appointed to look after the financial affairs of the family. Those assignments were given by the court system of Illinois.

Tried but True

One of the mistakes many people make concerning Emma is that they look at her only as the Prophet's wife without considering the human side of being a woman and a mother. When placing so many expectations upon one person, it is easy to lose sight of our ability to be compassionate and sympathetic. Many who are quick to condemn her choice to remain in Nauvoo are incapable of understanding her mode of reason because they have not walked in her shoes, or they lack a full knowledge of the many things which transpired after the heavy emotional losses of Joseph and Hyrum.

Emma's reasons for staying behind cannot be portrayed in black and white. They are complex and multi-layered. It is not just about polygamy, or conflict with others. While it is true that Emma struggled with polygamy, it does not mean that she denounced the Book of Mormon or the Church; in fact, she never denied the truth and authenticity of the Book of Mormon. On her deathbed she stood by the work that her husband Joseph had been called to accomplish, so it is evident that she still had a testimony.[17]

Trust issues, the bond that she felt to Nauvoo, a nearly invalid mother-in-law, the threat of yet another forced migration, and the risk of losing more children all weighed heavily on the broken heart of a woman who had given and lost so much already. What error was there in her staying behind? She had received all of the blessings of the endowment and sealing to her husband and her calling and election was made sure so there is no reason to believe she had lost blessings by not going west.[18] It becomes evident as one studies her life that her reasons for staying were more personal than an agenda of discontent toward others. Emma reflects this idea in her own words;

"I know the Saints in Utah thought I wasn't a very good Saint for not going west," Emma stated, " but I knew what my lot would be here. I did not know what it would be there. I have suffered until the Lord knows I have suffered enough. My husband and children are buried here; I want to be buried here."[19]

It is a simple statement which speaks volumes. Emma is expressing that she has suffered long and hard. Her heart is broken and she wants to be near her family, both living and dead. She yearned to spend her remaining years on the land that she and her husband, Joseph, poured so much of their lives into and she longed to be buried by his side. Even if she had endorsed polygamy wholly, I believe Emma still would have remained in Nauvoo because deep down in her heart and soul it is what she felt she should do. But let us pause for a moment and reflect upon that particular thorn which has rested in the side of the Smith posterity for generations: polygamy.

Polygamy in my family might as well have been labeled as a dirty word. It was considered just as hateful and off limits as the other inappropriate words we were never allowed to pronounce as children. The mere mention of the word was like opening a window in the midst of winter. An ice cold wind would blow through and cut you to the bone, causing faces to tighten and teeth to clench. Eyes would narrow, flashing with indignation and you would see before you the look of one who, if you were to prevail further upon the subject, was liable to shoot lightening from their eyes and cut you asunder! The description may seem amusing, but I remember those looks when the topic was ever broached. My son, Bryan, calls it the death stare. To a teenager it was a very scary sight to behold, indeed!

I became bitter about polygamy without even knowing the history behind it. I only knew it was a bad thing because it

Chapter One

was what I was taught. I reconciled this by one important measure; unconditional love. As I grew older and prayed for an understanding about confusion of the past, I was given to know that all of the things I did not understand would someday come to light in the Lord's timing, and a peace settled over me. I also knew that what was most important was to acquire a deep and binding love for all of those who have passed before us. I was satisfied. Far be it from me to be like Willy Wonka's Baruka Salt proclaiming, "I don't care how, I want it now!"

When the peace settled over me I knew then that I did not have to know everything about polygamy and why things happened the way they did. The reason it continues to fester among many is because people continue to pick at it, hindering the healing process. Put quite simply, if one would just walk forward and attend to the work they have today there would be no issues from the past to stumble upon. I was not there to see how these things unfolded; therefore, I can only love my ancestors and honor them by progressing and moving forward. I remember once, as I sat in quiet thought by the old Homestead in Nauvoo, asking my Grandmother Emma about these issues. I immediately received the impression that I was not to focus on the issues of the past. A sweet, soft voice came to me and said, "Go and do."

When Emma chose to remain in Nauvoo, it affected the family in many ways. Some seem to blame Emma for the family's bitterness against the LDS Church. They believe that she apostatized and urged her son, Joseph, to start a new organization. In the process of several generations, hearsay has been woven into truth, distorting and complicating the simplicity of reality.

While it is true that Joseph Smith III became president of the Reorganized Church of Jesus Christ of Latter-day Saints in 1860, the organization of that church had not been at the hands of Emma. Two men by the name of Zenos Gurley and Jason Briggs believed that a lineal priesthood should be over the restored church and that a son of Joseph Smith Jr. should be at the head. After searching among the many early break offs of the Church, these men formed The New Organization, later called The Reorganized Church of Jesus Christ of Latter Day Saints, in 1852.[20] Joseph Smith III was approached by some of the leaders of the new church in 1855 but "turned a deaf ear to their request."[21] By 1860, Joseph had changed his views toward the Reorganization, accepting the office of Prophet and President.

We have through the witness of her own son, Alexander, a true picture of Emma's character and how she was careful to allow them their free agency in belief systems.

"That mother, knowing her duty, taught her children to be noble men; taught them to be God-fearing men; taught them to recognize God and His laws; but never influenced their minds in the direction of the Church, giving as her reasons, when those boys talked with her upon the matter, that if the principles revealed of God, through her husband, were true, these boys would find their place in the great latter-day work, and would enter in upon it at the command of God."[22]

Many skeptics of Emma are not aware that much of the bitterness within Joseph's posterity stems from the children and perspectives they formed as they witnessed events unfold following the death of their father. Joseph Smith III details in his memoirs accounts which affected his outlook upon the LDS Church, Brigham Young, and those who had been some of his father's closest friends.

One incident provides the evident mistrust and disfavor that young Joseph III felt toward Brigham Young. When Brigham returned from the mission field following Joseph's death, the brethren held a conference in which it was decided that the legion should have a parade, probably to boost the morale of the people by showing the leadership as ongoing and united in the wake of losing their Prophet.

Correspondence was sent to Emma from Brigham Young requesting the loan of her late husband's favorite horse, Joe Duncan, along with the military trappings and finery. The horse had been sorely misused previously by two businessmen who borrowed him to travel to Fort Madison and had recently been restored to health.

Joseph III was not favorable to let the horse go but Emma told him to prepare Joe Duncan as Brigham had promised to take good care and return him directly after the parade. Hours after the horse should have been returned, young Joseph spotted George Q. Cannon riding Joe Duncan hard down the river road. Emma sent a message immediately to Brigham Young that the horse had not been returned. His reply expressed genuine surprise and he sent someone to find the horse and return it at once. When young Joseph beheld the condition of the horse he was incensed. Joe Duncan had been reduced to a "pitiable plight." Joseph felt a special bond to the

Hills & Valleys

horse because it had been his father's favorite and to see it so misused hurt immeasurably.

"To say that I was disturbed is to put the matter mildly. I was thoroughly indignant, furiously angry, and utterly heartbroken! All the while I was caring for him and trying to comfort him I was crying bitterly....I made a vow then and there, while washing that horse and giving him proper nourishment, that never again would I put saddle and bridle upon him for Elder Young."[23]

Joseph III indicates in his recollection that Brigham did send a note of apology, that the incident was at the hand of another, but feelings of hurt were impressed deeply and accompanied many other wounds that had already been etched into the hearts of the children. They had witnessed one too many scenes in which they felt their mother was being treated cruelly.

Peering Through the Haze

At the time Joseph was killed, his children were all thirteen years of age and younger. The dynamics of what occurred in Nauvoo and within the Church following the martyrdom were hard to comprehend for adults, let alone children. Many actions toward Emma may have seemed cruel to the children, yet were a natural procedure following the death of a prophet. For example, it had been told in my generation that the brethren had approached Emma and demanded things that belonged to Joseph, and in the process of time actually stole items from the home. It was one more thing that made me upset. However, when I began to do my

Chapter One

own research I found where fact and innuendo had been merged.

It is true that Emma was asked to turn over any papers pertaining to church business, which was well within reason for they were church property. They already had Joseph's journals, history, and books. Some items which did not pertain to church affairs were returned to Emma.[24] If they had not preserved the records and history we would probably have very little of it today. It is easy, however, to see how feelings could have been stirred to an embittered state. Emma must have felt as if everything was being taken away from her.

It is apparent how important Joseph's writings would have been to Emma when one considers the emotional attachment she would have formed to documents and other items while supporting and working side by side with her husband as he carried out the work of the Lord. One can understand Emma's feelings that these were items she felt belonged to her as his widow considering that she was involved with their history on such a personal level. But when all is said and done one must acknowledge what the children may have been feeling. There would have been some question in their hearts as to why the brethren wanted their father's belongings and they would have sensed how upsetting the matter was to their mother. But being so young they were incapable of understanding the dynamics of the situation.

While it is true that Emma did have a widow's right to her deceased husband's belongings, the Church also would have felt they had rights of ownership as well. Joseph was the Prophet and leader therefore the bulk of his activity, writings, and purchases were in behalf of the Church. The importance of these artifacts for preservation would have been the only motive the brethren would have had. Still, the rumor filtered down into the hearing of my generation that Brigham Young tried to bully Emma into giving up such artifacts and that he outright stole some of them.

I can see both sides; in essence they were both right. It is a horrible situation to try and reason out. From the time I was twelve and was around my father's family on a long term basis I had seen many artifacts such as books, apparel, and handwritten papers which I came to know had belonged to Joseph, Emma, and the children. When I became interested in the history of my family and asked what had become of those things I was met with answers such as, "I don't know," or "It fell apart so I threw it away." If those items would have been preserved years ago we would have access to much more than we do today. We have those brethren from the early Church to thank for what has been preserved.

The children occasionally were witness to visitors from Salt Lake City who at some point would try to persuade Emma to bring her family west. One such conversation was overheard by Joseph III, when Almon Babbit made a visit to the Mansion House on his way to attend to affairs in the east as an Indian Agent. Unable to convince Emma she should take her family to Utah, Almon told her in "plain terms that it had been determined to make her so poor that she would be willing and glad to come out there for protection."[25] Young Joseph must have been appalled to hear such a declaration and most certainly assumed that Brigham Young had sent this man to present Emma with an ultimatum, and it has been passed down through the generations that Brigham continually sent emissaries to try and bully Emma into going out west. Joseph later intimates in his memoirs that Almon Babbit's death, though attributed to an attack by Indians, was in his opinion most likely the work of those in power in the Salt Lake Valley.[26]

By reading the memoirs of Joseph III it is easy to recognize that he has had developed a keen mistrust toward Brigham Young and harbored bitterness against him. Polygamy, accompanied by events which transpired in Nauvoo after the martyrdom, have been heated topics of discussion for many generations of Joseph and Emma's posterity, at least in my family line. However, the most alarming rumor was that Brigham Young had Joseph, Hyrum, and Samuel murdered. I remember being a teenager and hearing my aunts talk of it. I was both stricken and influenced by the spirit of bitterness and hatred, which was entirely not of my nature. It took me many years to overcome those feelings, after which I became very aware of just how ruthless the adversary can be in his attempt to turn hearts against one another and divide the flock.

The rumor had its beginning in a letter that the prophet's brother William Smith wrote to *The Illinois Chronicle* accusing both Brigham Young and Willard Richards of having Samuel Smith murdered.

"I have good reason for believing that my brother Samuel H. Smith, died of poison at Nauvoo, administered by order of Brigham Young and Willard Richards only a few weeks subsequent to the unlawful murders of my other brothers, Joseph and Hyrum Smith, while incarcerated at Carthage Jail."[27]

Over the process of four generations following the martyrdom the story grew to include the accusation that Brigham was also responsible for Joseph and Hyrum's deaths. I have found nothing in all of my research that would suggest that Brigham Young would strike at the heart of the Smith family, especially Joseph for he often spoke of his great love for the Prophet. It was told by my father's family that Brigham Young committed this crime so that he could take the seat of power out from under Joseph, yet three years would pass after Joseph's death before he became the president of the Church. A man who is reaching hard enough for power to kill someone would have taken that position immediately. In a letter to Samuel's son, Samuel B. Smith, Joseph III indicates that the family was aware of this rumor;

"Your father was on his feet all the day of the murder (martyrdom), and all night and all the next day; and was so overwrought by his exertions that it brought on sickness as our Grandmother puts it; though I used to hear **whispers that he was helped out of this life** by some friends who feared his sterling uprightness and fearlessness of character. Had he lived Pres. B. Young could never have hoodwinked him."[28]

Upon hearing of William's public accusation Brigham Young replied;

"And William Smith has asserted that I was the cause of the death of his brother Samuel, when brother Woodruff, who is here today, knows that we were waiting at the depot in Boston to take passage east at the very time when Joseph and Hyrum were killed. Brother Taylor was nearly killed at the time, and Doctor Richards had his whiskers nearly singed off

Chapter One

by the blaze from the guns. In a few weeks after, Samuel Smith died, and I am blamed as the cause of his death."[29]

The death of Samuel Smith is one of great sadness. Known as the unknown martyr, he received internal injuries from being chased for hours on horseback after the mob spotted him en route to visit his brothers in the Carthage Jail on June 27, 1844. Samuel would approach his mother the next day in agony expressing his fears;

"Mother, I have had a dreadful distress in my side ever since I was chased by the mob and I think I have received some injury which is going to make me sick"[30]

The injury grew to become infected and his condition worsened until July 30, 1844, when he passed away.

Slander and misperceptions were widening the gap that was quickly growing between the Smith family and other Latter-day Saints. Libelous newspaper articles only added to the problem. On December 9, 1845, one particular article moved Emma to react swiftly. It was a letter that had been allegedly submitted by her to the New York Sun:

"The widow of Joseph Smith writes from Nauvoo to the NewYork Sun, that she is left with a family of small children, without any means of giving them an education, for there is not a school in the city. She adds: "I must now say, that I never for a moment believed in what my husband called his apparitions and revelation's, as I thought him laboring under a diseased mind; yet they may all be true, as a Prophet is seldom without credence or honor, excepting his own family or country; but as my conviction is to the contrary, I shall educate my children in a different faith, and teach them to obey and reverence the laws and institutions of their country."[31]

Emma responded by writing her own letter to the editor, denouncing the fraudulent address:

"To the Editor of the New York Sun; Sir: I wish to inform you, and the public through your paper, that the letter published Tuesday morning, December 9, is a forgery, the whole of it, and I hope that this notice will put a stop to all such communications."[32]

Whether or not the retraction was printed does little to lessen the effect of the words as they spread from person to person. The rumor that Emma Smith, widow of the Prophet Joseph had gone apostate would have been circulated wildly so soon after Joseph's death, as well as reprinted in other papers such as the Boston Cultivator. But regardless of the tittle tattle that was running rife in Nauvoo and the surrounding communities stemming from every manner of rumor mill, there were those who came to Emma's defense when her loyalty to Joseph was questioned.

Coming from a Mister Wood of the St. Louis Republican was the false report in January of 1845, that Emma was about to reveal an alarming exposé on Mormonism. This new shocking revelation was to benefit the paper with all publishing rights.[33] Coming to Emma's defense, John Taylor published in the volume six, January 15, 1845 edition of the Times and Seasons that Emma,

"...honored her husband while living, and will never knowingly dishonor his good name while his martyred blood mingles with mother earth."[34]

Chapter One

Clearly, even though there was evident stress regarding events which transpired in Nauvoo between 1844 and 1846, there were also good feelings and support from those in leadership.

On February 4, 1846 the Latter-day Saints under Brigham Young began their trek to the west while Emma and her children remained in Nauvoo to start over. Everything that she had known since she married Joseph had come to an abrupt change on June 27, 1844.

During the exodus from Nauvoo in 1846, riverboat captains had been warned not to help the Latter-day Saints in any way or their own lives would be in peril. During this perilous time, the Smiths boarded a boat called *Uncle Toby*, which was owned by a friend who risked his life by taking the little family up river to Fulton, Illinois where they stayed for six months.[35]

There is a scene in the *Emma Smith: My Story* movie where Emma says she will never cross that river again. It is a line that expresses exactly how she may have felt. After their return from Fulton she rarely traveled upon the waves that seemed as a crooked spine of a book that she desired to leave upon the shelf. Across that river lay memories of pain, persecution and loss. It is my belief that Emma sealed up the joyous pieces of those times within her heart but placed the volumes of pain upon that shelf, moving forward in a manner that she felt was right for her children.

Emma's reasons for staying were more personal than antagonistic. Whatever feelings existed between Emma and Brigham Young, however, they did have one aspect of common ground; they both loved Joseph dearly. Throughout the coming years Emma would become one of the most loved and respected citizens of Nauvoo due to her compassionate service to both friend, stranger and orphan. One must consider what would have happened to much of the historic value of Nauvoo had she not stayed and preserved some of the properties there.

Righteous Desires

Many writings have been published concerning the life of Emma after Joseph's death. Some are documented fact; most are derived from second hand reports differing here and there, a deluge of hearsay and perception. What does one do with this kind of chaos? In the first place, why must anything be done or decided? It is the past. I choose instead to absorb the richness that has been gained in my journey of discovery and the love I have developed for those early Saints. I desire to build upon their sacrifice so that I can have the fullness of the gospel today. There were things said and done between the Smith family and members of the Church after the martyrdom that were at times unpleasant and hurtful. The damage was dealt and received on both sides. It is more important to remember that our ancestors experienced these events, not us. They are on the other side and have reconciled all things; it is wrong for us to carry on the hurt and the pain. What matters the most is what we have in front of us today. I am someone who wants to learn from the hardships of the past, not repeat them.

There are many other passages from the past, both cruel and hatefully spoken on both sides of the fence that I could put upon these pages. But instead, I choose to remember the abundance of love that existed. I have mentioned only a few incidents so as to convey a picture of how division and contention was ushered into the family and the damage that ensued. After all what would the repetition of such murmurings serve except to stir renewed contempt and anger concerning events that have passed and should have no hold upon us? I call such things the Devil's brew, and he loves to stir the pot. I refuse to give him any ingredients, effort or energy that would serve up a poisonous dish.

Both the Savior and Joseph emphasized greatly the importance of unity. It is left to this generation and those who follow to let go of the negative deeds of the past and progress forward, looking to what we have today in the gospel. It is by no other means but a unity of mind, spirit, and action that Zion will be redeemed and her people gathered. How can that be accomplished when the children of God hang on to and dwell upon issues of the past?

These events I have spoken of happened to my own ancestors but I know the pure love of Christ and that love has taught me to forgive those who have done wrong to me and mine. It has also taught me to seek forgiveness for wrongs done by me or my family, and to let go. This is the only way the work of the Lord can be accomplished. It is the sure way to keep the fiery darts of the adversary deflected. We in this Gospel should know by now how the adversary works. What better way to attempt to divide the Church for generations than to pit two sides against one another whose heads were the two individuals most loved by Joseph? I refuse to let episodes of the past have the effects the adversary desires, for I desire unity. It should be the desire of every member of the Restored Gospel, of every human being.

Alexander Hale Smith

Chapter Two

"A smooth sea never made a skillful mariner."

—*Unknown*

Many have commented since the death of Joseph how sad it is that his posterity has become lost, fallen away from the fullness of the gospel. I wonder sometimes if we, as the product of human thought, fail to grasp that what may seem a stumbling block is actually a stepping stone depending on how one may process what is before them. The old adage, "sometimes things fall apart so they can fall together," may have some substance here. In making such a statement I do not want it to appear that I believe we should pull away from the truth any time we have an issue; indeed, in such times we should become steadfast in prayer and cling to what we know is true.

The events which unfolded within the family after Joseph's death were truly both dynamic and traumatic; a unique situation on many levels. For many, the element of oneness became lost in a fog of disunity and they reached out, grasping on to pieces of truth, surviving as best as they could with what they had. These were good moral and Christ-loving individuals whose motives were sincere.

It is important to realize that the family never became completely lost. The testimony of the Book of Mormon and the early restoration period remained solid in the hearts of Emma and the children. A thread of it has carried on throughout the generations. Instead it may be better to say they were held back by their inability to reconcile themselves with later doctrine and events which transpired in Nauvoo after Joseph's death.

It could be that the posterity needed a season of distance for some reason, maybe to come back in these times with a testimony that is solid and steadfast. In that season there have been storms upon the seas, the tempest raging with no mercy to offer, no compassion in the torrential winds and engulfing waves. There was always a safe place for them to land in the west, the one place they would not consider going. Instead, they pressed forward on a route they felt strongly they should follow, all the while carrying within their hearts and spirits a love for the Savior and a desire for peace. By taking the long route they had to master the tempest of the sea. Some still struggle but many have endured, cultivating their trials and turning weakness into strength. Doing so has allowed them to overcome the waves, finding a landing in that safe place; the fullness of the gospel. Having examined the generations which have preceded me while experiencing my own journey upon the sea, I have arrived at port equipped with a testimony strong and sure. Because I have battled many storms, I feel more prepared to face the storms ahead and I know there will be many.

As I spent years pouring through four generations of my Smith ancestors, I became acquainted with a loving people who had a true desire to follow the paths of righteousness, a people who loved and revered the restored gospel. Discovering the jewels of my heritage, I became aware that even though they fostered antagonism, they did love their Latter-day Saint kin in Utah, desiring peace and unity. These were two opposing sides standing staunchly for the same God. Regardless of their desires for unity, there would be none until they sat down together in council with the Lord on the other side of the veil. Only then would both sides learn of any error and be rewarded for their devotion to Heavenly Father and the Savior. I am sure that many wept and then embraced and all was healed as they began to work toward mending the hearts of those that they left behind; the posterity which would follow.

Alexander Hale Smith

There are three elements which shaped Alexander's thought process concerning Brigham Young and the LDS Church: what he saw as a child and how he viewed it, what he heard from others as he grew up, and what he saw and experienced in his adult years. Some of these situations were covered in the first chapter. But I wish to go a little deeper and offer an expanded view of the emotional impact from events Alexander experienced as he grew and interacted with saints in the west.

My great-grandfather, Alexander Hale Smith, was the eighth child of Joseph and Emma. With his jolly disposition, yearning for adventure, dark blonde hair and bright blue eyes, he has been described by contemporaries of Joseph as the child who was most like his father.[1] Born in Farr West June 2, 1838 during a time when the saints and the Smith family were weary and destitute as a result of harsh persecution,

Alexander's first years were surrounded by the stress and anxiety that attend a family who is in survival mode.

At the tender age of eight months old, Emma grabbed little Alexander up in her arms beside his brother Frederick to make the treacherous journey on foot across the frozen Mississippi. Her older two children, Joseph and Julia, held tightly to their mother's skirts as they treaded an icy surface toward an uncertain future. As he was clutched tightly against his mother's heart he may have sensed the emotions she would have been experiencing as a violent mob pushed the saints out of Missouri. He would not know, however, until years later the full extent of the danger they had faced that treacherous wintry day in 1839.[2] As they endured the perilous crossing, his father and uncle languished in a cold prison in Liberty, Missouri, threatened with death on a daily basis from attempted poisonings, violence from jailors, and exposure to the extreme Missouri winter.

While imprisoned, Joseph was mindful of his wife and children, desperate for their situation. The letters he wrote from Liberty express the tender love he held for his family.

"To Emma Smith on April 4, 1839, from the jail in Liberty, Missouri: "My dear Emma, I think of you and the children continually. ... I want to see little Frederick, Joseph, Julia, and Alexander, Johanna [an orphan who was living with the Smiths], and old Major [the family dog]. And as to yourself, if you want to know how much I want to see you, examine your feelings, how much you want to see me, and judge for yourself. I would gladly walk from here to you barefoot and bareheaded and half-naked to see you and think it great pleasure, and never count it toil."[3]

After Joseph, Hyrum and the other brethren who had been at Liberty escaped and made their way to Commerce, Illinois, which was later named Nauvoo, they set immediately to the task of rebuilding their lives. During the years of 1839-1844, Alexander would have been exposed to the bustling activity that would eventually transform the small town of approximately one hundred to a population of over twelve thousand, rivaling Chicago.[4] But the adventurous spirit which tends to amplify the tender ages of one to six years would have been turned toward agendas more appealing than the building up of a people. While his older brother Joseph may have been attentive to his father's work amongst the saints, it is most probable that Alexander spent his time near his mother's caring eye helping as he could but more likely catching frogs, exploring the outdoors, or throwing rocks in the river.

Joseph's death would take from Alexander and his siblings the love of a tender father. Though he was but six years of age, there was an acute awareness of just how deep the loss was. "Vague and terrifying was the effect on his youthful mind."[5] All of the children, even the unborn son who would be named David Hyrum Smith, could not help but be affected by the deep mourning that Emma processed. Children and mother embraced through the following months and years, supporting one another, gathering strength and forging a bond which was solid and true. Alexander considered his mother the "center of the universe."[6] During a visit to Nauvoo in 1863, Charles Derry recorded, "I never saw a family pay more respect to their mother…"[7]

Alexander married Elizabeth Agnes Kendall in his 22nd year. Called Lizzie by those who loved her, she was a short, petite, bonnie lass who had traveled to Nauvoo, Illinois from Marysport, England in 1843 when she was but a few months old. Lizzie's parents, John and Elizabeth Kendall, had converted to The Church of Jesus Christ of Latter-day Saints in England and were saving funds to migrate to America to join with the Saints in Nauvoo. In the fall of 1842 John, a painter by trade, fell from a scaffold while he was attempting to save other workers and died. Within months after Elizabeth's birth her mother gathered her children and joined other converts on the ship Ketoka, sailing toward a new future. While living in Nauvoo, Elizabeth's mother and Emma would become close friends.[8]

Lizzie's mother eventually remarried and had two more children before she died in 1850. Her children from her first marriage, John, Isabella, and Elizabeth were placed in homes when their step-father remarried. Young Elizabeth would be one of many orphans adopted by Emma Smith, a woman whose compassion knew no bounds when it came to children. From the time she was seven Elizabeth grew up in the Mansion house as part of the Smith family.[9]

"She was like some shy little plant transplanted into a strange garden. She grew into womanhood in the Mansion, and in the old parlor there she was married to Alexander in the spring of eighteen hundred and sixty-one."[10]

Theirs has been described by the children as a merry household filled with love, as well as the loneliness that comes with the absence of a husband and father whose work takes him often times away. But the members of the household, from large to small, understood the importance of their father's work and instead of malice for his absence bore him the greatest love and respect due to a father. His gentle laughter, jolly heart, and twinkling eyes were a source of merriment in the Smith home. Alexander was known to have said, "If you want to have a good time, take it with you."[11] It was a sentiment which has undoubtedly peppered the generations which followed, for there are many of us who excel in livening up a somber room when given the chance.

Alexander's talents were such that he could build almost anything with his hands. His children delighted in the toys he would make for them, and his wife Elizabeth was often rewarded by various contraptions fashioned by his hand which eased the burden of domesticity.[12] Known for his athletic abilities, Alexander excelled in swimming, running, hunting, rowing, wrestling and marksmanship. His proficiency with the gun was such that he was barred from the shooting competitions in Nauvoo, for no one could beat him!![13] But above all the call of wildlife and nature was the most deeply rooted in his soul, and Nauvoo became attached to his heart with a fondness so dear that it would beckon him in his last days.

A Man of Adventure

One story that I have come to adore concerning Alexander's love for the outdoors cannot be ignored in telling of his character, for it was written by his own hand and is such a frank expression of the free spirit he possessed. I could not help but chuckle when I read his account of what was supposed to be an outing of maybe an hour, which turned into nearly three days! His usage of the words, "the spell was on me," rang familiar to me for I have seen more than one descendant of Joseph with the wanderlust spirit, including my father!

The story was penned by Alexander as a result of a rest he was taking to bring relief to rheumatism in his back. His daughter Vida had spied him writing and inquired after the details of the narrative. He replied, "It's the river lust in me, daughter, the river lust; why I can see the whitecaps riding in, and the fret line on the shore, and I'm hungry for it, sick for the sound of the river. I want to go to Nauvoo!"

When Vida asked if she could see what he had written he gingerly gave it to her, saying that she could do what she wished with it. True to the character of one who loves a good story, especially one of family, Vida kept the narrative and recorded it for future generations.

In looking through Alexander's account of this adventure I tried to reason where I should edit to shorten it but found the tale would be much lessened in its richness if even one line was omitted, so I offer it in its entirety for the joy of those who find pleasure in indulging in the simplicity of a time that once was, through the musing of a true woodsman and pioneer.

"One evening, when a young man, I arose from my seat beside the fire, for the cool weather made a fire necessary to comfort, and passed to the door and looked out; my wife noticed that I was restless and remarked, 'what is the matter with you?'

Chapter Two

Now, that the reader may the better catch the thread of this little story, I will say I was then a young man of about twenty-four, was married and lived in the Old Mansion situated on the brow of the hill on the east bank of the broad Mississippi, whose beautiful waters shone in the light of the afternoon sun with enticing strong for me, for I dearly loved the old river. My wife saw the spirit of unrest was upon me and was uneasy because she and our baby boy had ere this been left alone for days while I was off on the river, or in the woods, no one knowing exactly where nor at what time I would return.

Our brown eyed, dark haired baby boy was a joy to her, and a comfort when I was gone; but her heart was always filled with fear when she knew I was on the waters, or when I was gone and she knew not where. I was a good enough sort, had few bad habits, but unfortunately for my wife's peace of mind I was descended from a great hunter, only two removes, and in my blood was the taint, a love for my gun and rod-and as the seasons for hunting and fishing came round, my blood became fevered for the longing for the woods, or river and lakes, and I could seldom resist the 'call of the wild;' and so my wife many times found herself alone with our baby for days. With this explanation the reader can understand with what uneasiness she asked the question, 'now what is the matter with you?' She had heard the call of the quail that afternoon, and knew that I also had heard it. Three separate times I had left my seat and went to the door and listened. At last I sprang to my feet, caught down my gun, and saying, 'I'm going to see if I can find those quail; I'll not be gone long,' I

Hills & Valleys

passed out, crossed the road, and was soon out of sight in the neighboring fields.

Now when I started out with my gun, I really had no thought going beyond that neighboring field; but the spell was on me, and I could no more be content to abide in the four walls of a house than could the little martins stay when the time to go had come. In the first field I did not find the quail, so in the next I must needs go. I knew that the evening meal would soon be ready, but little cared I while the impulse to roam was upon me.

My footsteps soon led me past the dwelling of a neighbor, one Sam Chambers, whose love for a gun and the fields was as great as my own. As I approached the dwelling, I shouted and Sam came out and as soon as he saw that I had my gun he said, 'wait a minute and I will go with you.' Now Sam was married and had a family, but the hunting nature was strong in him also; when he joined me his blood was fired by the same fever and unrest that made me reckless of time.

When he came he said, 'where to now?' I replied, 'Oh anywhere; let us go up the river..' So up the river we went. Field after field was passed through, until just before the sun reached the horizon we found ourselves some three miles and a half away from home and near the riverbank. Then I remembered I had a canoe which had been left a half mile above where we were. The proposition was made to go and get the canoe and ride home. It suited both, and we were soon in the frail vessel speeding towards home.

The canoe was a small one, barely able to bear up two full grown men, and when we were seated and had pushed off

Chapter Two

from the shore it appeared that two or three inches of the gunwale was above water; but both of us were expert boatmen and used to that kind of vessel so we felt no fear. The weather had been cold several nights before and ice had formed in the river north of us, and was now floating quite thickly in midstream. As we pulled into the stream some wild ducks flew past and settled in the water near the opposite shore. The river here was nearly a mile wide, and to reach the opposite side we hunters had to pass through the floating ice. But as it seemed very little out of our way, we at once proposed to run across and try for some ducks. True, by this time the sun was disappearing, but we did not mind that as the evenings were light as a rule, long after sunset; but unfortunately for us as we neared the farther shore a fierce squall, or gale of wind, suddenly arose and swept over the river and our frail craft would not live ten minutes in such weather so we hastily sought shelter on shore. With the wind came clouds and rain. The wind blew so fiercely it would catch up the water at the top of the waves and blow it in great sheets through the air. The night settled down in earnest and it became very dark. We were in for a night's stay on an island. So long as the wind raged there was no escape. To add to our discomfort we began to get very hungry, but there was no show for supper on that bleak island, no human habitation within miles and miles of us.

Through the island, which was large, some miles in extent, ran deep but narrow sloughs; the landing had been made near one of these. I remembered a deserted wood chopper's cabin a mile or such a matter across the island on the banks of this waterway, and I proposed to take to the boat and keep close under the bank and if possible reach the old hut for shelter for the night. And now began a voyage of danger, under the best of conditions; with the wind blowing as it was, it was a hazardous undertaking, but in the dark it was doubly so. The banks were abrupt, the wind from the west, and by keeping in touch of the shore with our paddles we slowly coasted across the island till the shapes of tall trees overhead told us we were near the shanty.

How often since that I have wondered how we ever made that trip and found the hut, but we did it. We built a fire in the hut and by its light we found, carefully laid up, a loaf of dry bread some wood chopper had left; and having killed a duck we roasted it over the fire and feasted on roast duck and bread, and chatted and talked till sleepy, then stretched ourselves on the wooden bunks in the shanty and went to sleep. It must not be thought that there was much comfort in the woodman's shanty, but it was a shelter from the fierce west wind. There were no blankets, nor even straw in the bunks. We were glad to be even shelter from the cold wind, however. It was a long, weary night, but daylight came at last.

As soon as it was light enough to see to shoot, Sam went out to see the river and if possible get a duck or two, while I roasted what remained of yesterday's catch, which was scant enough for two hungry hunters. Sam returned and reported the main river too rough yet to venture on with our light canoe. Here we were, two men on an island, one of many miles long, with main river on the east, and several wide waterways or sloughs on the west between us and the mainland. Thus we were obliged to wait until the wind ceased blowing ere we could leave the island.

Chapter Two

After breakfast, we both went to the bank on the main river to wait for the going down of the wind. It was cold; neither one had overcoat or gloves, and we were forced to keep moving to keep warm. Noon came and still the gale swept the waves aloft. Toward evening, to add to our misery, there came a fierce shower of rain and sleet and wet us through. After the rain the wind increased in force. We feared to leave the river, being anxious, if the wind ceased blowing as the sun went down, to hasten across the cold water. We gathered a huge pile of driftwood and succeeded, after many trials, in lighting a fire. Everything was wet and it was very difficult to get the wet wood to burn. The sun went down, angry and red. We watched the wind tossed waves from beside the huge fire we had built. The ground was too wet and cold to lie down on and weariness had overcome us, to say nothing of hunger which had become intense by this time, for we had been unsuccessful in killing anymore game. However, we gathered brush and piled it near the fire and lay down on that to catch, if possible, a little sleep. But the cold was so severe we had to keep turning to keep warm; one side freezing, the other roasting.

The long, wretched night passed at last and day came, but no cessation of the wind. Stormbound and miserable--wet, cold, and hungry, stiff and sore--we roused ourselves and sought for something to eat. One poor little duck was all we could find that day, and that seemed only to aggravate our hunger. It did seem strange, but the very ducks were hid away, or refused to venture to face the storm. We wandered up and down the bleak river shore and at last resolved to seek the old shanty and spend another night within its walls; but on further thought, we resolved to risk a move, one in the canoe and one on shore, and coast along down the river. On reaching the sloughs, or waterways, we both entered the canoe and crossed them. Several times the water splashed into the little boat, and as many times we were in danger of sinking. We could not had lived twenty minutes in the cold water if we had been plunged into it, even if we could have kept on the surface so lone; but by great care and skill, keeping close under the bank as much as possible, we finally reached the mainland and thus the town, some four miles below where we were held upon the island.

It was evening, just before dark, when we came ashore there, and recognized the boat of a friend who was looking for us. We soon found him and I got into his but while Sam paddled the canoe, keeping close to the larger boat; thus we crossed the wide river. It was late at night when I carefully let myself into my own home, and found my way to my wife's room. I found her wide awake, a bright light in her room, and as I opened the door and walked in she turned pale and for a moment was silent, then she said, 'You're a pretty fellow aren't you? Where have you been?' A little shamefacedly I answered, 'Aren't you glad to see me? I'm hungry! Can you give me something to eat?' And the baby looked up from the bed and laughed, 'Papa, Papa!' "[14]

I simply love this glimpse into an episode of the lives of my great-grandparents. And it is so easy for me to know the character of Alexander for in many descriptions I have read about him I see a duplicate of my father; the jolliness, the adventurer, the craftsman, the marksman, even the man who leaves for a few hours but is gone for days and walks in as if it were nothing and asks for something to eat. I am sure Elizabeth, in her short pause before addressing his return that evening with an edge of wit, was biting her tongue in an attempt to keep from scolding too much the pitiful sight of her hungry, wet, cold husband. I am also quite sure that they both had a good laugh later as he regaled his wife with the tale of a treacherous hunt which resulted in two little ducks that could barely feed him and his companion.

Crossroads

In 1860, Alexander's brother Joseph began his presidency in the RLDS church, a move which brought anxiety to Alexander's mind and heart. He had grown up in Nauvoo during a period where the persecution of the Mormons had all but ceased after his father's death. He attended the Methodist church, romped with the other local boys and reveled in the adventures of the Southern Illinois wilderness, bordered by that mighty river which throughout his life would so often call to his heart for a return visit.

The full extent of Alexander's childhood years, which had been spent in what he described as reckless youth, now led to this crossroad and it was time to pause and determine which path to take. It was not a decision he was ready to make. He examined his brother's workings within the RLDS church from a distance. Time and circumstance, however, have a way of bringing the human race to terms with indecision, often in the most grievous of measures.

The love and reverence which existed between the Smith brothers was bonded by a keen sense of loyalty and camaraderie. The strength of their existence rested within the unspoken devotion which linked their hearts together. They were innately aware of the fragilities of life and how circumstance could either add or take away from their number.

In the winter of 1862, the harshness of the Nauvoo climate threatened Alexander's wife, Lizzie, who had just given birth to their first son Frederick. At the onset of her illness, they were living at the family farm a few miles beyond the bluffs on Parley Street. Alexander bound her and the babe as best he could and took them to the Mansion House where Emma could care for her. Alexander's brother Frederick and his little family moved into the farm house to take care of it while Lizzie was nursed back to health. Not too long after his wife's illness commenced, the beloved brother Frederick, for whom Alexander's new son had been named, also fell ill. He had been suffering from consumption for some time.

Because Frederick left no written account of his life it is unclear how long his illness had been at a serious level, nor is it known why his wife took their daughter and left without notifying the family of his dire condition. But one day his brother Joseph felt to stop in and check on him. He found Frederick in a destitute state, alone in the midst of winter without food, water or heat. Joseph immediately took his brother to Emma, who nursed him as well as she could. Throughout the winter Lizzie would recover, but Frederick would die later in the spring. Once again Emma felt the inconsolable heartache of losing a child. Frederick, through his kind and gentle ways, had been loved by all who knew him.

"His was a peculiarly happy and sunny temperament that has won for him to the third generation a reputation for

Chapter Two

his many loveable qualities. His was the merriest heart of all the merry household. His soft brown eyes held no accusation nor severity in their gentle depths. Tearfully the grandmother gathered the little son of Alexander in her arms and thanked the fates that had prompted them to name him Frederick."[15]

Frederick's death at the age of twenty-six dealt Alexander a severe blow and he became concerned about the welfare of his brother's soul, since he had died without baptism. One day when he was in prayer expressing his concerns, Alexander heard the still small voice offering the following words of comfort, "Grieve not; Frederick's condition is pleasant; and the time will come when baptism shall be secured to him."[16]

At the time of Frederick's death, Alexander had been at odds with his brother Joseph's decision to join The Reorganization. Now he began to feel some stirrings within, the unspoken words of encouragement and confidence that are often whispered to us when we are standing at a crossroads unsure whether or not to proceed. Still, as his brother David prepared for baptism, he was cautious as he studied the whole matter out.

"When my brother, David, was baptized I refused to go down to the water and see him baptized. I stood on the hillside afar and watched his baptism. God was working with me. I was fearful to do that which was wrong in the sight of God. I did not fear God as a monster. I feared to displease Him. I feared to do that which would bring upon me the penalty of His displeasure. I had been taught from childhood by my mother to revere His holy name, and His holy word. And being a God-fearing man in this wise I respected and reverenced those that obeyed the commandments of God. But

I saw before me, if I accepted that work, the excommunication of myself from the world, the turning away of my friends, the leaving me alone, and the persecution that followed my father to his death. Can you blame me for questioning whether my brother was right in what he was doing, under these circumstances, when all the world seemed against us?"[17]

Twelve months before his own baptism, Alexander was speaking with a friend at work who had been pushing him toward joining the RLDS church. Alexander expressed his feelings:

"'There are some responsibilities, sometimes, that are placed upon men of a character that if they could refuse to accept them and still hold a good, pure conscience toward God, they would refuse to accept these responsibilities.'"

"'I see how it is. You will never join the Church until God lays His heavy hand upon you in sickness.'" The man replied. Within months Alexander fell severely ill and Lizzie sent for his brother Joseph for a blessing.

"He came and laid his hands upon my head, anointed me with oil. I was in that state of mind that I watched what that man said. I watched his prayer. I wanted to be satisfied that it was of God, that it was not the power of man, nor of the adversary. God was working with me." After the blessing Alexander fell asleep. His fever soon broke and he was up and about the next day, weakened but healed. On May 25, 1862 he was baptized. [18]

Onward and Forward

Alexander's emergence into the RLDS Church catapulted him to a position that many descendants spend their lives trying to avoid, for once that step is taken the participant is immersed in the pot of boiling controversy surrounding who is right and who is wrong. A man resolute in his devotion to God, Alexander defended his position with passion, encased by the heartbreak which accompanies familial division, standing on opposite sides of the fence from cousins and playmates of his early childhood.

Alexander felt he had little to offer in the areas of leadership. "...In no sense, in my own estimation, was I worthy to be made a teacher over members who had been in the Church nearly as many years as I had been in the world."[19] Despite his feelings of inadequacies he trusted in the Lord and moved forward when called to leadership positions.

On May 20, 1866 Alexander gave his wife fifty cents, all the money he had to spare, and bid her goodbye before heading to the Western territory on a mission. The destination of both he and his companion was the Great Salt Lake Valley. Their journey started afoot and penniless but as they trudged ahead with faith their needs were met sufficiently. At length they joined with an LDS emigrant wagon train in Fort Kearney, Nebraska. To avoid any problems which might occur, Alexander chose to remain incognito, calling himself Alex Hale. Both he and his companion were aware that they were being watched with suspicion.[20]

One night as Alexander prayed over their meal, one of the men in the camp approached the captain expressing his concerns that the strangers were surely apostates, possibly Josephites. "No other class of religionists continued to keep up service, have prayer and ask a blessing upon the food so long after striking the Plains," the man said.[21] After that evening there were a few attempts made to ascertain the identity of Alexander and his companion. At length the truth surfaced during a conversation between Captain Ricks and Alexander while they were riding. But by then many had come to know and trust Alexander because of his character so that when it was made known he was a son of their revered Prophet, suspicion turned to love and the two Josephites became a welcome part of the wagon train.

While on this trek, the adventurer in Alexander was magnified. When the wagon train came upon a hill called Sugar Loaf, he was not resigned to merely pass by, but sought instead to climb it so he could see with greater advantage the route they were following. Having been assigned as scout, he rode ahead, dismounted his horse, Billy, and led him up the steep slope of the hill.

"I wish I could describe the scenery as viewed by me upon this mountain among mountains, detached and alone it stood like a sentinel doing duty among his fellows, grand, noble and inspiring."[22]

As he gazed upon the etchings of God's architecture, a sound began to softly arouse his senses. The gentle breeze carried with it a choir of voices singing a tune familiar to him. As he saw the wagon train passing below him, he realized that the music was coming from them. "These were a band of good singers and they were singing We Thank Thee O God For a Prophet. I have heard the hymn sung by a good many choirs including the Great Salt Lake City Choir since then; but never have I heard it equaled as it was sung at the base of my little mountain."[23]

Chapter Two

Alexander would satisfy his visual desires of nature yet again when the wagon train came to Devil's Gate. Once again he chose to climb to the summit, a much more treacherous adventure than sugar loaf, but well worth the effort in his eyes.

"I could see the wagon trail winding its way around the huge rock in the dessert; and away toward the east the vast plain which seemed limitless; and to the South I could see occasionally the glint of silver as the river came in sight in its meanderings; while to the west lay a valley, a beautiful valley; and beyond, range upon range of rugged mountain scenery."[24]

The expanse of the trek from Fort Kearny, Nebraska to Salt Lake City, Utah afforded Alexander one adventure after another. The beauty and awe of God's nature unfolded before him in measures he had never dreamed of. But the trail was also filled with experiences which seemed to confirm to him rumors he had been exposed to his whole life. Alexander's journal reflects his disgust concerning the behaviors of some immigrants. He encountered instances of adultery, and disrespect. There was much contempt toward the elderly women from the younger girls and quite often profanity was used. When he approached one man by the name of John Hammer about the situation he was told matter-of-factly that it did not matter what happened on the plains for they were to be re-baptized once they reached Salt Lake. Alexander asked John for more information about what he termed as wholesale re-baptism.

According to Alexander's journal, he does not seek to know from John or any others, why rebaptism was required. He seems instead to have later formed judgment about the matter writing. "I did not understand it then. But I do now. The Church in Utah was a new church under the leadership of Brigham Young, and was really the Brighamite Church and during their reformation a change had been affected and all had been re-baptized out of the true order into the apostate organization."[25]

It had actually been common early in the restoration for the Latter-day Saints to be re-baptized for health and as a semblance of rededicating their lives to Christ and the gospel. After the exodus of Nauvoo and trials of the plains, rebaptism to these early pioneers was a ritual which signified their new beginning in a place far removed from the flaming torches of the mobs who crept through the cloak of darkness on the errand of the adversary. Re-baptism edified them and gave them strength and hope to move forward. The practice was not so much for salvation but rededication and it was not unheard of, for it had been performed as early as 1832 when David Johnson requested re-baptism because he, "lived unworthy of the communion of sacrament."[26] From that time forward, re-baptism was often employed for the edification of the Saints. According to Wilford Woodruff, fourth president of The Church of Jesus Christ of Latter-day Saints, they were not discounting their first baptism but renewing the covenants they had made and by extension their faith.

"I was baptized by regular authority in 1833, and I do not wish to say there was any necessity of being re-baptized in 1849 or '50, I simply wanted to renew my covenant."[27] Brigham Young was merely doing what the Saints had been accustomed to since the Church had been organized, so in that respect Alexander was mistaken in his summation that the Brighamites were a new order.

One also must consider that Alexander was surrounded by a multitude of immigrants who may not have had full understanding of the Church they had converted to. There is no doubt that they had testimonies and had been led by the spirit, but it is clear from John Hammer's statement that some had not yet grasped a comprehension of propriety concerning church standards. To say that it mattered not what they did on the plains for there was re-baptism ahead, completely disregards the significance of covenants and rededication.

Once in Salt Lake, Alexander was immediately aware of a shift in the people he had spent months traveling with. All of a sudden none of them knew him. When passing acquaintances from the wagon train, his salutations were met with avoidance. Though his uncle, John Smith, and cousin Samuel housed him and treated him well, there were several occasions which gave him pause to be concerned for his safety.

Because they staunchly stood up for their kin, John and Samuel Smith received silent warnings as well.[28] These individuals who acted in the cloak of darkness to affect fear in Alexander and his companion are to me products of their own design. I liken it to the general who has many soldiers whom he has instructed concerning proper behavior at their post, yet he is unable to watch their every move, or control ill behavior and improper conduct as it arises. Even today we are taught by our General Authorities to love those who have chosen different paths, to be their friend, and the better portion of people do. But there are some who of their own devices persecute those they see as fallen. It is most probable that when Alexander beheld such actions at the hands of certain men, he assumed they were acting by direct order of the leadership, or he viewed it as a breakdown of leadership. Either way it seemed to confirm his perspective that the Church under Brigham Young had broken away from its foundational teachings, especially concerning polygamy.

Many scenes of ignorant behavior crossed Alexander's path, further driving his passion and desire to do something to help what he viewed as a fallen people. Toward the end of their fifteen day mission, before leaving for California, Alexander fell into discussion with several whose testimonies seemed to contradict teachings he had studied in the Millennial Star and Times and Seasons. When he broached discrepancies with people, he was met with answers such as, "The books are a dead letter," and "We don't care anything for the books. They are not worth the ashes of a rye straw," and "We have the living oracles." Commenting on the Book of Commandments one individual exclaimed, "Oh, yes; that was well enough in its time but we can't be governed by those cast iron books. We have outgrown them. They did well enough for the Church in its infancy, but they are too narrow and strait for the Church now."[29]

When Alexander challenged one man about the testimonies of the Saints concerning polygamy, which in Alexander's eyes painted Joseph and Hyrum as liars for they had publicly denounced it in the Times and Seasons, he was met with the remark, "Oh, that's nothing; I hold the priesthood, which authorizes me to lie for the good of the Church." to which Alexander replied, "That may be sir, but of one thing I am certain, you never received that priesthood from God."[30]

One can understand the shock which must have coursed through Alexander after hearing and experiencing the things that he did on that 1866 visit. But how many of these people with whom he conversed truly understood the concepts of their own beliefs? And who was this man who so flagrantly boasted he could lie for the good of the Church? Once again the condition of the people Alexander was surrounded with must be examined here. There were a large number whose conversions were so fresh that they may have unintentionally spoken out of ignorance. Did they know enough about the true tenets of the Church to accurately convey the reality of its teachings, or did they barely have a grasp on the basic teachings and fill in the blanks with their own views? It would have served Alexander well had he taken these reports to the leadership and simply asked if they were true. It is the same issue every church has to reckon with even today, when their members voice opinions or convey their own perceptions which are not necessarily acceptable by the leadership of the Church itself.

In the face of such perceived spiritual atrocities, Alexander's resolve to plead his cause to the people of Salt Lake City was strengthened, for he felt as if they were being misled. In his heart he held a love for the people and merely felt that he was doing the right thing in trying to get them to see they were in error. He mourned for their souls for he truly thought them in peril. It is much like the evangelicals today and how they feel they must rescue us, for they feel we are on a path destined to hell. It is out of their love for us that they do these things.

A Bitter View

Alexander would go on more than one mission to the west. Each visit brought both wonderful and terrible experiences. Those journeys I will leave to the pages of time for the reader to investigate at their own will, for I have sought here only to touch on a few instances which formed in the mind of this gracious, gentle man, and the perceptions he had of the LDS Church and Brigham Young. So embedded were the portraits of his experiences that he still carried them as late as 1901 when he was sixty-three years old. Preaching to a congregation in Tahiti, Alexander spoke vehemently concerning the history of his family.

His words carry the sting of pain and anguish concerning a time when he was but six years and older. One has to wonder how many of those memories were tainted by innuendo and misrepresentation. Once again I include the fullness of the article, for how can one know another in just five minutes, when five days would secure a better understanding. Therefore I offer here the bulk of his sermon preached on November 10, 1901 in Tahiti. Of his mother and the condition after Joseph's death he stated;

"She was left with five children to support and maintain; four boys, and an adopted daughter, and the struggle was not an easy one, especially under some of the conditions which may relate. I relate them because they had a tendency to form my opinion about religion and what the Church should be. I can only relate a few of the instances to show you the heritage of shame—as the world looked upon it; but as under God and the fulfillment of His declarations, I now esteem to be a heritage of the greatest riches that He could possibly have placed upon me. Still, through all my manhood, from childhood to manhood, I have had to carry and see the marks of the finger of scorn pointed at me by the world, because I was a son of Joseph Smith, the Prophet."[31]

Alexander believed his father intended young Joseph to become head of the Church. Many RLDS believe Joseph III's blessing in the Liberty Jail by his father constituted his right to the office of Prophet. However, at the time Joseph received the blessing from his father he was not yet a baptized member of the church so he could not have been ordained. It would have gone against the process by which the organization had been founded. Alexander believed that the Council of the Twelve's knowledge of Joseph III's blessing prompted attempts to kidnap his brother and take him to the West.

"I wish to return in my thoughts to the time of the visitation of my mother to my father in the jail in [Liberty] Missouri. For I had learned since coming upon the islands here that there have been statements made that are foreign to the truth, and I would like to set the minds of the people at ease relative to that statement.

At the time my father was in the jail with others, it was expected that perhaps he would be killed. That seemed to be the intent of the people, and his thought for the welfare of the Church was that it might be provided for in the future. The testimony of those that were with him in the jail was that he called to him, upon this occasion, his oldest son, Joseph; he took him in his arms and placed his hands upon him and blessed him, and under the influences of the Spirit of God prophesied upon him and declared that he would lead the Church, that he would be the successor to the position which he held in the Church, under the divine influence of the Spirit of God. Mark you, at this time the boy had not been baptized, was not by baptism a member of the Church; but in blessing was considered a member of the body.

Wheeler Baldwin, Alexander McRae, and Lyman Wight, if my memory serves me right, were witnesses of this blessing of the Prophet, had under these circumstances, blessed and set apart so far as it is possible for him to do, his boy to take the place in case he should be removed—when he came to years of accountability......there was an effort made by the Church [leaders] to take the oldest son of the Prophet with them when they left Nauvoo and went westward. The object of taking the eldest son was well known. It was a well understood principle in the Church that he would succeed his father. It was talked in their councils; and when it was talked in their councils the matter was hushed up and they were told not to tell it to the world, because the world would kill him as they had killed his father before him.

They were driven from Nauvoo, and in their move westward they desired to take with them that portion of the family of the Prophet that was designated as being essential to the organization of the Church. They sought my mother. The tried to persuade her but she told them, "No." She could not indorse what they were doing. They then sought to steal away the firstborn. They placed a guard over my mother's house, and for two weeks, fourteen days and nights, that guard watched around the house with the intent and purpose of stealing the firstborn, and taking him westward. They told my mother that she must comply with their wishes. And in order to compel her to do so they placed around her house a guard to prevent anybody bringing food to her, and told her they would starve her to comply with their wishes.

These things were calculated to have their operation upon my mind. In the fall of 'forty-three or the spring of 'forty four [1843 or 1844], there was baptism in front of the city, at Nauvoo. On the riverside there was a large concourse of people. I remember well the circumstances. My father had been baptizing in the river. As he came up from the water he said, 'Is there anyone else that wishes to be baptized?'

From a cluster of boys at one side of the congregation, my oldest brother sprang out. Running down to the riverside he took off his hat and threw it behind him and said, 'Yes, father, I want to be baptized.' And my father took him into the water and baptized him. He was confirmed afterwards under the hands of Lyman W. Babbitt, then an active elder in the Church. At length called into his father's office and in the presence of James Whitehead was blessed, set apart and ordained, so far as he could be ordained, to the position that he would be called upon to fill. You, who have studied the law, will understand that my father could not ordain him to the position of prophet, seer, and revelator, nor to the position of the president of the Church, because he was yet alive and occupied that position."[32]

Had the family gone west with the Saints it is possible that Joseph would have succeeded his father. However, by becoming prophet of an opposing church all possibility of leadership of the western saints became void.

Hills & Valleys

Alexander was in his elder years when he gave this sermon and still after so much time his words were absorbed with bitter feelings about events he was not even old enough to comprehend at the time of their passing. I asked my cousin Gracia Jones, who is the historical advisor in the Joseph Smith Jr. and Emma Hale Smith Historical Society, what she felt about the content of the sermon. I offer here a wonderful summation from her concerning Alexander's feelings.

"I don't have to point out all the misstatements in this article to show how very little Alexander Hale Smith possessed in terms of knowledge regarding what happened after the martyrdom. The value of this to me is giving us a view of how the boy Alexander came to think about what he believed had taken place. He has testified here that his mother said and did things which are surely not on record and which she surely did not do—but which he fervently believes she did and said. Joseph III does the same thing, but not as flagrantly as does Alexander. They are the main reason the leaders in Utah blamed Emma—their broad statements place her as the source of their false beliefs.

In reality, their teachers were the dissenters who tutored them. One comment I can't resist making here is regarding the story of why Joseph is said to have blessed his son when he was in the Liberty Jail to be his successor—the reason given by Alexander is that he was concerned about what would happen if he should not survive. In reality, it is my understanding that Joseph fully knew they would come out of that jail, and he was not talking about his own demise and concerned about succession in the leadership, but was concerned about the condition of the Church and the need for

Chapter Two

the priesthood to be humble and righteous so the Lord could bless them. (See D&C 121—etc.)

It is true Joseph III was blessed in Liberty. But he himself testified in public that he was not ordained, but blessed by his father. Alexander here is stretching the point to suit himself and nobody would ever question his right to say what he did as he was accepted at that point as the authority he had become. This talk gives us a vivid picture of a child, deprived of his father, left rudderless until he finds his way into a frame of mind to join his brother in the Reorganization.

I want to comment also on the fact that when I was in the temple in Cardston Canada when Alexander and Elizabeth's endowment and sealing was performed, and when I was proxy for my grandmother, their youngest child, Coral, and for her sister, Eva Grace, I was privileged to receive absolute assurance that at least those four had accepted the ordinance work done for them that day. If I did not have that confirming testimony, reading these things would be extremely hard to bear. But I know absolutely, they have embraced the Gospel of Jesus Christ and are on the same page with those of us who are presently attempting to bring the fullness of the true Heritage to the descendants. As for the 'posterity' being 'the eldest son' that I think is a narrow view. Posterity is all who descend regardless of which child they descend through. But, in reality, the posterity will ultimately be those who will receive the true gospel and the endowments, as Elder Packer prayed for in the December 23, 2006 program."[33]

While examining the pages of history it is easy to see that there were things said and done on both sides of the fence which were wrong or misleading. Though his perspective of the Saints in Utah and Brigham Young may have been skewed by the influence of those around him, Alexander's love of the Savior was sure and strong. He devoted his life to a faith he felt was true and was known to all as a gentle soul. His intentions were righteous and I have always believed that that the Lord takes a good look at our intentions when considering our actions.

"Alexander's involvement in the RLDS church during his lifetime would include serving on the Board of Directors of Graceland College; he was an apostle, the patriarch to the RLDS church, and served as a counselor in the presidency. His entire heart and soul was committed to service to God, His church, and His kingdom. His testimony of the Book of Mormon, the Bible, and the Doctrine and Covenants, resonated across the nations in sermons of faith, and the expectation of Christ's Second Coming."[34]

A Sail on the Horizon

When time had circumnavigated the fullness of his life and the ship became weary, the Lord provided that Alexander should visit the old home place en route to a conference in 1909. The whitecaps of that grand old river called him back one more time through the doors of the home he had once professed should be the place of his passing; the dear old mansion in Nauvoo.

The account of Alexander's passing was memorialized in writing by his daughter Vida. So touching in its eloquence, expressing the love that he shared with his dear Lizzie, I could not attempt to use my own inadequacies to relate it. Instead, allow the voice of one who viewed the scene and knew firsthand the love of her endearing parents. Such description endorses the very embodiment of true love and devotion.

"The summer of 1909 was hot and dry, and the heat was unusually trying to father. The tilling of his garden, heretofore such a pleasure to him, was burdensome. Sometimes in the evening he sat on the lawn into the night trying to cool his heated body. Never had he suffered so intensely with the heat. Very early in the morning (his custom was early rising) he did a turn in his garden, fed the chickens, and Lady Grey, the family house cat, followed him to and fro about the place and even to the sidewalk as he took his usual trip to town, sure of his kindly interests and ministrations of food. Always did the domestic animals receive kindly care from him," I will add here that this conduct of affection toward animals seems to run throughout the family starting with Joseph Smith Jr, himself and maybe even beyond. I only know that my siblings and I have always had a singular connection and love toward all of nature, especially animals.

"If the roses bloomed or the leaves changed or the robins called for spring or geese flew south for winter, it was a matter of interest to the father. Turning over the papers before me I find his schedule of reunions for the fall of 1909. Of course Nauvoo District was one. No excuse, small or great, counted against Nauvoo, but the heat was not less there. He urged mother to go, but it was impossible; she could not spend the money to go to Nauvoo, although she sometimes had the sweet old longing for the place as it 'used to be.' Ah, how often the impossible happens! That day when father started from the big, cool, white house under its shade of maple and pine trees, he came back twice and kissed the little

Hills & Valleys

woman sitting by the open door, and she laughed at his sentimentality but watched him as he turned away down the sunny village street..."[35]

While in Nauvoo Alexander fell ill. According to family tradition through my grandfather, Alexander had enjoyed a dish of boiled cabbage at the Moffet's and became ill soon afterwards, unable to digest the meal due to some intestinal blockage. He lay in pain for several days. At some point Vida arrived in Nauvoo and was greeted by her uncle, John Kendall.

"Still and breathless the river seemed to wait, and the sands of the shore were hot and shining in the morning sun as I hurried up the bank and around the corner where once stood the old (Red brick) store, and was soon climbing the old stairs that my earliest footsteps had known. Bending to kiss the dear face, how gladly he greeted me, but looked past for..., 'You want mother?' I inquired, and he nodded, the blue eyes full of tears. The time for speech had passed.

Reader, do you know the exquisite agony of such a discovery? Promising to get mother was easy, but all that terrible day he watched eagerly for her face, and once Uncle John asked, 'Have you heard from Lizzie?' And at the sound of her name a glad light leaped into the eyes. The sun went down; not a bit of air stirred; the summer winds that should have come drifting over the river were still, and sleep had fallen on the father of our home. It was the little moment of repose before the long flight of the spirit. He awakened. The twilight stars were coming, but the room was darkened to keep it cooler. Before the lamps could be lighted, we turned him a little. I put my face down by his and he nestled his close in a movement like an affectionate caress--and the last sands of

Chapter Two

time slipped quickly out. The glass stands unturned, although this is not all. Once that day when I was in the hall, he had called out with a sudden vigorous, vibrant tone, 'My Daughter!" and clung to my hand and kissed my face.

I knew that somewhere on the road en route to Burlington was my mother. Slowly the night wore on, the household sounds were stilled. Not a sound soothed to ear. I went down into the old garden where my father had romped in childhood. I paused at the well whose waters were sweet to him to the last. The stars lay untwinkling against the sky; the hot, sandy soil steamed in the night air; not a leaf moved. Then far away I heard the sweet, faint song of the river, gleaming in the starlight; across the street in the old burying ground slept the only ones of his kindred in the old town. I slipped back into the dim old parlor and leaned against a chair.

In this room my father and mother were married forty-eight years before. In the room above lay the silent form of that father alone...In the morning we crossed the river and met mother. Sweet and smiling she came down the steps. In her hand was a wilted little bouquet of garden blossoms sent by some of the children to Grandpa, and she carried also some fruit she had selected from the home place for the sick man. 'Ah!" she cried, 'I know that Alex is better or you would not both be here.' Dear little mother--yes, he *was* resting.

Just as the sun was setting, flooding the river with bright beams of pink and crimson, the ferryboat with the funeral party crossed to the Iowa side of the river bearing the body of my father over the beloved waters for the last time. More than seventy years before he had crossed it for the first time, nestling close in his mother's arms, as heartsick and desolate she had crossed on the ice coming from Missouri. Strange are the ways of fate."[36]

Thus, these are the memories I choose to carry. Not the slips and slants which adhere to us and bear record of our follies through ill human behavior. I look always to the desire and intention that lay within. Let me speak from my heart. Truly, what is the measure of a man, or woman? What constitutes their worth? Shall we recall all of their failings? No. That is not the way the Savior has taught us. Instead we are to look into the hearts of those who surround us and we seek to embrace that love which is the embodiment of our Savior. We take that love and spread it as though it were a blanket.

At length only good can come of this kind of love, evolving with every good turn until any residue of darkness has fled. As my great-grandfather lay examining his final hours upon this earth, yearning for the heart that was one with his, it probably did not matter what heated words had passed between him and Brigham Young. Such passing verbiage would be rectified as he reunited with his family on the other side. What defined the man was his character, his honesty and good intentions, his integrity and his devout love for family and the Savior.

No matter how ugly our past was at times, it is over.. We can't help that now. But how I process it determines what it is now and what it will become. That is the importance of knowing as much as we can about our past, the good and the bad. No matter what it is we must examine it. Nothing should be left unaccounted for that might jump up and hit us in the face in the future. What we do not manage the adversary will use to his own advantage. So we must look at these things, come to peace with them, forgive, and let go. Then we must

Chapter Two

move on, releasing any ill feelings from the bad and magnifying the good as we progress onward. That is what I am doing in my generation, just as my grandmother Emma impressed upon me while I stood on her home ground in Nauvoo, "Just go and do."

It is most important that we release issues of the past to allow room to focus on what we have before us today. We cannot move forward while second-guessing the past else we would stumble continually.

Alexander Hale Smith Family
Front row from left: Vida, Alexander, Elizabeth (Lizzie), Don Alvin. Back Row: Emma Belle, Fred, Joseph, Coral, and Arthur (my grandfather). Ina was in Australia when this picture was taken. Eva Grace died in 1893.
From family collection.

Hills & Valleys

Mom's Parents:

Arthur Marion Smith

Minerva (Minnie) Catherine Smith

Chapter Three

Peace is seldom found by an anxious heart.

—*Kimberly Jo Smith*

My grandfather, Arthur Marion Smith, was the eighth child born to Alexander and Elizabeth Kendall Smith on February 8, 1880 in Halifax County, Missouri. He came into this life in his parents' bedroom, which also served as the town post office. His mother, Lizzie, was the Post Mistress in Andover. Years later, upon writing of his birth, Arthur could not resist the ever present Smith with:

"Of course I don't remember much...but I am sure I was there. I have full confidence in my mother...she told me a lot about the occasion." He wrote, claiming also that due to the location of his arrival, he was the only one he knew of that came by special delivery. [1]

Arthur felt strongly about his heritage, having been made aware from an early age of his history and the patriotism which ran deeply in many of his ancestors.

"Where did I come from? Well, I just don't remember that either, but I do know that while I may not have had anything to do with the selecting of the time, place, or my parents, I am grateful for the powers that may have determined these things for I have long been proud of my country, state, and parentage."[2]

Alexander and Elizabeth's existence in Northern Missouri was meager. But living in a remote rural area in those days afforded young Arthur many valuable lessons on life and spiritual matters. He experienced from a young age the blessings which come of following the laws of God and living a moral life. The love he bore his father was deep, though he sorrowed that the loving, gentle patriarch of the home was often away in service of the Lord.

"I was only a year old when my parents moved to Independence, Missouri. We lived on South Spring Street, the first house on the right hand side of the street, just off of Lexington Street. My father was active in the ministry of the Reorganized Church of Jesus Christ of Latter day Saints, and thus was away from home most of the time. As a child I remember him only on special occasions. One such time was when he returned home, bringing with him the first gift I can remember; at this time he took me up on his knee and rocked me to sleep singing, *From Greenland's Icy Mountain* and the song has been dear to me ever since."[3]

Arthur's childhood years would expose him to the truthfulness of the power of God and the trial of persecution. He would cut his teeth upon many experiences which passed before him. Not exactly sure about the timing of his conversion, Arthur wrote that it was more of an absorption, because of the family he had been born into and church work which surrounded it. He received a witness to the healing power of priesthood at the tender age of five when a malady had struck their community.

Arthur, his brother Joseph, and baby sister Coral had fallen desperately ill. The doctor had given up all hope for

Chapter Three

Coral, telling Lizzie that she should prepare to let her daughter go, but the mother would have none of it. She knew that her daughter should live and she waited desperately for her husband who had been sent for. Arthur had heard the conversation between doctor and mother from his room.

"No!" Lizzie cried, "I will not lay her down!" Arthur could see from his position, the tall figure of the doctor, who had been trying to convince Lizzie to lay the baby down for she had died. "I will not let her go, she must not go!" To which the doctor silently picked up his hat and satchel, leaving the humble farm house.

Arthur then heard the cries of his sorrowful mother, "Alex, Oh Alex, why don't you come?" Within seconds Alexander rushed through the door with Joseph Luff and they immediately laid hands upon the babe's head to give her a priesthood blessing. Arthur would gain a solid testimony of healing that night. "...Scarcely had they ceased the prayer that I heard her draw a quivering breath, and my mother's cry of joy." Alexander then went to the bedside of Arthur who looked into the loving face of his father saying, "If you do the same for me, I know I will be alright." The next day Arthur was up and playing about the house. Arthur would recall the event of his sister's healing as the first evidence he knew of a heavenly Father whose mercy and kindness was ever present.

"It was stamped upon my memory, and through the long years, and they have been many, through the trials and troubles of a long life, the memory of that night remains an undimmed picture which has held me up at times when I was under burdens hard to bear and I found it difficult to keep my faith, when it seemed the easier way was to follow the suggestion given to Job by his wife, 'doth thy still retain thy integrity? Curse God and die.' "[4]

It is well worth mention here, that Coral would grow up to marry and have children and many grandchildren, one of whom is my dear friend and cousin, Gracia Jones, who was the first descendant to join and remain in the Church in 1956.

As always in the case of great spiritual experiences, the adversary is never far behind with his stumbling blocks of darkness and hate. One year after Arthur received such a powerful witness of God's healing power, he found himself under the attack of prejudice on the school playground. He was but six years old and had looked forward to the experience of school with great anticipation but on one occasion an older boy approached him roughly, calling him a Mormon.

"Now I may have heard of this name before, but I had not registered it with anything of a disgraceful nature. Yet, I recognized in the manner of which the word was spoken, that it carried with it an intent to insult. When he repeated it the second time I resented it with all of my might. Just what the outcome would have been I do not know, for there were older ones who stopped us. But I do know that I went home with a bloody nose and a broken heart."[5]

Six year old Arthur ran home to his father in an attempt to find out what a Mormon was. He does not detail exactly what his father told him, but it is clear from the discussion and later perceptions he would grow with, that the image was not favorable.

Chapter Three

"It was then I learned the story of the Book of Mormon, and the stigma of shame that had been placed upon it and the task that had fallen upon the children of Joseph Smith, to free his name from the stain of Polygamy. From that day on I have always resented being called a Mormon."[6]

Thus at the tender age of six, the radiating core of prejudice and bitterness had taken root in a tender heart. A young mind that did not even know the extent of its history had already programmed itself against a people it knew nothing about. Not too long after the playground experience, Alexander and his family moved back to Lamoni, Iowa. When Arthur was eight years old he attended a prayer and testimony meeting at the Old Brick Church where he experienced something which was so moving he was baptized the same day.

"As I sat by my father, a man in a buckskin coat came and sat beside us and with him was an Indian, also wearing a buckskin coat. After a few had spoken a man stood up in the northeast corner of the room and began speaking in tongues. Now I was watching the Indian, fascinated by his dress and the evident fact that he was a real Indian. Suddenly he was leaning forward in his seat and listening very intently. The interpretation to the tongue was given by another brother sitting on the south side of the room. I do not recall a single word which was said but the full significance of the whole thing was made manifest to me after the meeting was over. I saw this Indian go up and speak to the man who had spoken in tongue, but the man did not understand a word the Indian said. Then the Indian spoke in English, stating that the language used in the tongue was the same as the Indian's and the interpretation was correct but he could not understand why the man who had spoken it, was now unable to understand it."[7]

Discovery and Loss

Arthur describes his youth as relatively happy. He and his siblings were raised to respect the values and ethics of hard, good and honest work. Earning a living by the sweat of the brow was something of merit. The rural expanse of Iowa beckoned him to many hours of frolic and adventure. He was, after all, his father's son.

Throughout those years he would be exposed to discussions in passing concerning their past history and the early restoration work. Of his heritage, he had a mixed recipe of humility, goodness, pride and frustration which would turn out a cake that would rise or fall depending upon the climate of discussion.

In speaking of his parents, it is clear that Arthur's heart holds an endearing love for Nauvoo and its history, yet he seemed to harbor an image of desolation and darkness as well.

"...Among the wreckage and the ruin of that once beautiful city, my mother and father grew to maturity, tutored and schooled by the thrice told tales, and legends of a glorious day that had ended in heartbreak and sorrow...Mother was an able defender of the Gospel, having been raised in Nauvoo and knowing of the stirring times within that city..."[8]

Arthur was also educated upon church history by those who often called upon his parents.

Chapter Three

"Much of my education concerning the Church was the result of tales to which I listened with eagerness although my understanding of these historical facts was that of a child."[10]

When he was fourteen years old, Arthur began working for a man by the name of Charles A. Wicks. It was a hard job hoeing in the Iowa cornfields during intense summer heat. One day as they sat under an apple tree enjoying the ease of the shade and a fulfilling lunch, Charles joined them and began to talk about Church history. Arthur knew very little at that age beyond the most basic tenets; the first vision, organization and the persecution which followed. Mr. Wicks began to relate to the boys that many mistakes had been made early in the restoration work and he gave them a pamphlet called the *Book of Commandments*, which told the story of the destruction of the printing press in 1833 in Independence, Missouri. Arthur took the pamphlet to his father for he was disturbed by what the man had said.

On a warm summer evening, Alexander began to explain to his son about the destruction of the printing press which was in the process of publishing the laws given to the Church by revelation. As pages were being strewn into the streets a man gathered as many pages as he could and hid them. There are several stories which lay claim to gathering the pages in the street when the press was destroyed. Mary Elizabeth Rollins Lightner in her journal talks of how she and her sister gathered an armful of pages and quickly ran away with some of the mob pursuing them.[11] Alexander expressed to Arthur that a man had gathered the pages. It could be that many were involved with gathering pages, or maybe not. I only know that it is an example of how stories evolve and

Hills & Valleys

become inaccurate at times in the retelling. I wondered as I researched my family history how many times something like that happened. In our youth, we as individuals tend to believe things we are told by family without question. It is a normal response. But it is vital that at some point in our lives we search for the truth ourselves because we may absorb it with a different perspective, finding that error or misunderstanding has painted a distorted view of what should be a balanced landscape.

As Arthur edged toward adulthood, he began to question more and more what he viewed as inaccuracies. When he did inquire of those in authority, he was often disappointed and suspect of the evasion of certain questions.

"I started to attend Sunday School under the tutelage of Church historian Heman C. Smith but I did not learn much here; I was asking too many questions and not always satisfied with the answers. I was not in this class long before I was 'honored' with a class of my own boys to teach. I enjoyed this until I learned I had been given this group to get me away from the history class where I and another boy were asking too many questions, which embarrassed the historian."[12]

Arthur was so discouraged by what he had experienced that he quit attending church altogether, but his faith was still intact and he was waiting for a church to emerge which did not include the offices which he felt were not a part of the New Testament church.

One of the things which bothered him in his early twenties was the question of presidency in the organization of the Church. He could find no proof to support it in the Bible, only the Doctrine & Covenants.

As the 18th century waned into memory, Arthur began to learn the art of book bindery, while working at The Herald Publishing House, which was owned and operated by the Reorganized Church. He became very accomplished at his newly acquired talent, building for himself a small living. On June 15, 1904, Arthur married Estella Almira Danielson, a beautiful woman who was very well loved in Lamoni. The couple lived there until 1908, bringing into this world two sons, Verl and Karl. In 1909, Arthur and his little family moved to Colorado to try homesteading. During these early years of marriage Arthur seems to have pulled away from religion as far as being an active participant in any organization.

The years in Yuma, Colorado were harsh for Arthur, Estella and their children. During their first year in Yuma, Arthur's father Alexander passed away. The new homesteader had staked his claim in the vast Colorado wilderness, building a crude sod house to offer shelter against unforgiving winters. The growing seasons there were not very long and the stress of meager living in small quarters probably worsened the consumption that Estella developed. It was during their time in Yuma that Estella gave birth to two more sons, Alexander, and Kenneth, with her husband and possibly a neighbor being her only attendants.[13]

In 1914 Arthur decided to give up the idea of homesteading, moving his family to Kansas City, where he procured work as a street car conductor. The pay was sufficient for their needs and for the first time in years they were not struggling so hard to survive. However, because of

Estella's failing health it was decided that she should go to California to visit relatives and recover. Young Kenneth and his baby sister Elizabeth, who had been born in 1914, accompanied their mother. On March 18, 1916, shortly after she returned from California, Estella gave birth to Arthur Granger Smith. I must interject here, this same Arthur just passed away as I have been writing this narrative on March 22, 2012, at the age of ninety seven, the last of my father's brothers to leave this world.

Estella's health, already diminished by consumption, was further compromised after Arthur's birth and she lived but three months, passing from this life on June 23, 1916. It was a severe loss for all who knew and loved her. The Lamoni newspaper honored her devotedly.

"The heart of the whole world feels the shadow when the mother of little children falls into last sleep. It seems like this loss lies outside the accepted verdict that all must die....a tragedy, a mistake of destiny."[14]

There are no passages in Arthur's memoirs which express the depth of his loss. Such sentiments I have retrieved from their children and the report is one of a glowing affection between mother and father, which settled into a dark loneliness that could only be relieved by moving forward. Arthur's son Kenneth took the loss incredibly hard. "The blow was terrific and made a deep and abiding mark upon my life."[15] But he goes on to say that through this experience his mind was opened to the workings of the Lord.

One evening as Kenneth lay in bed, his pillow drenched from ceaseless tears, his father comforted him.

Chapter Three

"There came to me in the darkness one with the gentle touch of a mother, and the low sweet voice of a father."[16] Arthur explained to his son that, "mother was surely in paradise and would gain the highest glory God had for man. That story and the inflection of that voice has never left me."[17]

After Estella's death, Arthur and four of the children moved in with his mother, Lizzie in Lamoni. The two younger children, Elizabeth and Arthur, stayed with their Grandma Danielson, also in Lamoni. Arthur would remain in Lamoni until the death of his mother on May 7, 1919, after which he moved with his family to Des Moines, Iowa and began working once again in book binding.

A New Life

During his time in Des Moines Arthur met Minerva Catherine Smith, who would become my grandmother. Minerva, or Minnie as she was called, was from a completely different line of Smiths who hailed from Charlestown, Indiana. Fourteen years younger than Arthur, Minnie would become his dear companion, wife, and mother to his six children as well as bearing five of her own. They were married May 20, 1921. According to one of my aunts, Grandma's family was Presbyterian and when she and two others sisters joined the Reorganized Church in Des Moines they were shunned by their family.

By 1924, Arthur and Minnie were living in Minneapolis, Minnesota and had added a new daughter, Georgia, to their family. Arthur had taken extension classes in order to teach the art of book binding in the vocational high school there. Two more daughters arrived; Lorraine in 1924, and Myrl in 1925. The burgeoning family attended the Reorganized Church in Minneapolis until the Church conference of 1925.

Frederick Madison Smith had been presiding as leader of the Reorganization since his father, Joseph's death in 1914. At the conference of 1925 there was an upheaval of enormous proportion as a result of Frederick incorporating Supreme Directional Control. By instilling this principle, all power would rest within the presidency. There was a split immediately after it was introduced in 1924 to the Joint Council. By 1925 the controversy had spilled over into the membership and when the resolution passed, hundreds of members, including Arthur and Minnie, left the Reorganization. Arthur had befriended Daniel McGregor, a former missionary of the Reorganized Church who had become affiliated with The Church of Christ Temple Lot.[18]

The Church of Christ Temple Lot's headquarters sit upon the plot of land in Independence where Joseph laid the cornerstone designating where the temple would one day be built. It was organized in 1862 by a man name Granville Hedrick, indicating the origin of the name Hedrickite.

When I was growing up, The Temple Lot Church taught that Joseph Smith Jr. was a fallen prophet after 1832, so anything beyond that date is not accepted by them as divine revelation. They do not believe in a high priesthood, nor do they endorse prophet or first presidency offices. Instead, they run their organization as a council of twelve apostles. Aside from their claim that they have remained the most true to the original foundational teachings of the Restoration, they also feel it is their duty to preserve the temple lot until the Savior

Chapter Three

returns or so orders the temple to be built. In respect to the latter, The Temple Lot Church has done a remarkable service.

There is an interesting story that my Grandfather Arthur told years ago. He had not been in the Church for too long when it was announced that the time had come to build the temple. Arthur was on the building committee and noted that hardly a day's work would pass before an argument of some proportion broke out among the committee members about how this or that should be done. At length they managed to pour the footing and build the foundational walls in the area that would be the basement. One day the men were on the grounds arguing furiously about something. One of the men heard a commotion behind them and as he turned, beheld the foundation walls crumble. He said he thought he saw a dark movement pass over it just as he turned. Arthur said that the men were so shaken that the hole was filled in and the project abandoned.

On July 1, 1926, Arthur transferred his membership into the Temple Lot Church. Finally he felt as if he could put his concerns about errors in church organization to rest. Between 1926 and 1927 he was called to the offices of Elder and Apostle. Eventually, church assignments required them to move to Sioux Falls, South Dakota, where the family would be stationed as Arthur and his friend Archie Bell covered their missionary responsibilities throughout Montana, North and South Dakota, and Western Canada. In 1930, the family moved to Independence, Missouri where Arthur could devote full time to church work. There, along with his other callings he became Secretary of Church affairs. He also became assistant editor to the Church publication, *Zion's Advocate*. While fulfilling these new assignments, Arthur was also called to be a missionary for Missouri, Kansas, and Nebraska. Somewhere in the midst of all of his appointments they managed to have yet another daughter in 1929, named Barbara.[19]

In 1933, Arthur was assigned to the states of Missouri, Oklahoma, Tennessee, North and South Carolina, Arkansas, Louisiana, Alabama, Florida, and Georgia. Of the work he was assigned to in the Temple Lot Church, Arthur valued missionary responsibility above anything else. He always left on foot for his missions with no money, or plan; just a direction he knew he should go. His son Kenneth loved hearing about his father's journeys.

"He told a very interesting experience about hitchhiking down through the flooded area of the Ohio River Valley states, having just enough change in his pocket to pay for his ferry boat way across the wide river into town. In determination he approached the loafers on the town square and preached to them. They took up a collection which was enough for his next meal."[20]

My father, Joseph Fredrick Smith, Arthur and Minnie's last child, was born January 3, 1935. By the time my father was born, the family had moved onto some land in Ava, Missouri, which belonged to dad's half-brother, Alexander. My grandmother's life became very hard, for her husband was often gone and she lived nine miles or more from any town deep in the rural Ozark Mountains. Their move to the Ozarks rode upon the sorrows of the depression. Though their living conditions were not the best, they did have what they needed to endure the hard times. They raised pigs and Jersey cows, selling the milk to make ends meet. Their existence was inadequate at best, not having electricity in the home until my father was in his teenage years.[21]

In 1942, there crept into The Church of Christ Temple Lot a period of maladministration concerning the financial affairs of the Lord's Storehouse. As secretary, it fell to Arthur to try and repair the damage which had been done and rebuild confidence within the organization, but conditions only worsened. In 1943, for the first time since 1927, Arthur was absent from General Conference. Contention within church business administrative departments and rebellion among council members had pushed him to his limits. He gave his resignation to the 1943 conference and announced he would not be able to do any missionary work for the next year.[22]

Arthur was kept on the council on inactive status. He took a job in the Detroit auto industry but soon after signed up to help in constructing the Alaskan Highway. It was hard work but for Arthur it was an answer to prayer. He was thrust into the wilds of Alaska, free from the constraints of organizational turmoil. Anytime he was in the woods or mountains he was at home. During this time, while Arthur soothed away his ministerial concerns in nature, world conditions were brewing. More and more, war seemed imminent. When his time in Alaska ended in 1945, he headed home and labored as he could, for the war overseas had limited ability to travel and work. But soon he was assigned more work in the missionary field. For the next twenty years Arthur would bask in his love of missionary work.

Every calling became a part of Arthur's soul; he especially loved the missions he served in Wales. But the satisfaction he felt as he served his God was overshadowed continually by the administrative duties which seemed to hold him captive. Part of those duties entailed solving disputes and lawsuits which still permeated the membership as well as some of the leaders. He grew tired of finger-pointing over trivial matters, quarrels and accusations of misconduct, some of which had been pointed in his direction. According to his daughter Georgia, Arthur said near the end of his life that he felt like he had wasted most of his time and that if he had it to do over again he would join the LDS Church because at least they were an honest people.

On March 6, 1965, Arthur walked into his little cabin on the hill in Ava, Missouri. He had been home for just a few days, having returned from a mission. We were there at the time and I was three years old. Mom was in the kitchen helping prepare the evening meal when someone alerted Grandpa Arthur that his pigs had broken free from the fence. He hurriedly went outside and rounded them up, securing the place where they had escaped.

When he came back in, he called to my mother, asking where Grandma was and if there was any coffee on the stove. As she went to pour him a cup he sat down in his chair in front of the fireplace he had built years before. When mom came in to give him his cup of coffee, she saw that he had gone to that peaceful sleep, head lowered as if he had just been napping, home with his kin from long ago where finally he could see the order of things and worry no more. He was eighty five when he died.

As Apostle, Secretary, and Elder of the Temple Lot Church, my grandfather served over twenty seven missions between 1926 and 1965. Though he differed in various

Chapter Three

doctrinal measures with his cousins in the Reorganization and LDS Churches, holding his own valiantly in a debate when challenged, it is very clear through his writings that he held a love and respect for his kin, acknowledging that in their own ways the paths they had chosen held great purposes. He wrote that he joined the Temple Lot Church for personal reasons.

"I joined the Temple Lot Church for personal reasons in spite of the ties of kinship that still draw me toward another group of restoration. In this I do no violence to the memory of my father whom I remember as a courageous man, unafraid to stand boldly for that which he believed was right regardless of what the consequences to himself might be; neither does it discredit those of my family relations who are still carrying on in other factions or divisions of the restoration, in their efforts to continue to build in the organization of their father's."[23]

Though he may have formed negative opinions when he was young, I have yet to find in all of Arthur's journals and church publications any evidence where he railed bitterly against the LDS church or Brigham Young. He was very clear and adamant about points of doctrinal differences and where he felt the Temple Lot Church was right on these issues, but it was all very academic. It is apparent he did not have a condemning spirit. My mother said for all the years she knew him that he was a very kind man, extremely loving, devoted to his wife, and tirelessly faithful in his beliefs. It is evident that there was a degree of antagonism and some bitterness throughout Alexander's and Arthur's lives concerning the differences of the churches but not to the degree of hatred that I was witness to in my generation. It has only been recently while writing the account of my family that I have discovered that the element of hatred toward The LDS Church was introduced by my grandmother, Arthur's second wife, Minnie.

As fair as Arthur was in his summation of free agency, the chain of antagonism within the children he had with Minnie festered in bitter retribution against those who were not members of their church. Something shifted in my father's generation and the thrice-told tales Arthur spoke of hearing in his youth became legend. Hardly resembling their infancy, some of these tales evolved into a darkness which would threaten what little light remained.

Grandma's childhood was very hard and there was much abuse in the home at the hands of an alcoholic father. It hardened her heart in many ways. She would relay to my mother shortly before she died that she had always struggled with being jealous, spiteful and bitter against things or people whom she felt were in the wrong, especially concerning church membership. Her lineage also reflects the influence of the Amish, who are known for shunning their own members who fall away and isolating themselves from the world. Although I knew Grandma Smith to be a loving soul, it was those dark elements she labored with which influenced her own children against The LDS Church at an elevated level. The mix was like fragile glass when it receives too much heat, shattering and sending cutting shards everywhere.

When grandpa died, it made the situation even more volatile, for it was his presence that brought calm and stability when opinions and sharp tongues got out of hand. The scale had been tipped and it would take a pure heart to bring balance once again, but at a great price.

Chapter Three

Arthur Marion Smith

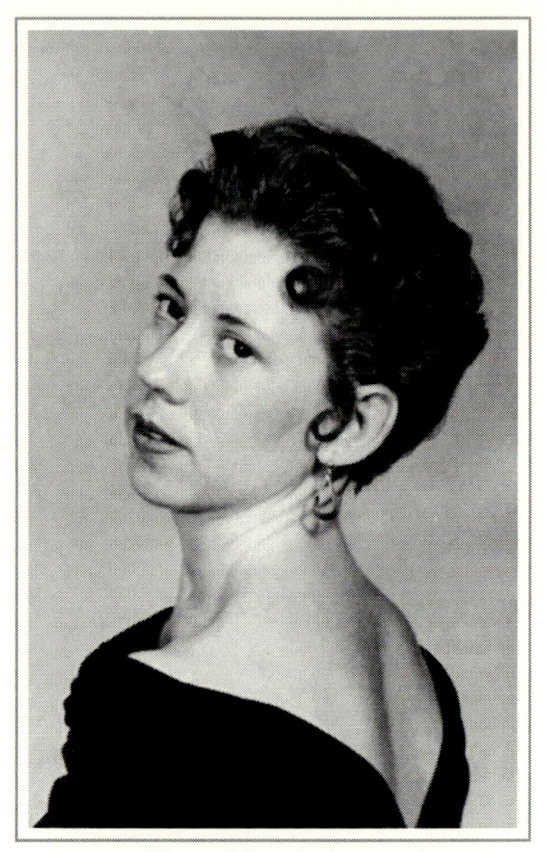

My Mother, Mary Sue Roberts Smith

Arthur and Minnie Smith wedding picture

Chapter Three

Georgia 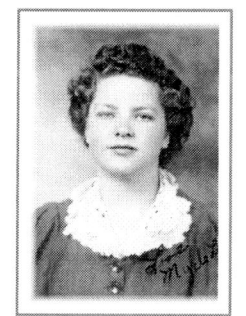 *Lorraine*  *Myrl*

Barbara  *Joseph*
(My Father)

Chapter Four

Storytelling

We all have influences from both parents. Therefore I could not give an accurate account of my heritage without examining what my maternal ancestors were doing in the 19th century; after all, they make up half of my existence! That part of my heritage is filled with stories so colorful it boggles the mind! It is a tale mixed with mountain adventure, moonshine, religious fervor and good folks. My mother's side of the family was made up of kin who were righteous to the bone, good honest people who would do anything in the world for those in need. Then there were those who were outright gun- totin' hillbillies who loved you if you were their friend, but would just as soon shoot you if they thought you were their enemy!

As in every family, there is a mix of good Christian virtue and those who struggle to walk a straight path, but when you pair those qualities with mountain life it flies in all kinds of directions! Honestly, when I look at the history of both sides of my family and view what has come to pass in four generations, I am amazed that any of my family survived with their sanity intact.

Over Hill and Holler

My mother's maiden name was Roberts and they hailed from East Tennessee, where the mountains are both amazing and breathtaking. Visitors who travel there every year are walking upon the ground my ancestors settled. My 6th great grandmother, Martha Huskey Ogle, was one of the first settlers of what is now Gatlinburg. The generations following her would spread into mountain and valley lands, carving out their lives and establishing societies in Pigeon Forge, Cades Cove, Townsend, Sevierville and Maryville, where I was born.

It has been indicated through family that our Roberts line came over from Wales, or possibly Scotland, in the early 17th century. My third great-grandfather, Benjamin Roberts, was born in 1767 in Pennsylvania, then migrated into Virginia, North Carolina, and then by 1820, Sevier County Tennessee.[1] Several of this family line fought in the Revolutionary War in battles such as Kings Mountain and Bunker Hill. My grandfather Roberts' third and fourth maternal great grandfathers, William and Moses McCarter rode alongside the Swamp Fox, Frances Marion, a soldier who was portrayed as The Ghost in Mel Gibson's movie *The Patriot*.[2]

While one generation fought for a united states, two generations down were divided on whether or not to destroy the Union with civil war. Some of my ancestors fought for the South, while others, like my second great-grandfather John Roberts, signed up with the 9th Tennessee Cavalry for the Union.[3] His desires were such that he did not want to see the Union his grandfathers fought for torn asunder. John would later relate to his grandchildren how the Confederate soldiers and their kin would hide in the mountains and shoot any Union soldiers who rode through to visit their own families. Whenever he was on leave, John would stop near the mountain en route to his home and dress as a woman so that his life would be spared.[4] John's grandson, Ray, was my pappaw, southern slang for grandpa.

Ray Cates Roberts, or Pappaw Roberts, was an amazing giant of a man standing over six feet tall with tan skin from his Cherokee roots. He was deeply spiritual and had the gift of visions and dreams, which he shared often with his children, acknowledging the hand of God in their lives. These experiences were perceived by Pappaw as personal spiritual direction, serving to reinforce the devotion and dedication to the Lord that he had rendered most of his life.

Mountain preaching was different than what can be heard today. It was a very direct "cut to the bone" sort of talk that put the fear of God in the listener. It instilled in my people knowledge of right and wrong and the consequences of hell which followed if you were on the wrong path. Though many adhered, there were those who, even though they were good folks, walked on the wild side.

I love a good story. And I have heard many about these mountain people, some I have to tell here. Even though it is hard for me to comprehend some of the antics that went on, it was their way of life. My pappaw had a sister named Jean and she lived close to her sister-in-law Della. These two women married brothers, who were very close and got on well. The women, however, couldn't stand each other. The two families lived in mountains close to where Dollywood is today and they had a particular hankerin' for moonshine. It was common in that day for mountain folks to make their own remedies for ill health and they used to make rock candy and dip it in moonshine for colds. Aunt Jean knew that Pappaw Roberts was well-known and loved as a fine man throughout the mountain and that he was good friends with the local sheriff.

One day she told her husband to tell the sheriff that Ray Roberts' sister-in-law needed some medicine. Uncle Ben carried the message to the sheriff, who went back into a big store room filled with jars of confiscated moonshine. He took one off of the shelf saying "This is from a good batch," He got the sign-out sheet to follow procedure when checking anything out of the office. Uncle Ben knew that the shine was not for any medicine because Aunt Jean also asked him to get some 7up on the way back to mix for a drink.

Aunt Della never missed an opportunity to get Aunt Jean into trouble and as much as she did not like her sister-in-law, she paid frequent visits just to snoop and see if she had any corn liquor in the house. It was no surprise to Aunt Jean that following one of Aunt Della's visits, the law would be on her steps saying there had been reports of moonshine on the premises.

Sure enough, one day Aunt Della set the law onto Aunt Jean, saying she had moonshine in the house. In those days, if one drop was found in the house the occupants were arrested. When the cops knocked on the door, Aunt Jean ran and grabbed her last two jars of moonshine and tossed them into the Warm Morning stove. When she opened the front door the cops were just about to question her when, BOOM! The moonshine exploded, tossing the heater several feet into the air. Needless to say, the evidence was gone so they had nothing to hold her on! There was never a dull moment in the mountains.[5]

Chapter Four

Pappaw Roberts was a good, religious man but in his young adult days he wasn't beyond taking a nip or two just for leisure. One day he was with some of his friends and they ran out of moonshine. They knew where they could procure more way up the mountain. The mountain road was narrow and the old car took up most of the road, sputtering up the way until they reached a steep incline where the embankment on the right side was high. All of a sudden a white horse jumped over the embankment and onto the road. The embankment was so high that a horse shouldn't have been able to clear it. The man on the horse was white as well, and Pappaw said it was almost as if you could see through both horse and man. The car came to a dead stop for just a few moments. The three occupants sat frozen in amazement, then silently but hurriedly they began to go backward until they found a place to back in and turn around. No one said a word until they got down the mountain. Then they began verifying if they all had seen the same thing.

Aside from being a religious man, Pappaw, like many other mountain folk, was superstitious. He took the vision as a warning and that was the last time he touched a drop of the drink. Pappaw was called the peacemaker because there were certain members of the family that could not get along. Everyone loved and revered him. On March 14, 1933 he married Bessie Kate Noland.

The Noland Clan

Our Nolands come from an ancient family that reaches far back to the U'ineills and ruling clans of Northwest Ireland. The Nolands came to America in the 1600's, making their home in the Carolinas and then Tennessee.[6] During the Revolutionary War, some of my Noland ancestors served under George Washington. General Gilbert du Motier, marquis de Lafayette, who played a pivotal role in France's involvement in turning the tide of the Revolutionary War in favor of the Continental Army, was highly regarded for his service and it is believed that my ancestor Peter Lafayette Noland was named after the French General. Peter's grandfather, Hugh Rogers, married George Washington's niece, knitting the family tightly into the fabric of the War of Independence.[7]

The Nolands owned a ferry on the Potomac by which they built a sizeable mansion called The Noland House. George Washington dined there and the property was used as a military depository during the Revolutionary War. This mansion is still standing today and is one of the oldest Colonial buildings in the historic regions of Virginia.[8] As the war came to an end, the Nolands used the land grants they had received for service to procure land in Fines Creek, Haywood County, North Carolina. It would take a false accusation and running from the law to get them into Tennessee.

Over the Mountain

In 1881, my great-great-grandfather Peter Lafayette Noland was accused by a woman of rape. The trial transcripts clearly show he was a man well thought of, while the accuser had some of her close family testify against her dependability as an honest person. Peter endured the trial, assured that justice would clear his name, but he was found guilty and sentenced to hang. He filed for an appeal and won based on

Chapter Four

evidence that there was fraud, perjury and tainting of the jury. But in the court of appeals he was denied a new trial and his previous sentence was commanded to be carried through as ordered.[9]

Knowing he was innocent and about to be hanged, Peter and his wife concocted a plan to get him out. One day when she came to visit, she traded clothes with him. When it was time to leave, the jailor opened the door and Peter slipped out posing as his own wife. He hastened to a prearranged destination where a horse was waiting for him and by the time their ploy was discovered he was long gone. They released his wife and she went immediately to her children, who were packed and waiting. They crossed over the mountains into Sevierville, Tennessee.[10]

It was later proved that Peter had been framed and his name was cleared but by then they had no inclination to go back. Had he remained in North Carolina he would have hanged before his innocence had been proven. Thus, they stayed in Tennessee and on October 5, 1906, Peter's son, Mark Leander Noland married my great-grandmother, Laura 'Noda' Hickam. Mark, though a good man, was hard and very stern. Noda, was very kind and soft spoken, well- loved by all who knew her.

Grandma Noda hardly ever came down the mountain, but one day in the spring of 1963, when she was 79, Noda's daughter and son-in-law talked her into riding in their old Chevy truck down the narrow mountain road to go to the grocery store. They met another car along the way and Noda's son-in-law edged too far over to the side of the dirt road causing the ground to give way and the car tumbled down the side of the mountain. As it fell, the door by Noda swung open casting her part way out, then as the Chevy rolled, the door slammed at her waist, killing her instantly. Her husband was never the same after her death. They had been married fifty seven years and had ten children, three of whom died in infancy.[11] Their daughter Bessie Kate Noland was my Mammaw.

    My mother has for many years believed that Mammaw was abused during her childhood due to the history of behavioral issues throughout her life, manifesting in severe manic tendencies as she grew older. But no one is sure who committed the abuse. My mother told me that there also seemed to be a manic disorder which ran through some of the Noland family. If there was abuse, it doesn't appear that Mammaw's parents were the cause, but throughout her childhood she was surrounded by men who were rough, heavy drinkers and her father was a prison guard who at times brought prisoners home to stay all night. By the time she was an adult, Mammaw was prone to episodes of fits. Her nerves were a wreck and she would erupt in tears without warning. Pappaw never knew what to expect; one day he came home to find a for sale sign in the yard.

    But there was a side of Mammaw that was genuinely good and when that side was active she was fun to be around. She gave continuously to those in need and was very religious. She was constantly humming or singing spiritual songs. Still, whatever happened to her as a child destroyed any ability to have a real loving relationship with her husband and children, and they would feel the brunt of her illness.

Chapter Four

A People of Faith

Alongside the crazy stories from our past were the great ones. There were heroic stories of those who first settled the Smokey Mountains and the preachers who established churches throughout 'hill and holler.' Many of Pappaw's relatives were Baptist and Methodist preachers. His second great-uncle William Roberts was responsible for building the Roberts Methodist church in 1839 located in Sevierville where a portion of my Roberts ancestors are buried. From these great sermons echoing across the Smoky Mountain peaks came an understanding of Heavenly Father and knowledge of the Savior and His role in our lives. It was well-established that one should know and recognize the Holy Ghost, realizing the importance of always following the Spirit when prompted. People who learned the gospel in the mountains had a solid foundation which created in them a firm relationship with the Savior, one that was both deep and personal. Pappaw Roberts was such a man. He knew when the Lord spoke and he followed.

Though many of the churches in the mountains did not teach about tithing, Pappaw had a clear understanding of it by the time he had married and started his family. He knew that if he always paid his tithing that they would never want and though they were poor, they were never without the necessities of life. All of his life he searched and searched the scriptures, hungry for more. He once told my mother that he knew there was more out there and he was desirous to find it.

Approximately thirty miles south of the Smoky Mountains in East Tennessee, there is a small and lovely town called Maryville where my mother Mary Sue was born

Hills & Valleys

January 7, 1938. From the time that she was little, my mother was a good person with a sweet spirit and a pure heart. Always wanting to do good, she exhibited a natural, pure love for people and family, and an ache to have that love returned. She was especially close to her father and yearned to be close to her mother, which was hard given the immense mood swings of the latter. Because of the many demons that Mammaw struggled with from her past, one never knew when to expect an outburst of anger. When it happened, some or all of the children would get a beating. At times, the outburst would be unleashed through a belt, but most often with whatever she was holding when she came unglued, including wooden spoons and the flat of a butcher knife.

Mom was targeted more than her siblings. It was a vicious and confusing cycle for a child because Mammaw was the epitome of Christian virtue and charity, and that part of her was not fake. Then there was the dark side that came at any given moment that my mother lived in fear of. It was an environment which made it hard for a child to feel normal or relaxed. Only years later, when my Mammaw was dying at the age of eighty, would it be found that she had been schizophrenic for all of those years and nobody knew. Despite the abuse she suffered, mother carried within her a happy and jolly disposition. I am amazed at the capabilities of endurance that she harbored, for it was not only her mother that terrorized her, but one of her sisters as well.

There were three siblings in the Roberts' home. Ailene was the oldest and one that Mother loved dearly. Betty was a sister that Mother sought to love whole-heartedly yet found only another source of abuse. Some of Aunt Betty's children were terribly abusive to my siblings and me as we were growing up. We would learn from our cousin in later years that Aunt Betty had taught them to hate us, coaching them in their abuse. In her older years we would find that Betty suffered from the same manic disorders that ran in the family.

Max was the youngest and mother shared with him a camaraderie that knew no equal. Uncle Max said that in all of their lives they had only had one argument and mom said it was started by Aunt Betty! Uncle Max called mom Boots. No one knows why, mom doesn't even remember, but it was a nickname that caught on early and stuck. They did everything together, including getting into trouble. Mom had learned to walk on eggshells in fear of getting beaten by Mammaw, but still there seemed to be openings where she and Max could not resist a little adventure.

On one such occasion, when Max was eight and mom was twelve, he asked her to put him in the agitator, a term by which the earlier washing machines were called. Agitators had no lid and there was a roller device attached where the clothes were put through to wring all of the water out. Max wanted to see what would happen if he was inside when she turned it on so they filled it with water and she lifted him into the basin. When she pushed the plug into the outlet the agitator went wild, jostling Max to and fro in a frenzy, beating him half to pieces. He yelled at her to turn it off, but she had become excited and answered back to him that she didn't know how, and then it registered to her to just pull the plug. He got out quite shaken, but unharmed. No one ever found out about it, but there were many times that their ploys often placed them beneath the heavy hand of their mother.[13] To hear them talk of it today, one would think the adventures were worth the beatings. I have sat on Uncle Max and Aunt Pat's porch for over twenty-five years nearly every Thanksgiving and heard all of these stories told, followed by a chorus of laughter, and even as I laughed there was marvel at the fact they were even alive to tell such tales!

Mom can recall that from a very early age she felt flawed in some way. There was a sense that she was a failure. Why else would her mother carry so much hatred toward her? Though she was happy in many ways, there was always the question of why her mother did not love her. Why did her sister hate her? What did she need to do to change? This caused mom to have a very low self-esteem and little confidence.

I have come to believe that the adversary knows our missions in life. He knows what good we are capable of achieving. He does everything in his power to try and thwart progression by looking for open doors such as trauma, especially when we are children. Thus begins a downward spiral as we start believing thoughts that he whispers to our minds when we are suffering. Little sentences start filtering into our heads such as, "you're not good enough," or "you're dumb, no one will like what you do," or "why try, they will just laugh at you," and the worst..."nobody cares." Generally when small children start processing such thoughts it leads them to become bitter and angry. As they grow into adolescence that anger is intensified, especially if they do not seek help or have a strong spiritual environment. Drugs, alcohol, and promiscuity can become part of the downward spiral. For my mother, there was an element in her life that helped to prevent her from going in such directions; having a knowledge of Heavenly Father, the Savior and the Holy Ghost. It was not only having that knowledge that saved her, but understanding it and implementing it in her life.

Leaning on the Lord

Even though she struggled with a disorder, Mammaw Roberts' faith was very strong. But it was Pappaw Roberts who had the most spiritual influence upon my mother. His soft-spoken demeanor, devotion to the Lord and spiritual conscience impacted my mom so deeply that she yearned to follow the spirit in all things without question. She knew that no matter what anyone said, one should always go the way they are directed by the Holy Ghost because He is one who will never lie or mislead us.

Mom also saw Jesus Christ as more than the Son of God and the Savior, but as a personal friend. She knew that she could confide all things in Him and that He would never leave her side. It was an understanding of the atonement and how to lean upon it when in need. Because of such knowledge and understanding, Mom was able to endure the trials of her childhood. The things she encountered were never easy, they were just easier to handle because of her relationship with the Savior. It is much like how we feed our bodies. We know that if we prepare for a rigorous day by eating all of the food groups, edifying our bodies with proper nutrition, we will not become faint and can go the distance. But if we only eat junk, we will collapse and go no further. Mom had sustained her spirit with a balance of knowledge and understanding, embracing it fully. At a young age, she learned the value and meaning of the scripture

John 15:4, "abide in me and I in ye," for the Lord was always with her, so long as she was with Him. Wearing her faith as if it were a suit of armor, Mom struggled to maintain a balance of sanity as she passed from childhood to adulthood. As if the continual abuse of her mother and sister were not enough, she was struck by a car at the age of nine.

In 1947, Mammaw and Pappaw Roberts managed a small market on Walland Street in Maryville. On weekdays, Pappaw worked at the Alcoa Aluminum plant and Mammaw managed the store alone. One particular day while walking on the road beside the market, Mom stepped into the path of a car which clipped her at the waist and drug her several feet before she became detached, rolling toward the side of the road.

Adrenaline rushing out of fear that her mother would beat her for causing problems, Mom ran into the market and wedged herself between the brick chimney and an ice cream freezer. It was all anyone could do to pry her away so she could be taken to a nearby clinic, for there were no hospitals in the area. When they were finally able to get her to a doctor it was determined that there were no broken bones so she was sent home. Had she been examined at a hospital, they would have been able to discover some internal injuries which would cause problems later in her life. As for Mammaw, though the incident scared her, she showed no outward emotion of sympathy and no means of comfort. Mom was basically told that what she had done was stupid and she was not allowed to complain of any pain.

By the time Mom reached her eighteenth year, she was ready to get out on her own and establish a new life for herself. She still had very little self-esteem or confidence. Her deepest desires were to love and be loved and to please the Lord, but there was always a feeling of inadequacy that lay just beneath the surface. It was just enough to make her feel as if she could not amount to anything, emotions echoed by her mother's sharp and cutting sentiments which seemed always to confirm that the inadequacies were very real.

Just at the edge of the independence which comes with maturity and graduation, it was my mother's chance to step onto a new path of growth and learning. That path would begin with a young man who loved my mother with all of his heart.

Chapter Four

Bess Noland

Ray C. Roberts

The Roberts family from left: Max, Betty, Ray, Bess, Sue and Ailene.

104

My Father, Joseph Frederick Smith

Chapter Five

"A Loving Heart is the Truest Wisdom"

—*Charles Dickens*

With her traumatic childhood behind her and the world fresh and new ahead, Mom was anxious to plan the wedding which would bind her to a man she had fallen in love with. The engagement had taken place in May of 1956. It would seem that I should say that the intended groom was my father, but indeed it was not. His name was Jim Reveal, a navy man from Illinois who was stationed at the air force base just behind the Knoxville airport. They met through a mutual friend during Mom's senior year and fell in love. A kind man who nearly worshipped my mother, Jim was a Baptist minister and he and his father were in the process of building a nice new home for the newly-engaged couple.

Just months before the wedding, Jim was given leave to visit his parents in Rock Island, Illinois. While he was gone, Mom made an appointment for a physical in order to get the marriage license. During her visit to the doctor she received horrifying news. The damages from the car hitting her when she was a child were far more extensive than any of them could know. Her tailbone had been thrust forward into the birth canal. The doctor told her that she should not have children for it would be life-threatening. Mom was devastated for they both desired to have a family.

Chapter Five

The ride from the doctor's office proved to be one of darkness and pain. Everything seemed altered somehow. Here was the one chance Mom had for happiness and she felt it slipping away. Once again she felt as if she were a failure. Considering her options, Mom entered upon a decision that tore through her heart. She would break off the engagement, for she wanted Jim to be happy. She knew he wanted a family and she could not provide him with one. When he returned, she would break the news to him.

After arriving at her parents' home, she told her mother of her intentions. Mammaw was livid. She wanted this marriage badly. Jim was a Baptist minister who could give Mom a very good life and a fine home. Flying into a rage, she ordered Mom to go pack her things and prepare to spend some time with her sister in Independence, Missouri. Mom was numb with fear. She always did what Mammaw demanded or faced her heavy hand so without a word she went to her room and packed some belongings through silent tears. When Pappaw got home he was told only one thing by Mammaw, that they were driving Mom to Independence.

As they left, Mom told Aunt Betty to make sure that when Jim arrived from leave he was apprised of her whereabouts. She was to have him call Aunt Ailene's house so they could talk. That evening they left for Missouri. My mother was in a state of disbelief and felt completely powerless to do anything about the situation.

Jim arrived home from leave a few days after Mom left, expecting to have a happy reunion with his fiancée. Instead, he was greeted at the door by Betty, who told him my mother did not love him and never wanted to see him again. She also conveyed to him that he was not allowed to contact her. To have left for a brief period with the joys of life at his feet, only to arrive back and have such news dashed upon him would have been such a blow. He was so devastated that he asked immediately to be reassigned. By the time Mom learned what had happened, he was gone and she had no idea how to contact him. When she returned to Maryville, Tennessee she found that Mammaw had given all of her belongings in her room away.

Mom was horrified and filled with pain. After some time had passed, she called Jim's mother to explain what had happened. She longed to talk with him and clarify what had come to pass. But Jim's mother said that he had married someone else only months after he received the devastating news. At that point, Mom knew she could not interfere with Jim's life and she buried the sadness deep within her heart. It did not surprise her that he had married. He had once told her of how much he loved her and that if she ever broke up with him he would marry the first girl that came along.

With a heavy heart, Mom returned to Independence where she took up residence with her sister Ailene. Aunt Ailene was an amazing woman with many accomplishments. While living in Independence she was a nurse and excelled in the culinary arts. A woman of society, she thrived at participating in community functions and called Bess Truman one of her dearest friends. With Aunt Ailene's demanding schedule, mom's presence in the home became an asset. As she threw herself into caring for her two nephews, the pain of lost love began to ebb away.

Chapter Five

Just across the street from Aunt Ailene lived a young woman named Deanna Bell with whom mom became friends. Deanna was a member of The Church of Christ Temple Lot, a faith my mother had never heard of. As their friendship evolved, Deanna began to talk of a man she was dating by the name of Joseph Fredrick Smith and how her father was not favorable to the match. On one of their outings Deanna showed mom a picture of Dad in an army uniform and she acknowledged that he was quite the handsome man. At the time this was all unfolding, my father was stationed in Germany with the army. This was a prime time in my mother's life. It was the first time she had really been allowed to spread her wings and experience freedom. In this new place she could become independent and learn to express herself without fear.

Always looking to have fun, Mom began to go out socially with Deanna Bell. They would go to the movies, horseback riding and shop. One day Deanna called Mom to see if she wanted to go for a ride. When Deanna arrived, the young soldier from the photo was sitting in the driver's seat. Deanna and another friend were sitting in the back. Mom should have known then and there it was a set up! From that point on, every time they arrived for an outing it was the same; two girls in the back seat, Mom and Dad in the front! This went on for a couple of months until one day my dad called and asked Mom if she wanted to go to the movies. The conversation went as follows:

"Would you like to go see a movie?" Dad asked.

"Not if you're going to bring the whole community." Mom replied.

"Well, I didn't think you would go with me if the girls weren't along." From that day, Mom and Dad were a couple. After a few months of courtship, Dad went and bought a 1956 Mercury, drove to Aunt Ailene's to pick up Mom and asked her to marry him.

You can imagine how ecstatic my mother was. Finally she could start her life and build a home that did not have the trauma and chaos that existed in her childhood. But there was something that my mother didn't realize. If one would like to escape trauma and chaos, the last thing they want to do is marry into the Smith family, for it seems to follow them everywhere!

Dad's religious views at this time in his life had been placed upon a shelf. Having been baptized into the Temple Lot Church by his father at age twelve and ordained an Elder when he was eighteen, he had sought to move in the direction of The Temple Lot but ran into difficulties.

"I entered the service of the Lord with great expectations, only to come head to head with disputation among other ministry that soured my feelings somewhat."[1]

These disputations and other disappointments in my father's life are what led to his joining the armed services in 1953. After serving his time, he came back to Independence, anxious to partake in the Lord's work but once again was confronted with activities he felt did not correspond with the teachings of the Lord. "I felt that I could leave the work of the Lord in the hands of more able men."[2] Thus he prepared for marriage and a new life ahead. But settling into marriage before he was settled himself without goals and a plan would result in a very fragmented future.

A Whole New World

The first Smith family member that Mom met was my Aunt Lorraine, who was distant but kind at first. She called Mom "the blue-haired little Baptist girl." In those days it was the latest thing to bleach a white streak through part of your hair. Mom partook of the new fashion while she was in Tennessee but Pappaw told her that it wasn't fitting, that only trashy women did that. Mom tried her best to use a color dye that would make all of her hair the same color again but first it came out green, and then blue!

My father's family was mortified that Dad was marrying a Baptist, but this one had blue hair! Much of it was not funny at the time but we have found ways to laugh about it. I would have liked to have known Mom then, when she was young, when she had goals and enthusiasm, before reality set in. If you were to ask me what makes me think that my mother was brought together with my father for a purpose, I would tell you what she brought into this family, what it cost her and the result of that cost; a generation of descendants that did not have hatred and bitterness.

Mom had walked into marriage before she had an understanding of the destruction abuse had wrought within herself. Carrying wounds that she had buried deep within, she gave herself completely to my father. Only now is it clear to see that it took someone broken and pure-hearted to bring light into this family.

Mom and Dad were married on March 1, 1957 at The Church of Christ Temple Lot in Independence, Missouri. Although the first meeting months before with the family seemed to go well, the nightmares soon began. It started when Mom decided to move the marriage date from June to March because her parents could not come in the summer. All of a sudden the whispers began circulating among some of the ladies in the Temple Lot church that mom was pregnant. The source of these rumors was some of Dad's family. Today such a rumor is waved aside with little care, but in the fifties it was a scathing tale which could cripple a woman's reputation, causing her to be outcast. Mom was devastated and it cast a shadow over her happiness. The majority of Dad's family were kind to my mother, but she would find that a few of her future in-laws despised her. She was Baptist and not of their faith, and she had corrupted their little Joe by influencing him with blue jeans, country music, and movie theaters. All of the hurt cut deep. Already pulled down in resistance from her childhood, Mom did not have the emotional strength or wherewithal to just get in their face and politely tell them that she was there like it or not, letting them know she would not be pushed around. She questioned her self-worth, trying to reason why her husband's family and her own mother seemed to hate her.

When my mother had moved to Independence before meeting Dad, she did something that most victims of abuse are guilty of; she escaped without the closure of understanding why she had been abused. It is so easy for us all to jump into another phase, just wanting to start over and forget what happened before. But it is not easy to forget because effects of abuse attach to the victim. They lie dormant, waiting until we are weak, tired, or sad. When we are in any state of existence where our emotional guard is down, the unresolved residue of past trauma filters in. Then we become depressed, and do not understand why.

Mom had jumped from one kind of abuse to another. She entered into marriage with no idea of how to stand up for herself, nor did she consider that she had any self-worth whatsoever. BecauseMom was so fragile, she was ill-equipped to handle the load which would come with marrying my father and dealing with the contempt some of his family had for her. Though Dad was and is a good man, he was carrying so many unresolved generational issues that he could not remain settled or satisfied. His spirit was restless. Once children came into the picture, our father was far removed from us; in our midst but not really there. I remember being very young and loving him so dearly, but in those days I did not understand everything that was going on and how my mother suffered.

Here is a woman who I can attest has the purest heart and soul. I have never seen her blow up from anger, or raise her voice in scathing language. She is compassionate beyond measure and would not hurt a soul. She has a steadfast belief in God and the Savior, Jesus Christ, and has been witness to many spiritual miracles in her life. She leans on the Holy Ghost and follows the guidance of that quiet voice. Out of all of Mom's trials, the one thing that has stayed constant is that she always follows the admonition of the Spirit, no matter what anyone else says. She also has a natural desire that everyone should get along, a peacemaker like her father before her. Now picture what the opposition from the adversary would be if such a peace-seeking, pure heart was placed with a descendant of the Prophet Joseph whose family for generations had been torn asunder by contention and division.

Because of my mother, my siblings and I have hearts that are open to the truth when it comes our way. Caution stemming from fear which had trickled down from the traditions of my father's family caused me to push it away, but as I was pushing there was always a presence drawing me to learn for myself. I knew the feelings stirring within me were good and at length, I trusted that spirit. I learned that from my mother. That is why I say she had to pay a cost; the opposition against such an alliance was relentless.

Endless Trails

I could write a whole volume on our many moves and the events which caused much pain, but what would it serve? As I said, my father has changed over the years and to me, pulling out all of the details would do nothing but alter the good changes that have evolved. I will touch on a few things, but it is enough to say that those days were painful, hard, deprived and emotionally cruel. Suffice it to say there was enough stress for my mother to have a nervous breakdown on more than one occasion..

It was a constant circle of moving, getting settled, Dad changing his mind, losing his job, losing everything, and then moving again. Many times we stayed with relatives. There would be approximately forty moves before I was twelve. Our environment was never stable. The only constant was the love

Chapter Five

and goodness of our mother. My brother called those early years the most nomadic of our lives.

"My home life was filled with uncertainty, broken promises, instability...Constantly moving and being an outsider gave me license to think and dream bigger. Being insecure and unstable made those dreams a lot more complicated to pursue. Living through tough things taught me how to navigate through almost anything. Living outside of any accepted group whatsoever made it impossible for me to fit in, even when I wanted to."

"The one thing that I always remembered was that Jesus was about love, and Mom was about love. And that seemed good and pure and good and pure had to be better than bad."[3]

In Dad's defense, it is apparent that he married before he knew what he wanted in life. He also knew very little of what my mother stood in need of as far as love and affection. Being raised mostly by his mother and sisters, and having a father who was not present in the home often, the only family life he had was one comprised of hardships surrounded by a lifestyle below the poverty level. Although there was love in my father's home, there seemed to be that element missing which is drawn from the pure love of Christ. All that he knew when he left home was that he wanted to experience things he had not been able to while growing up. When he married Mom, they had not taken the time to really know one another, to see if their strengths and weaknesses had the elasticity to withstand trials and contrasting personalities.

When it came to contention and verbal insult, Dad's way of coping was to either tell the offender off or let it roll of his back, forgetting the whole matter one way or the other. This is a process which works well yet contrasted and worked against Mom's way of internalizing contention and turning everything toward herself. He could not understand why she didn't suck it up and get past it. He quickly grew weary of what he saw in her as weakness, unable to comprehend why she could not pass off the verbal assaults of his family and go merrily on her way.

Regardless of being told that she shouldn't have children, Mom found herself pregnant within a few months of their wedding. The news lifted her spirits. Though she was frightened of what could happen because of the risk, she was excited at the prospects. Such excitement rode on expectations of having something of herself that she could shower with love and devotion, motherly affections she had been robbed of as a child.

At the time they were living on Truman Road in Independence, Missouri. Mom was working at Kansas City Bank & Trust and Dad had been working at Westinghouse but quit after only a few months and went to Colorado to look for work, leaving Mom behind at Aunt Ailene's until he secured employment at Martin Plane and Missile. In the year 1957, they would move five times between Colorado and Missouri.

My brother, Timothy Granger Smith, was born March 5, 1958, in Denver, Colorado. Mom had actually admitted Dad into the hospital the night before for liver infection and she stayed close by at a friend's for she had started labor. The next day she was admitted. Dad was allowed to go into the labor and delivery room but he passed out and had to be taken back to his room! All went well with the birth and both mother and son came through without a problem.

Chapter Five

Unhappy with his job, Dad quit and they all moved back to Independence. Unable to find satisfactory work, he enlisted once again with the Army. He was stationed in Maine but Mom was not able to join him because he was not on military family housing property. So she went back to Independence and stayed with Aunt Ailene until November 1958, when Mom and my brother took the train to Maine. This was a happy time for my mother, even though her life was lacking stability. From the time her son was born, she felt she had a new purpose in life.

While in Maine, Mom became pregnant once again and Dad was not making enough to care for them all so she packed Tim and some belongings to take the train to stay with her parents in Tennessee. More than anything, she did not want to stay in her mother's home because it was so stressful, but she did not want to burden her sister in Independence yet again.

Mother and son were in a dismal situation but it has been during such times in her life that she has witnessed miracles. There were only ten dollars to make the whole trip and Mom worried about how she would eat, though she had food for Tim. While waiting in line at the train station, Mom said a beautiful older woman approached her and offered to buy them breakfast. Mom, who did not want to be a burden, said that they had money and would be fine. The lady then asked Mom if they would join her for breakfast so she would not have to sit alone. She obliged and after being seated, the woman ordered something then talked Mom into ordering food. The two women conversed cheerily back and forth and then after some time the woman stood to leave, placing a twenty dollar bill upon the table and moving it over toward Mom.

"We will be fine, we have some money." Mom said, and then, being distracted by my brother, turned to attend to him. When she looked back up the woman was gone. She had only looked away for a moment and there had not been time for the woman to walk out of her sights. Though she looked all around the place where they had eaten she never saw the woman again. It was then that my mother realized that an angel had attended her and Tim on that day, reminding her that even when things seem impossible the Lord sends those who help.[4]

While in Tennessee, Mom did her best to keep her spirits up. It was wonderful for her to be around her father, but there was still the continual degradation from her mother. One day when she was seven and a half months into her pregnancy, she was playing with Tim outside and she fell, her tailbone smashing hard against concrete. Though she was jarred and would be sore for the next few days, Mom did not realize that she was injured internally.

Seven weeks before her due date, Mom was awakened in the early morning hours in pain and saw that the sheets were drenched in blood. She was hemorrhaging badly and very weak. Her father and brother rushed her to the emergency room where doctors assessed the damage, finding that the fall against the concrete had caused the afterbirth to tear, thus causing the hemorrhage. After some time elapsed, a doctor came out and faced Pappaw with grave news. They could only save one person and chances for that were even small. Pappaw had to choose whether to save his daughter or

Chapter Five

his grandchild. He reasoned that there was already one child at home and it would seem cruel to rob him of a mother so Pappaw told them to do all they could to save his daughter. It was a choice that ripped at his heart.

On July 18, 1959, my sister Candance Sue Smith was born weighing 3.5 lb. Both mother and child survived but my mom was told that there should be no more children and that her husband should consider having preventative surgery. When Candy was six weeks old, Dad drove to Tennessee and picked his family up so they could live with him in Maine. When he was apprised of the situation, he refused to have the surgery because he said it would be a sin.

During this second stay in Maine, Mom began to notice a distance forming between her and Dad. She stumbled upon an alarming document as she was cleaning one day that seemed to confirm her suspicions that all was not well. Instinctively, she picked it up and began to read. It was a letter Dad had begun to write to one of his cousins in Independence, Missouri and in it he commented that if they had not started having children so quickly, he may not have stayed in the marriage. Mom was devastated and when she confronted Dad with it he told her it was nothing. He explained that the letter was written in a moment of frustration and that's why it was never sent, that it was in the past and she should not think of it anymore. Still she could not help but feel that Dad did not love her fully and there seemed to be what she perceived as jealousy aimed toward their children.

Though hurt and saddened, she tried her best to forget what she had seen and move forward. But it was difficult for she internalized the whole issue, blaming herself and feeling as if she had even less worth. She viewed herself as more of a failure for not being able to fulfill the measure of the kind of woman she felt he wanted.

As Mom began to lose more self-confidence, it seemed as if Dad was pulling farther away, becoming an inactive father, present yet absent in the home. His thoughts rested on a thousand directions he wanted to go and since his heart did not seem to be wrapped around his family, it went on a walkabout that lasted over thirty years, dragging us part of the way with him

The timing of my arrival in this world would shift the situation into an even more despairing existence for my mother. A surging gulf of indifference emerged between my parents, coupled with devastating choices with which Mom would be faced, a mixture which created a tide of loneliness and depression. With both parents co-existing as Dad moved them from one place to another, Mom sought solace through her faith, while Dad tried to find himself. El Paso, Texas would be a trial by fire for my mother, and the hopes of my safe arrival rested within her distraught heart.

Chapter Five

Kimberly Jo at 9 mo. 1963

Chapter Six

"If I could have but a single breath of peace
I would exhale contently"

— *Kimberly Jo Smith*

Between 1960 and 1961, the little Smith family moved from Maine to New Jersey, Independence, Missouri, and El Paso, Texas. After Mom learned of her pregnancy while in El Paso, the fears of losing a child and possibly her own life resurfaced. She perceived by Dad's response to the news that he was angry and there was little communication between them. As Mom's fears began to escalate, she made an appointment to see a doctor in El Paso in order to make sure her new child was healthy. It was a three mile walk from her house to the doctor's office so she put my two year old sister in a wagon and started walking. My brother, then four, trailed along beside.

The walk was one of reflection and despair. Surrounded by loneliness, every step was filled with communication with the Lord. Why did things have to be like this? In her mind she was doing everything she knew how to be a proper wife and she loved her husband so. Her heart was breaking. These thoughts weighed upon my mother like an anchor, and the weight became as burdensome as a sinking ship.

Chapter Six

After the exam, the doctor explained that because of her injuries as a child and the near death of both her and my sister during delivery, she should terminate the pregnancy. Mom was stunned to hear such advice. The emotions of her past fell upon her in waves. Not good enough for her mother, not good enough for marriage and now not good enough to carry a child. With every step of the long journey back to the small house, the doctor's words coursed through her over and over again, each cycle building in weight and darkness "Terminate the pregnancy," he had said. The next thing she knew she was nearly home, pulling the little wagon, children chattering away as they had been before. She didn't even recall leaving the doctor's office. My brother and sister sat down on the floor in the living room and began to play. Mom lay down upon the couch, exhausted and bewildered. She felt alone, completely alone. There was not a soul with whom she could share the grief that such news had just brought her. All she could do was lie down on the couch, hopeless. The environment seemed to become as a haze and she looked dazedly at her children as they played, so numb she could not even remember their names.

Racked with fear, she considered what the coming months would bring. How could she face possible death, leaving two children behind? Who would care for them and instill the things she knew to be good and right? She had experienced first-hand the sting of bitterness and hatred in some of my father's family and she feared that her own children would grow to have such inclinations if they did not have the right influences around them. She also knew that abortion was not the answer. It was a choice she would not even consider.

As the winds of change permeated my mother's heart and mind, life outside of the little home was experiencing its own changes. It was 1962 and John F. Kennedy was president. Gas was 31 cents a gallon, and the cost of a stamp was four cents. The population of the United States stood at 186,537,737 people who were warily holding their breath in fear as fragile international relations were leading up to the Cuban Missile Crisis. My dad was stationed in the radar division of a military base in El Paso during a nationwide crisis of fear. But the only fear my mother knew was whether or not she would live through her third pregnancy.

As she reflected upon her situation and the lack of support and love she had in her own home, my mother did the only thing she felt she could do. She went to stay with her sister Ailene in Independence, Missouri. It was her intent to leave my father and never go back for she truly felt he did not love her.

Another doctor's visit in the Midwest would bring more devastating news to my mother. It appeared that the child she was carrying was a tubal pregnancy. Mom was told of the serious risks and that in such cases if termination was not initiated, it could mean certain death for the child and possibly her as well. Once again she was advised to get an abortion. A renewed fear filled her heart and mind as she struggled to balance the stress of how she was going to provide for herself and her children. With everything seeming to spiral downward, my mother turned to the one place which always kept her from losing complete hope: her faith.

Being sensitive to the Spirit, Mom had felt the Holy Ghost at certain times around members of The Temple Lot

Chapter Six

Church and she had been present during blessings in which the spirit was very strong. Mom realized that there was much contention in the Temple Lot Church and she felt something was missing there, but she did believe that one could be healed through the laying on of hands if they had faith. One day she called on someone to administer to her. Upon the next visit to the doctor, they were surprised to find that the baby was in the uterus as it should be. This miracle would serve to increase my mother's strength of spirit for the trials that lay ahead.

Pressures from some of Mother's family members made it impossible to stay in Missouri, leaving Mom to feel she had no other choice than to go to back to Tennessee and live with her parents. It was an added stress. Mammaw was hard on my mom, as always. With doctor's orders directing her to stay in bed, Mom instead found herself physically exhausted much of the time due to cleaning and taking care of her children to avoid the abuse of her mother. If it had not been for her sister-in-law Pat, who was her best friend, she would have fallen to pieces under the strain.

It was during such turmoil that I arrived on August 7, 1962. Mom was in labor for only four hours and I was the easiest delivery of all three of her children. It was a calm end to long months of worry and stress. I guess I felt she needed a break! When I was four weeks old, Mom moved to White Sands, New Mexico to try and repair her marriage.

Trials in Missouri

Four months after we had all moved to White Sands, Dad decided he had experienced enough of the army and tried to get out on a hardship discharge, claiming that he needed to take care of his parents. He was turned down; only his wife could get him out on a hardship. Mom called the Chaplain and asked him to make a house visit after which he reported that the family home was neat and clean, the children were well-kept, but there was little food and means to care for the children. The Chaplain recommended an honorable discharge due to hardship and Dad was released. For Mom, it was a hope of starting over, but those hopes were dashed when she realized that they would be moving to Missouri.

As a child, I loved being in Missouri around Dad's people. Of course I did! I was the baby and Grandma's favorite. But being young, I did not know of the negative effects that their treatment of me was having on all of my cousins and even my brother and sister. My brother, Tim, told me of these times, revealing a side of some of my father's family, who for some reason caused division. It may not have been their intent but it was the result of their actions.

"I remember how the four of us seemed like a team, like a tribe," Tim said, referring to Mom and us three kids, "like it was us and the rest of the world. Except when we would go to Missouri, and the Smiths would take you in, and turn against Candy and me. I still don't understand that. But you were accepted and loved. I don't have enough rear-view vision to understand, and it doesn't matter now anyway. When we were in Oregon and Montana, there were no families to tear us apart. We were close."[1].

One of the key elements of letting go is contained in what my brother said; "It doesn't matter now." But it did at the time and caused hurt feelings to become embedded amongst us as a family. But there was a positive side to their possessiveness. Being taken into their affections enabled me to see another side of Dad's siblings. I beheld the good side of his family, where Mom had been exposed to the dark and cold side; the bitter side that had grown crisp and hard over the years. Being very young at the time, I was not aware of some of the cruelty which was going on toward my mother. But I would see those things in time and it was a great source of grief to me.

The trials of Missouri would be the turning point for my mother. Dad was rarely at home and Mom's health had deteriorated significantly. Early in the marriage, Dad had promised Mom that they would never live too close to his people for she had expressed to him that they were cruel to her. Not all of his family treated her in such a fashion, but there were those who had been ruthless in their assessment and treatment of her.

At least four times we lived right in the midst of Dad's family in the direst of conditions, having to rely upon their charity. Each time, Mom would spiral downward, despairing that Dad did not care enough for her, did not love her enough to shield her from such pain. Each time he could not understand why she did not just stand up for herself. He was unaware of the scars she carried that had debilitated her. At the same time, Mom did not know Dad felt trapped. It was a vicious circle and because no one communicated their feelings, neither could be a source of support for the other.

When I was three, Mom weighed 95 lbs. and we lived in an old rock house that did not have running water. The bucket in the well was heavy when filled and Mom was so weak she could not heft it alone so at times we would have to wait for Dad to get home to have water. Often she would have to load all of the dishes into the trunk and drive to grandma's to wash them. These were hard days and in those years in Missouri Mom would suffer three nervous breakdowns, losing her hair and staying in bed most of the time. I used to sit on the bed beside her and play quietly.

We existed below the poverty level and my mother was surrounded by in-laws she felt hated and despised her. In truth, there were three individuals in Dad's family who did hate Mom; they seemed to despise her goodness. But the majority of Dad's family just had a hard time understanding why she was so weak and unable to function. They were not aware of how she perceived their feelings. They had no way of knowing about her past abuse or that Dad had not been supportive as a husband in many ways. There was no way for them to know that her silence was a cry for help. So once again lack of communication gave way to distorted views and all parties made judgments for themselves, concluding those judgments to be fact.

Those years in Missouri caused a shift within my mother. The turning point came when I was four and she went to Tennessee to visit Pappaw, who was ill with cancer. She left me with Grandma because I loved her so much. She knew Grandma loved me dearly and I would be well cared for. But while she was gone, Grandma and one of my aunts had taught me to think that Grandma was my mom and I began to believe it, addressing her as "Mom." I was even told that my mother was not my real Mom. After Mom returned from Tennessee and heard me referring to Grandma as "Mom," she asked who

Chapter Six

had told me that. The answer would be the final factor which determined my mother's direction where my siblings and I were concerned. She had only one goal in sight by that point: the welfare of her children.

Mother felt an inner desire to see us raised with sound reasoning skills and a positive outlook on life, especially considering the things she had witnessed and endured throughout her childhood and marriage. She was also resolute in wanting to ensure that we did not absorb the tendencies of bitterness and hate she had witnessed in some of Dad's family.

Looking back on those days it is easy to see that Mom set out goals concerning her children, staunchly moving forward to see that those goals were met. In truth, she was in survival mode, throwing herself into the one thing she knew she had power over. Because Dad was not an interactive father, Mom became the ruling factor over our welfare. After regaining some strength following her last breakdown, Mom embraced her role as both parents.

To my mother's credit, she never once spoke against our father and always reprimanded us if we spoke out of line to him or about him in her presence. At this point in her life, my mother only knew that she had married a descendant of Joseph Smith. She had no knowledge of the history, nor did she have any intimation of the contention which had forged the attitudes and thought processes of the family she had married into. She only knew that her children must know the Savior and His pure love as she did. Although she was just following the guidance of her heart and the Spirit, Mother had unknowingly charted a course that would bring even more opposition her way; raising a generation of Joseph and

Emma's posterity who learned the pure love of Christ before they encountered the bitterness of the family. Having such teachings would empower us to be able to view the onslaught of contention with meekness and balance, something I am sure the adversary did not want.

The Lonely heart of a Wounded Child

It was difficult having a father who could not settle upon one geographical area for more than a year at a time. My early childhood was one that I learned to structure within myself, for the environment around me was always subject to change. I have always loved my dad. I didn't quite understand why we moved all of the time, or why he seemed always to be put out about something. I was always drawn to the lighter side of him that emerged around other people. It was a side of him I was very familiar with because I have that side in me; the happy-go-lucky, sometimes prankster who wants to be friends with everyone. Because I bonded with that part of him, it created a love which overrode the parts I didn't understand.

I did not know what lasting friendships meant and it was seldom that I had a best friend until I was in high school. In many ways, I pulled back from becoming very close to others because there was an almost certainty we would have to leave. There was also no sense of home. None of us could relax and view our dwelling place as a home because we were never sure when we would be told to pack to go somewhere else. My brother recalls:

"We were sleeping on couches and cots and floors. Sleeping in cars by the road. sleeping in relatives' places, some of whom had this kind of whispered attitude; tight lipped

Chapter Six

smiles I later knew to be conclusions that we were burdens, nomadic mooching desperate burdens."[2]

In 1969 we moved to Hubbard, Oregon, and shortly after to Woodburn, Oregon. I remember very little about our time in Oregon. There was a strawberry patch in the yard of our house on 1505 East Blaine Street in Woodburn, and just down the street was a small, old abandoned Bama processing company where berries were once sent to be washed, weighed and prepared to be sent to the main jam factory. On some days we would go down and play upon the pallets that were lying by the loading dock in the back. It was a big empty area with lots of odds and ends lying around to tempt kids like us who didn't have anything else to do.

There were different nationalities in Woodburn: some Hispanic, African American and mostly Caucasian, but just after we had moved there a large group of Russian immigrants had settled in. I was captivated by their brightly colored clothes and their language. They kept to themselves mostly for they knew little English.

While living in Oregon, Dad was working at a naval shipyard in Portland and he would bring home scrapped metal and wiring, the casings of which we would burn and strip in order to salvage the copper to sell for extra money. I did not know just how poor we were or how hard it was for our mother emotionally to try and pull things together so that we had food on the table every night. My mind was always somewhere else. I felt very deeply and was attached to certain things, especially where music was concerned and most definitely anything to do with history. When I was seven years old and attending school, we were just learning the basics of our early American ancestors. The story of the pilgrims and Native Americans stirred something within me.

At the time, I only knew that as we studied about those cultures and times I ached inside to know more. I wanted to know them intimately, to hear more and more stories about their lives. They seemed familiar to me, like family I met long ago but had not seen for many years. As a child, it was not easy to identify the process of what was happening in such an instance. Now that I have the fullness of the gospel, it is easy to look back and understand exactly what I was feeling. It is true that our ancestors in many ways call out to us so that we may come to know them and their stories. That knowledge is for our benefit, that we may know what their trials, sacrifices, joys and sorrows have purchased for our good. Our gift to them for such sacrifice comes through temple work. So they reach out to us so we may know them, yet help them as well.

There is also the fun side of experiences which unfolded as I learned of my ancestry as an adult. There were ancestors whose culture explained why I have always been drawn to things like Celtic, European and monarchial history;, ancestors who had passed their talents of music and art down to our generation. I even found two ancestors who wrote poetry in the form that I do.

When I was nine, my love for music was strong and I enjoyed listening to both country and pop. At the various locations throughout the United States we had lived in, Dad would take part in bluegrass parties, or jam sessions and he had taught my sister and me how to sing, including harmony. I was fascinated with the quality of sound which was created when there was a proper blending of voices. Harmonies

Chapter Six

captured my ear and reached into a deep place that seemed to welcome them like an old friend.

The Osmonds, David Cassidy, The Monkees and The Jackson Five were on the minds of every preteen and teenager and I was no exception. During the time we were in Oregon, I was still in my David Cassidy/Monkee phase but my favorite group was quickly becoming The Osmonds. I was like all of the other teenybopper girls who felt they were supposed to marry Donny. While *One Bad Apple* was soaring to the top of the charts and I was just getting to know about this family of singing brothers, my life became altered in a way that no child should ever have to endure.

In Woodburn there was a couple who lived down the street from us and I used to go there on occasion because the woman was so kind and would read me stories. She used to make cookies all of the time and give me some. On three separate visits, her husband molested me. The third time I went to see his wife but she was not there, and he coaxed me inside after which I was molested for a third time. I never went back again and was afraid to tell anyone for fear of getting into trouble. Mom noticed I was walking strangely and after telling her that I was in a lot of pain, she took me to the doctor. In those days the medical community was not as alert as they are today concerning signs of abuse.

The doctor diagnosed me as having fissures, tearing in the rectal area due to difficult bowel movements. He recommended more fiber in the diet. I breathed a sigh of relief. The whole time I was being examined I was afraid that what happened to me would get out and I would be in so much trouble. There are parts of the abuse I do not remember fully and I wonder if the man had threatened me in some way. I only know that I was terrified to tell anyone.

In gauging the downward spiral I experienced in the years following the abuse, I can clearly see that the adversary impressed upon my mind a sense of worthlessness in order to keep me from the path I should be on. Had I not been distracted and my whole being shifted by my abuser, I would have had more confidence in myself. I would have been more focused in school and able to absorb all of the knowledge which surrounded me. I would have embarked upon music and speaking in public earlier.

This is why I know that the adversary knows our missions and purposes, because after the abuse I was hit and debilitated in every area that I now excel in. I stopped singing, I would not do anything in public, and I would take a zero throughout all my school years instead of giving oral reports. I looked down when I walked and would not look people in the face. My self-image suffered severely. I hated myself and thought I was ugly and stupid. This destructive thought process drained me to the point where I had no energy whatsoever. I withdrew to my room and that is where I spent all of my spare time, becoming lost in writing, reading, and music. I jokingly like to tell people that my vocal coaches were the Bee Gees, The Carpenters and The Osmonds because I spent many hours listening to their songs and learning how to harmonize with their unique tonality and blends.

Food became my best friend. The more I hated myself, the more I ate. It was the only joy, aside from music and reading, that I had. I was made fun of at school and did not have the inner strength and confidence to just let the remarks

Chapter Six

roll off my back, throw a comeback comment their way or laugh it off. Every verbal assault rang like truth within my heart and it eroded my spirit.

There is one thing I did not lose, nor did I forget. The example of my mother's devotion to Heavenly Father, His Son Jesus Christ and the Holy Ghost showed me that I would always have three friends who would love me no matter what and I leaned on that. Whenever I felt alone, I talked to Jesus like He was my best friend, sitting right beside me. Though I heard no reply, I felt His presence and knew He heard me. Knowing that I had those connections kept me grounded. As in my mother's case, having that relationship on such a personal level enabled me to refrain from unhealthy activities that some victims of abuse get caught up in. There was something in me that just did not want to cross those lines and disappoint my Father in Heaven. But I could not help but be tempted by other things that damage the spirit as well.

Affected by the exposure to morally corrupt things before I was even old enough to comprehend their meaning, my body had experienced feelings that I was neither mentally nor emotionally prepared for. Those physical aspects which had sensed and experienced premature awakening through abuse never forgot, and would reemerge despite my desire to be free of them. Though I kept my virtue intact, never dating until I was 19, and married the only person I had ever dated, I was haunted by a tug-of-war of emotions. The side that moved me to do things which I felt were wrong won on several occasions and I learned the price of crossing those lines, even though I was convinced that it was okay. After all, it was just me, and society was teaching that it was natural and healthy. No matter how often society proclaims something to be right and good, if there is guilt following, or if one's spirit is troubled upon considering certain activities, it is a good indication that it is not a good choice.

Anyone who walks close to the Spirit, and has felt its influence, especially from childhood, knows when it has left. Let me tell you, it is the saddest thing, beyond all description. In an instant your support team is gone. My three friends who were always with me would be with me no more in those times until I made supplication, and I was left with only the darkness resulting from what I had done. I was very young, only 10. There was no structured religion I belonged to, only those early teachings. I had no outlet to learn about the repentance process. I only felt the hardness of that darkness and the deep desire for that light to return. Those three dear friends who I knew loved me, had left me because of things I had done against myself. In their absence I would eat more food, would suffer for days in guilt and pull myself out of it, only to fall victim again. No one knew. I was suffering through this hell on my own, a vicious cycle which would plague me until I came to understand that only I could put a stop to it.

The Power of Prayer

One can ask the Lord as many times as they choose for help and He is always willing. But what we as humans fail to grasp, especially at a young and ignorant age, is that sometimes help is not given until we make an effort first. The more effort we make, the more help comes and the strength to maintain a healthy state of existence begins to flourish. That strength only remains so long as we endure and overcome. In time, I learned the true power of prayer and that the Lord is always willing to lift us up if we make an attempt to stand on our own. Having that knowledge and understanding eventually enabled me to become whole, until I had no lasting effects of the abuse I had suffered. This process took many years because I was so slow in understanding and stumbled along the way, but I learned that the Lord is patient and full of mercy. Because of this type of healing, there is not one piece of residue from the abuse left in me. It is as if it had never happened, like a distant dream I am aware I had, but do not feel. Only having the Savior in one's life can erase such trauma. I was so grateful to know the Savior in such ways, but I would gain a deeper knowledge of Him after I discovered a very special man, my great-great-grandfather, Joseph Smith.

Chapter Seven

"Be not the slave of your own past, rather be its champion"
— *Ralph Waldo Emerson, Kimberly Jo Smith*

In 1973, we moved to Hiram, Georgia, a great contrast to the climate of Woodburn, Oregon. Still, I found the move to be one that was very agreeable. Moving to Georgia meant that we would be closer to my mother's people in Tennessee, and the Smokey Mountains had always been one of my favorite places to visit. It was that very culture which had impacted my life the most. A trip to the mountains meant we would pass a huge sign in a small town called Townsend, Tennessee that had always fascinated me. It was a cutout billboard of a Cherokee Indian dancing in full regalia.

I had always felt an innate attraction to the Native American people and when I was in the Smoky Mountains there seemed to be a heightened awareness, even a familiarity toward the environment. The intermingling of these singular and personal emotions within me were fascinating, yet confusing to me. I did not know at the time why I felt so deeply a connection to these people. It would be years later, as an adult, when I began to know more about my mother's side of the family and our Cherokee heritage, that I would come to an understanding of why I experienced the range of emotions that would course through me when I was in those mountains.

Chapter Seven

This was the deep side of me, the side that talked with Jesus like He was my friend walking beside me. The side no one else knew of. The part of me which was older, having an understanding that that there is much more to our existence than what we see with our eyes, yet void of the knowledge and tools necessary to carry that understanding beyond indescribable emotions and strange familiarities. None of my family knew the dimensions in which my thoughts traveled. I did not feel like anyone else around me in that respect. My mind was wrapped around histories of people who lived long before me. I seemed to see beyond the surface concerning things and people around me, yet I held those thoughts to myself for I felt as if I would be laughed at. It was a hard existence, for I craved to talk with others about deep subjects, but I did not know who to talk to.

Around the time of our move to Georgia, The Osmonds had released their newest album called *The Plan*. I was like all of the other teens awaiting the arrival of their new work. What I wasn't prepared for was the effect it would have on me. It was the most unusual but expressive album I had ever heard in my life to that point.

I still recall that first moment when I pulled the album out of the sleeve, placed it on the turntable of the record player and set the stereo needle on the first song. I was instantly surprised. This was not *One Bad Apple* or *Puppy Love!* As the album cover fell open into the palms of my hands, my mind was opened to something I had never encountered before. It would be my first introduction to the Plan of Salvation, though I had no idea at the time that was what I was seeing before me. As I looked at the visual images of the pre-existence, childhood, eternal marriage and returning home, I heard the words "Let me take care of you and keep an eye on you...." I looked over to the record as it was playing and then at the illustrations before me, realizing that this was something completely different. There was purpose in it beyond the simple thrill of dreamy, feel-good music. The moment left me feeling removed from everything while I tried to sort out what I was experiencing. I was very aware of a presence that was both comforting and enlightening, but there was a struggle within me that I did not understand.

It was the middle of summer and the humidity in Hiram, Georgia was at its usual brutal level, enticing most children to be out swimming or playing with the water hose. However, I could not bear the heat like my siblings and friends for it made me extremely tired and weak. Although I had listened to *The Plan* many times, I chose one hot afternoon to open those emotions up once again and examine them, in wonder of what I was feeling. I thought I was alone in the house so I left my door open. The song *Are You Up There* was playing and when it got to the verse, "*Maybe I'm a pessimist, then maybe I'm not*", my father paused in the doorway and sarcastically remarked, "Yeah, they're pessimists alright." I remember feeling alarmed as I looked up at him and felt uneasiness and intimidation in the presence of my father. There was an essence there that I had never seen or picked up on before. Though I didn't know a lot about spiritual matters, I recognized a shift and it did not feel good.

I wanted to act as if I had not heard him but there was a strong desire to ask why he didn't like the Osmonds. He had never really commented on them before except to say they were hippies, but my father felt that anyone whose hair touched their collar fell into that category. The moment that he spoke the words, I perceived that it was personal. His look betrayed a sense of disturbance and I wanted to know why.

Unspoken Connections

I had seen the word Mormon before but I really didn't understand it completely. Until that hot summer day in our house, my exposure to it was limited to my link with the Osmonds' music and their family. I asked my father what his problem was with their music and he replied with a sour tone in his voice that they were Utah Mormons.

My father's response was bitter and hateful; it hit me like a ton of steel, and the sweet, peaceful emotions and desire to know more were all ripped away from me. I became embittered against the word Mormon for reasons I did not understand and concluded that it was a bad thing.

Those feelings did little to upset my love for the Osmonds or their music. It created boundaries, however, that I promised myself never to cross. They seemed to be good people and I loved their music but because of Dad's reaction that day as well as things I would hear later while growing up, I formed the opinion that they belonged to a bad church and I would never investigate that side of them.

A couple of months after the incident with my father, we took a trip to Ava, Missouri where my Grandmother Smith lived. Grandpa Smith had passed away twelve years earlier. It had been a long time since I had seen Grandma and I was excited to make the trip. My grandma lived in what many people refer to as the boonies, nine miles out of town, in a little log cabin nestled high on a hill. She loved flower gardens and her yard was filled with all varieties of blooming color. My favorites were Hyacinths and the many species of Irises which bordered her yard. Many of the Irises had been brought from missionary trips to Wales that she and Grandpa took. I remember that she had a little white wrought iron arched entry that seemed so charming to me as it stood at the forefront of the flower-laden yard. When I first caught sight of the scene it was like beholding the cover of a story book. Little did I know that as I walked through the gate and opened that book, a story would indeed begin to unfold before me and it was a story that would take years and volumes to comprehend.

Walking into Grandma's cabin was an adventure to me. I had not been there since I was little so I looked around intently as memories began to flood back into my mind. Grandma loved doing crafts; quilting, needlepoint, macramé hats and handmade flowers. I walked studiously through the front room admiring all of her treasures as the adults sat and talked amongst themselves. Walking from the living room into a smaller sitting room, I couldn't help but smile for my eyes fell upon a shelf which contained a large collection of interesting salt & pepper shakers. As I turned to look at the wall to the right I took in a breath. The light from the sun peered through a window falling softly upon two portraits which hung on the wall; a young fair- skinned man, and a woman with dark hair. For a moment it seemed as if time stood still. My peripheral vision fell out of focus and all that I could see were these two images.

Chapter Seven

My heart was wrapped up in all manner of emotion and I did not know why. A feeling that I can only describe as lightness filled me as I beheld the images before me, especially the man. There was a familiarity which was deep and instant. The gentle, fair-skinned face housed eyes that seemed to hold stories in their backdrop hues of gray and piercing blue. Both faces reflected a history that spoke volumes, reaching out and embracing me in unknown depths. Even at such a young age I could feel the extreme emotions that must have coursed through this man's life. I went to find my grandmother and asked her who the people in the portraits were and she replied, "Those are your great-great-grandparents, Joseph and Emma Smith. Joseph is the one who started the Church." "What Church?" I thought to myself. I had no idea what she was talking about. All that I knew in that moment was that a door had opened when I saw those portraits and I was never the same after.

I recalled very little about that trip for my mind had been wrapped up in this man named Joseph and a church he had started. The image I was forming in my mind was that of a little white church in the mountains with a quaint congregation. After all, that is what the churches in the Tennessee Mountains were like. I had no idea how huge the history behind this man was. During our visit we attended The Church of Christ Temple Lot with Grandma. As I sat in the small meeting room filled with cousins, aunts and uncles I had not seen for about ten years, I heard a sermon that was quite different than any I had ever heard before. While I do not remember the topic of discussion I recall the speaker quoting from a book I had never heard of before. Names like Nephi and Moroni sprang into my hearing and I wondered about their meaning. We only stayed a short while in Missouri and then returned to Georgia.

On the Move....Again

By the time the summer of 1974 emerged, I had settled into life in the South. It was, after all, my favorite part of the states and so close to my favorite relatives. Sometime in June, my siblings and I were told that we were going to have to move again. It broke my mother's heart. This meant another move, move number who-knows-what. For the first time we really had a home, a house, and food on the table. We had become self-reliant. But my father insisted that things were so bad that he felt the end times were upon us and it was necessary to move to Missouri to be closer to Independence.

I did not understand any of it. I knew nothing of church history, or Joseph Smith's life. I had barely learned he was my great-great-grandfather. He was a man in a portrait that I felt very drawn to, but I knew nothing of him. I paid little attention to much of anything because once the realization had hit me that we were moving yet again, I pulled inside myself. This time we were leaving Aunt Pat, Uncle Max and cousins I had come to love so dearly. Just when I had started to relax we were being uprooted again. I withdrew even deeper into myself and paid little attention to the whys and wherefores of our situation, seeming always to be in a daze. I thought often of the man and woman in the portraits, longing to know their story while I gazed out the window of our car as we traveled the long stretch of road that led to Missouri.

Chapter Seven

The summer heat was broiling when we left our home in Hiram. It was storming. Not just any storm but a brilliant electrical storm with high winds. As we entered the interstate, strong winds blew against us with nearly unimaginable force. It was early in the day but the darkened storm clouds made it appear to be evening. We were in two different cars. Dad was driving the car with all of our belongings, and the rest of us were in the other. Every now and then our car would swerve from the force of the wind and it was terrifying because of all of the lightening and hail. The radio announced a tornado warning for the county we were driving through. I was terrified of tornadoes. As I looked quickly out of the windows, I spotted several clouds that threatened in darkened swirls to hurl themselves to the ground. Then I looked behind us and there about five miles away were a couple of funnels which had touched down. They were not moving to the left or the right which meant they were either moving toward us or away. I did not care to know as I sank down in the seat while we sped down the highway to outrun the storm, passing through in safety and arriving two days later in Missouri.

Ava, Missouri is nestled in the heart of the Ozark Mountains. In the summer of 1974, the little cabin on the hill which had been built by Grandpa Smith meant something different to each of us. For my brother it was another reason to be angry with Dad because of being uprooted yet again. Surrounded by lush wooded acreage it unfolded a new adventure for my sister. For my mom it was a prison. It was another means of escape for Dad, and for me it was solitude, at least for a time. Here I would be exposed to the heart of many things; the core of bitterness in the family, a hatred toward a church and people called Utah Mormons of whom I knew nothing, and the love of a great man who reached out to me in unspoken words urging me to move forward and learn of his story.

Joseph and Emma. Their images were etched into my memory and now I was able to look at them as often as possible, yet the pleasure of seeing them was always weighed down with a sadness of sorts. There were times as I studied those images when tears would slowly fall down my cheeks in trails. While other teens my age were engaged in social activities, coming into their own, and in many cases veering into avenues of frivolity with devastating effects, I was being pulled into a realm immersed in a history I did not know or understand. Even without a comprehension of my family history, there was one thing that I was sure of. It was connected to me with a depth I could not ignore.

The first time I recall asking my father about Joseph, I received a lesson about a man who started a church and another man named Brigham Young who took that church and corrupted it. Even as he was speaking, I felt uncomfortable. I have always been such that I want only to hear good tidings. The minute darkness creeps in I either withdraw or I will add my own depth of humor to try and swing the mood into a different light. The more questions I asked my father, the more I quit asking.

In those days, the Ava, Missouri branch of The Church of Christ Temple Lot was conducted in the home of one of my father's sisters. I used to love to go, only because I would see Grandma there for she had moved into a trailer behind my

Chapter Seven

aunt's house, allowing us to live in the cabin. I couldn't express to anyone a thing I had learned in those meetings because much of the time my mind was elsewhere. My gaze was often out the window in another time with another people. But it was during the meals after church service that I did pay attention.

At the table in my aunt's home, there were discussions which ranged from the economy to gossip about people and other churches. My father's people had good hearts and could be a delight to be around at times but when the topic turned to church, the atmosphere shifted significantly. It was like sitting at the captain's table on a ship. One could be enjoying a meal in a delightful manner and then the tide would turn and all of a sudden the plates would sail off the table and into the floor.

The conversation would indeed turn like the tide. One minute I would be laughing at something and then someone would bring up another church, immediately moving countenances to tighten, especially if the name Brigham Young was mentioned. Where was it coming from, and why were they so upset about these things? I had attended other churches and had never felt such indignation and condemnation toward other people or religions. What was the core belief of the church I was attending? Who were Utah Mormons and Brigham Young? What had they done that had brought the wrath of this family to surface? I didn't know and it perplexed me. I was so intimidated by their discussions that I was hesitant to ask them to expound upon their aggressive feelings.

Over the years, within the midst of exclusive and prejudicial meetings of the minds, I was educated as to the history of the Church according to them. Basically all other churches but The Church of Christ Temple Lot were condemned to hell. I felt confident in my newly adopted perspectives seeing as how that was the church I was attending. Even though I had no idea what it taught, at least I knew I was going to heaven! That was all I needed to know according to the family, that I was in the true church and must never belong to another.

I had no idea on earth what "the Church" was about, nor did I understand the meaning of the "true church." No one offered explanations or teachings about the complete history of The Church. No one ever spoke a word about Joseph, and when I did ask, no one really wanted to get into it. I only knew according to them that there existed a people called Utah Mormons and that long ago their leader, Brigham Young, had Joseph, Hyrum and Samuel murdered so that he could become prophet. When I heard these things it created bitterness within me toward this Brigham Young.

It has never been my nature to hate at all, in fact Brigham Young is the only person I have ever actually hated. Even though I did not know of my ancestor's history yet, my love for Joseph was such that it angered me to learn this man named Brigham Young was responsible for his death. The moment that knowledge set in, I vowed to keep a distance between myself and those Utah Mormons. Many times I would hear how well-trained their missionaries were and how, if I was not careful, I could be snookered into their organization.

It was a terrifying prospect. I was well versed in how horribly they treated their wives, and if one of the women

Chapter Seven

tried to leave the Church, they would be marched straight up to the top of the Salt Lake Temple and pushed into the Salt Lake! No sir! I was not about to let that happen! But I did not trust myself to be strong enough to withstand their powers of persuasion. After all I just wanted to get along and be friends with everybody. So to avoid getting "snookered" I was determined never to speak to a Mormon or even be in the same room. It seemed to be a well-devised plan, for I was not aware of any Utah Mormons living in Ava at the time. I felt completely safe and was assured that I would not be ensnared by their crafty ways! I would simply stay in Ava my whole life!

Every Sunday I received such education. After some time, my siblings and I tired of the contention within those gatherings and eventually ceased attending. There was nothing spiritual about them. I felt more of the spirit staying at home. But those few years of attendance had impacted me in ways that were dark and heavy. Twenty-five years would pass before I discovered for myself which path I should be on. Until then, I would be bound by the walls that had been built generations before me; walls of bitterness, doubt, fear, and ignorance. It would be a path of great learning, a road that stretched for miles.

Chapter Eight

"O What Grace Solitude Brings,
That Which Allows the Soul a Place,
and the Spirit a Voice to Sing"

—*Kimberly Jo Smith*

I loved the odd times that I would find myself alone in the cabin. Grandpa had built a kitchen and bedrooms onto the back side and the kitchen stepped down into a study, which had now become my mom and dad's room. We called it the fireplace room because there was a nice, big rock fireplace. We were quite poor and the only heat was the fireplace and a wood stove which was in the cabin part of the house. Our back bedrooms were freezing in the winter and dad would heat big stones in the fireplace, wrap a towel around them and we would put them at the end of our beds under the covers so our feet would stay warm. It sounds like something one would read about in a pioneer story, which is exactly how it was. I can remember many times when we had to heat all of our water for cooking and bathing because the well would run low or freeze in the winter. But for me, as frustrating as the circumstances were at times, there was uniqueness to that place.

Often times I would find myself alone in the cabin and it gave me a chance to look at my grandfather's belongings. In

Chapter Eight

the study there was a large trunk, like one would have used in the old days to pack their belongings in preparation for traveling by ship. The first time I opened it was like gazing into a treasure box. There were old books, letters and pictures. Some of the pictures were tintypes. In those images, I looked into faces and eyes that seemed to reach out to me. It was as if something clicked into place when I looked at them and I ached to know who they were. I had no idea what the books were, but they were dated mid to late 1800's. There were old pamphlets as well as hand-written letters between Joseph Smith III and Alexander Hale Smith. As old documents and pictures passed through my hands, they left imprints of emotions: identity, heartache, longing, and love.

From the moment I lifted the lid of the trunk my life became altered again. First the portraits, then the items in the trunk; it was like stepping stones toward something I felt was huge but was still beyond my view. All of this framework seemed to be going up, but it was hollow. I had no way of knowing what manner of house it was. I only knew it was beautiful, even wondrous to me. I could barely see the outside, yet longed to know what was inside that affected me so profoundly. Every chance I had to myself, I would go through that trunk in an effort to find a doorway to that house. But I desperately needed a map and it would take years to find it.

We lived at Grandma's house for a short while when Dad decided he wanted to expand the rooms of the cabin. The cabin part of the house was divided into four rooms on the inside. Dad wanted to make it one large room. He talked of many plans to improve the place, yet he was hardly home, most often working or looking for odd jobs. One day, disgruntled over our circumstances of poverty, Tim took a sledgehammer and knocked all of the walls down. I imagine every swing expressed a good measure of his anger over our situation. When Dad returned home that evening, the walls of the four rooms lay in rubble. He shook his head, walked back out, got into the truck and left. At length, the cabin was made into one large room but never quite completely finished.

Dad has always been the kind of person who does not like to work for other people. He rejects the authority of others and feels he always knows a better way. It doesn't mean he is bad, it is just the way he is and he was never able to harness his talents and capabilities into an area that satisfied him on a long-term basis. After being in Ava for less than a year, he decided to get involved with cutting timber in Idaho, which placed him where he loved to be the most: outdoors. His plan was to send us money on a weekly basis. The rate of pay was a hundred dollars or more a day so it should have been a good financial arrangement, but we rarely saw money. Mom began working ful- time at a restaurant called Hutches for a mere sixty dollars a week and they allowed her to take home food which had not been served, yet could not be held for the next day. Many times it is the only way we had food. When that source was not available, we either had potato soup or pancakes. At times, we only had the desserts Mom would bring home. In the summer, my sister and I worked for Hutches for ten dollars a day. I remember having one pair of bell bottom pants for the school year and I had to wash them out every night.

At length Mom went out to Idaho to see what condition Dad was in because we had not heard from him and she had the feeling she should go and check on him. She found him in his trailer with a full beard. He looked like a mountain man who had been reclusive from society for a long time. My perspective is that he was depressed because of his inability to find his place in life. He still felt trapped. Mom stayed with him until he finished out his time and they both came home.

Solitude

While Mom was gone I spent time working on a book that never really went anywhere, but it kept my mind occupied. Many times in that little bedroom in the cabin I would write poetry and short stories. One of my favorite television shows was *Little House on the Prairie* because I loved Michael Landon's portrayal of Pa Ingalls. He was the Pa I knew my father could be if he could just find what was missing in his life.

Though my time was spent in solitude, it was spent wisely, for in those days I was escaping. I still had not overcome the effects of the abuse I had suffered and the weight of those effects grappled with my desires to learn about my history; who Joseph and Emma were and why I felt so connected. It was a tug of war that left me emotionally spent. Though there were not many days that I did not gaze at those portraits and long to know the people in them, I spent my teenage years avoiding that quest of knowledge. To that point, it had only wrought confusion and fear. I threw myself into other things such as world history, writing and singing to those records. Such activities kept me busy to the point that I didn't have time to think of the old scars. I did not have the energy to try and unravel my father's heritage. Still, even in those days of wandering through the confusion of life and the threats of my past, it seemed I always felt the closeness of the man in that portrait.

These were also days when I leaned on things my mother had taught me about the Savior. I knew he was the Son of God, I knew He had died for our sins. But there was something else I had come to know of Him. He was my friend. I had learned He would never leave me alone unless I gave Him occasion to through offense of the Spirit. I loved reading passages of the Sermon on the Mount which reiterated things I had learned from Mom.

It was during those days of isolation that I came to understand the atonement. Although I would not have been able to put it into words at the time, I understood that in order to remain one with The Father, the Son, and the Holy Ghost, I should always strive to avoid activity which would draw me away from them. In truth, the Lord was the one who helped me through those years. I was ever aware that He was mindful of me and my desire to have Him with me caused me to be aware of my every thought and action. Many times I stumbled but He was always close and cared enough for me to help me up again if I would make the effort to reach out.

I was in my own little world, aware of the hardships we were under, yet far enough removed that I didn't feel the sting of it. To those around me I appeared sad and distant and there was some truth to their perspective, yet I was also gaining knowledge in my solitude, the kind of knowledge which comes with quiet ponderings and musings. I noticed that as I had my little conversations with the Lord, there were answers to questions which came to me in simple, soft, whispers.

Chapter Eight

It isn't that I got all of the answers I wanted. I still could not understand the reasoning for the instability in our lives, but my eyes were opened here and there giving me an understanding that all was in the hands of the Lord and if I simply made the right choices and tried to be as good as I could, then doors of further understanding and direction would be opened unto me. I only knew that honing my writing ability was important, and even though I was not striving to sing in front of people because of my fears, there was a desire in me to sing as often as I could to myself. I became lost in books, writing stories and music. I missed out on many things during my teenage years because I had escaped so far into the stories I was writing. It was a safe place and from the negative things I saw my friends becoming involved with, I felt it was a better place. It was not the healthiest attitude, for in some ways it limited my ability to grow, but it is all I knew and all I had to work with.

There was no adult in my environment to advise or help me. In the first place, I had not shared the source of pain which had debilitated me in so many ways. Mom knew something was wrong but I was not opening up and she was constantly in survival mode with little time or energy to try and bring to the surface the issues which had caused me to withdraw. Dad was seldom home, being gone months at a time and when he was at home he really wasn't there and probably would have been the last person I would have opened up to about such a topic. A daughter approaching a father about that type of abuse is hard. I also felt that he would not take anything that I said seriously. Often times he would tell us that we would not amount to anything, a statement many parents may say when frustrated with their teenage kids, but I took it to heart and allowed it to lie upon the pile of self-hatred that had been festering for so many years.

I could not have approached my sister, Candy. Although we are close now, we did not have a close relationship at the time mainly because I felt inadequate around her. She excelled at everything and was completely opposite of me. She was slim, popular, active, into sports, organized, and beautiful. I wasn't jealous but there was a keen sense in me that people preferred her company over mine and that cut deep. I felt lost, as if I had no footing on which to start me in a direction I needed to be going in society. Candy perceived my inactivity in life as being lazy and often told me so. Everything negative she had to say about me I believed, so I became those things. There was a part of me that felt helpless, for inside I wanted to be doing all of those things that she did. I wanted to be very active but the energy and confidence was not there.

Just like everyone else around me, my sister could not have known that my physical weakness and withdrawal was due to the exhaustive depression which had fallen upon me. Because of the abuse I had suffered, food became one of the few joys that I had and overeating had caused me to be overweight, therefore driving the depression even further. I was convinced that I had no self-worth and little worth to anyone else so my own little world was more appealing to me and not so critical in my eyes.

If I had talked to anyone it would have been my brother, Tim. I adored him and still do. Intelligent, compassionate, gentle-natured, and even-handed, he would have counseled me in a way that I feel could have brought me out of myself and I would have thrived with the confidence which was needed to excel and move forward in a healthy manner. But so great was the fear that he would find me ridiculous and laugh at me, that I held my silence.

Many times I ached for my family to know who I was inside but there was a feeling that they would not understand that deep side of me, the side my talents seemed always to be addressing. Then there was the fear that they would laugh and scorn me as if I could not measure up to anything of good value. That place inside of me played host to many stories and I longed to be in foreign places to see the ancient castles and ruins which had decorated my writing in flares of imagination and wonder. Then there was the music.

Music: Therapy for the Soul

By 1975, my appreciation for music covered a variety of genres such as Rock, Country, Bluegrass, Gospel, Classical, and Celtic. But what I loved to do was sing to music. Over and over again, the songs of the Carpenters, The Bee Gees, the Byrds, the Moody Blues and the Osmonds could be heard, sometimes loudly, from my bedroom. I learned to harmonize with all of those unique voices. When dad was there he would exaggerate saying, "you could see the walls warping in and out from the noise." My mind was wrapped around how the notes and chords would travel into all areas of emotion and I began to write stories on paper which enveloped the harmonies of strings and vocals. Over a decade and a half before music videos emerged, I was creating them in my mind.

Though I had spiritual assurance that I was not alone, the human side of me felt isolated and damaged. The therapy that music offered would cushion the loneliness I had felt for so long. I loved listening to Mom and Dad's Southern Gospel and Bluegrass records. There was a sense of home in the lyrics and sound. Among the other genres of music I loved, there were songs that were upbeat and happy which I could identify with. A number of songs were the only link I had to reassure me that there were others who had gone through circumstances which had disrupted their lives in a traumatic manner. The pain expressed in those songs were not explicitly evident so much in words; the music itself told the story in unspoken volumes, each sound resonated pain, release, solitude and peace. I would sing along with lyrics such as, "I am alone again, you can't believe the tears that I've shed, I'm an abandoned train," and "When do I know if there is an answer why, I wonder if I know where I begin, How do I stop myself from gonna cry, I wonder if I know where I fit in,"[1] expressing exactly how I felt. But then as I would get those emotions out I would move on to happier lyrics;

> *"Something you can't hide says you're lonely*
> *Hidden deep inside of you only*
> *It's there for you to see take a look and be*
> *Burn slowly the candle of life*
> *Something there outside says we're only*
> *In the hands of time falling slowly*
> *It's there for us to know with love that we can go*
> *Burn slowly the candle of life*
> *So love everybody and make them your friend"*[2]

Such lyrics conveyed to me knowledge that seemed a natural part of me. The desire of wanting to love everyone and be a friend to all was a characteristic embedded deep within. As I sang along there was a release of my own pain and sorrow followed by a peace that assured me that life does go on. The sun rises and sets every day and what passes in between can bring healing and progress, or depression and darkness depending on how we process trauma in our lives. The choices we make determine whether the candle burns slowly or quickly. So I wrapped my life around melodies which kept me floating above water as I swam toward a land of hope I could not yet see, struggling upon waves of confusion, pain and slivers here and there of happiness.

The Cabin in Ava, Missouri

Chapter Nine

"Not until we are lost do we begin to understand ourselves."
—Henry David Thoreau

My freshman year. I had spent a lot of time thinking about it. High School. Yes, that surge of one moment in your life when you pass from middle school into the big league. By then I had some desire to be a little more social in that I loved to take part in dance routines so I tried out for the dance squad, or as it was called in those days, the pom-pon team. When I was in high school there were cheerleaders and pom-pon girls. The pom-pon girls did all of the dance routines at halftime during the sports events. When I was called as part of the team after tryouts I was ecstatic.

I soon found that being a part of the in-crowd was not really my cup of tea. The other girls on the team were all nice, but I did not feel like I was a "part of the group" because I wasn't involved in the same social party scene that happened on the weekends. By only having a limited exposure to their gatherings, I was left void of the camaraderie they shared. Though I had crushes on guys, I didn't date and was happy about it, for in time I saw one too many of my friends go too far.

For me it was a joy just to take part in the dance routines. That is why I tried out in the first place. As much fun as I did have, I found it to be an experience lacking fulfillment. The price that came with popular groups was not worth the purchase, for there were hidden costs that emerged if one was not careful in their choices. I recall one of my friends coming over on a Friday night to visit me. I was a little surprised because she usually went out every weekend. She had led a wild life and allowed herself to be taken advantage of many times. When I asked her why she wasn't out, she told me she wanted to come to our place because when she was with me she stayed out of trouble. It felt good to hear her say such a thing and I was grateful I had maintained the standards set by my mother. All throughout my freshman year I would watch one too many friends get involved with sex, drugs and alcohol. At length I asked myself, "So...this is it?" I decided I had a better time in my room with my books and music. It would have been nice to have been connected to a church that had a good youth program.

    I found out at the end of my freshman year that we were moving again. This time I was the one who was devastated. I wasn't the most popular girl in school but I did have a lot of friends. I did not want to move again, especially in the middle of high school. But I had no choice. Mom felt we should move to Idaho because Dad wanted to continue logging out there. She wanted to be close to where he was logging so that she could care for him and keep things balanced. Still trying to manage effects of the abuse I had suffered in Oregon, and dealing with the normal chaotic emotions which come with teenage years, the move brought out a side of me that was not very pleasant. In Missouri I had made friends and found outlets. Being uprooted yet again caused me to become angry and withdraw even further within myself.

Bear Tracks

Before we made the move to Idaho in the summer of 1977, my sister had married and moved to North Dakota. As we prepared to make the trip west my mood was even more dampened when I learned my brother and I would be spending the summer in a tent, while our parents slept in the camper shell on the truck. When we arrived at the campsite which would be our new home, I half jokingly told my brother he could sleep in the front of the tent so if a bear came in, it would get him first! I had this nightly ritual of going to sleep as I listened to the all-night mystery theater on our shortwave radio so every bump in the night or screeching owl caused the hair to stand up on the back of my neck.

One night there was some noise in the camp by our picnic table. A young bear was looking for food. At length it made its way into our tent and was chewing my brother's hair. It was my brother's habit of swinging his arm if someone tried to wake him, and he did just that. By then Dad had awakened because of the noise and from the camper began to holler and the bear took off. I slept through the whole thing and when Tim awoke the next morning there was hair all over his pillow! By then I had had it. I was already angry because Dad had hauled us off again and here we were exposed to wild animals with little or no protection. Anytime Tim said anything, I smarted off to him and at length he threatened to throw me into the icy mountain river water. I made the mistake of daring him and he hoisted me over his shoulder and cast me in. I must say it did much to make me think before I spoke. Before long we rented a place in Boise and I registered to attend my sophomore year at Borah High School.

In every area we lived, there was something to focus on and dream about. In Boise it was Star Wars and the Bee Gees. I was Luke Skywalker in the scene where he has just argued with his adoptive parents about going away to Jedi training. He had knowledge within him that this was where he needed to be. He felt as if he were to be part of something big but didn't know what or how. He walked out and gazed into the dusk at two large moons, wondering where in the world he fit in. I remember watching it the first time and that one scene enveloped me completely.

Once again, I became lost in music. I simply loved the Bee Gees and their harmony. I refer to the older songs before the disco craze hit. I became lost in those songs because they were about life. Every song told a story in lyrical journeys of pain, abandonment, sorrow, love, happiness, joy, and hope. The cycle of life could be found in all of those songs and as I sang along with them I felt as if there were others just as lost as I was. There was a sense that if I just kept singing, I would get to where I belonged. By mid semester, work in the timber had slowed to a crawl and we moved to Douglasville, Georgia. I would finish my sophomore year at Lithia Springs High School. As we settled in Douglasville at Aunt Pat and Uncle Max's, I actually felt as if I belonged somewhere. For my mother it was different.

The Struggle of Where to Fit In

In every move we had made there was always the burden of having to rely on others. What was most difficult for Mom was living with relatives. She had no sense of home and it bothered her that we kept imposing. Even though we knew we were welcome, my mother's family was concerned with how inconsistent our lives were. Time and time again we had moved and Dad was getting to the age where he needed to be settled on some career in order to have a retirement. While we were at Uncle Max's, Dad worked in construction and Mom worked at a factory. By then my brother had graduated and my sister had married. I was facing yet another new school and worse, coming in between semesters.

I love my Uncle Max and Aunt Pat. Of all of my relatives, they were the ones I longed to be around the most. They made sense, were structured, and felt like home. They were both concerned about me because I watched too much television and confined myself to my room. They had no way of knowing that I had been molested, that the effects had caused me to be so withdrawn that I had no energy at all. I was tired all of the time, longing to be interactive, feeling like I had no input, but loving to be in their midst.

No matter how I tried to pull out of the heaviness, there was always this voice telling me that I was not up to par, or good enough to qualify for anything. That fear of being laughed at was ever present. Because I had been brutally made fun of by a few boys in elementary school, I had the perspective that everyone looked at me the way they did. The problem was that every move brought new and fresh assaults from the mouth of inconsiderate classmates who were ignorant of the effects of verbal attacks. I was exposed to a handful of idiots who had bad things to say and I had not been there long enough to make friends who would be a support system until after the damage was done. Then would come another move and it would happen all over again. There was never enough time and stability to build myself up.

There had been some progress in Missouri during the three years we were there. I had gained enough confidence to try out for pom-pon, I had become part of the choir and was just discovering myself and my potential when it was all shut down by another move. I was physically, mentally, and emotionally tired, scared to date boys, addicted to food, and disgusted with myself. I hated myself to such an extreme that I felt no others could like me. Even though I had friends, I felt alone inside. I had one friend in which I confided all things and I knew that if anyone loved and accepted me it was Him. It was the love of the Savior which held me up to where I could tread water, and tread I did for the next few years. Throughout all of that pain, not one day went by when I did not hear or feel the voice of both of my parents' heritage calling out to me. One side I did not heed for the fear which had been installed within me. The other, my Tennessee mountain folk, I wanted to throw myself into but I had little information to go on, only visits to the mountains. So in my room I remained.

While in Douglasville, I made new friends and relaxed into life again. I became good friends with a family by the name of Wade. Their daughter Cindy and I went everywhere together. I started to attend their Baptist church, feeling some attachment there, yet something was missing. I had brought the name Joseph Smith up to the youth pastor once but did not let on that I was a descendant. He gave me a good long speech about the evils of this man and Mormons, so much so that I refrained from even thinking about it for some time. I chose simply to throw myself into the joys of being around my mother's people and my friends. I joined the high school choir and was asked by the teacher to do solos at competition but I refused immediately, inadequacy invading my senses. I could not bring myself to stand before people alone. My grades suffered because I would take zeros instead of do oral reports. This fear of public exposure would be continual throughout high school.

The spring and summer of 1978 brought a fresh outlook for me. My Aunt Pat was very creative in many ways. One was ceramics. In her basement she had a large number of ceramic figures and she taught me how to paint them. I absorbed it like a sponge, spending many hours in her basement. It was a new comfort that I could embrace. Just as I was beginning to open up a little, there came yet again another move. Some of Mom's greatest sorrow would emerge within the summer months of 1978, yet she would also be shown that miracles come to those who pray, believing that those prayers will be answered.

On the Run

Dad had grown frustrated with Georgia so he left once again to go to Idaho and work in the timber. We stayed behind, enabling me to finish school. I did not want to go west. I had made good friends and started to feel alive for the first time in a long time. Toward the end of spring semester Mom drove to Maryville, Tennessee to help care for her father who was dying of cancer while I stayed with my uncle and aunt. By this time, my sister was divorced and had moved to Idaho and was attending Boise State University. Her marriage had been

Chapter Nine

marred by physical and emotional abuse. Suffering from flashbacks as a result of drugs her husband had given to her, Candy lost complete memory of who she was, disappearing in June of 1978. Mom flew to Boise and with the help of my brother started looking for Candy.

Uncle Max flew me to Missouri in July and I stayed with my Grandma Smith. After three months of searching for Candy, Mom returned to Ava, Missouri broken- hearted. She got me enrolled at Ava High School and tried her best to function. Having exhausted all efforts to try and find my sister, Mom turned to the Lord in prayer. In that prayer, Mom asked for something, anything that would tell her that Candy was alive and safe. At midnight the phone rang. It was Candy. She said, "I do not know who you are but this phone number came to me while I was in church." Mom replied, "I know who you are." Candy hung up the phone when she heard the words, then called back. Mom told her that she was her daughter and after a long conversation, Candy agreed to let her and Tim come and visit. In that visit Mom found out that Candy had been found by some college students only sixteen miles from Mammaw and Pappaw Roberts' home in Tennessee.

Three female college students had noticed Candy under some pallets on campus. She could not walk, talk, or hear. Each one of these students was attending college to be a nurse and all three had experience in areas helpful to Candy. They took her to their place and nursed her back to health, but she had no idea who she was. At length, she began to attend a Maranatha Church.

Mom and Tim stayed for a week to visit with Candy and they talked her into going back to Missouri with them.

She agreed on the condition they would bring her back if she was not happy. After a couple of weeks Candy returned to Tennessee, but called Mom soon after in fear. She felt that her life was in danger for she had carried a Book of Mormon to church with her and the pastor stood before the congregation and rebuked her, commanding her to leave the building and never return. Mom and Tim went to Tennessee and picked Candy up, then they all went to Idaho. I remained in Missouri with Grandma Smith. While in Idaho, Mom tried to work with Candy on regaining her memory. Through discussions, my sister would reveal things as they began to surface. At first she did not remember how she got to Tennessee under those pallets, but after time, she began to recall some of it.

Candy remembered that she was going to Boise State but then there is a blank space of time. Then she recalled hitchhiking and going from Boise to Denver, California, then Knoxville, Tennessee. She had no money. She remembered hanging out at fast food places and if people would leave their food on the table instead of throwing it out, she would get it, or find food in trash cans. Then she was found by the college students in Tennessee.

Though Candy regained her memory, the experience seemed to bring to the surface an inability to find a balance in life. Dad was having a hard time reconciling himself to the whole situation and he told Mom she needed to take Candy and go back to Missouri. After a few months, Candy seemed to be working through the transition much easier and when she felt strong enough, she went back to Boise and applied for college again.

Chapter Nine

When Mom and Candy left for Idaho, I begged to stay in Missouri and finish my junior year in Ava. I got to stay and though I loved my Aunt Myrl and Uncle Earl, and had the ability to go to Grandma's house nearby, it was not home. I did not know what a real home was. My home was in the music and books I had around me. The environment I lived in was far removed from what I was used to. My aunt lived in a small trailer so there was not a lot of room in their house. But they were the best people, jolly and fun-loving. They were always willing to help anybody at any time.

There was no real sense of belonging because some of my cousins resented my being there and I was aware of it. Once again, I escaped by staying in my small room in a little trailer, always knowing I was meant for something but feeling less than nothing. I was writing stories about other times and other places, where the damsel in distress, being me, always got rescued by a dashing Mr. Darcy.

A Trip to the West

My junior year of high school flew by and during the summer of 1979, I rode out to Idaho with my sister's boyfriend. It was his intention to surprise her and I was to spend the summer with Mom and Dad in Boise. The venture for the young man would prove to be one of heartbreak, for while he was there, Candy broke the news to him that she was a Lesbian. Dad's reaction was to cut off all relations with her, but Mom said that was not right. Though it broke Mom's heart and she did not understand how it had come to such a point, she continued to love and support Candy as her daughter. This action would prove to be worthy in the future and

Hills & Valleys

became a witness that all things can be healed and moved in a positive direction when the pure love of Christ is employed.

In August of 1979, I boarded a plane bound for Missouri. Tim rode his bike all the way to the airport to tell me goodbye and as the door of the plane shut there was communication to the pilot to hold the plane. They allowed my brother to board and say goodbye and those around me witnessed the love of a brother toward his sister, none of them aware of the tattered lives which had formed such a solid bond. As the plane took off, I was aware that I was heading for the final year of my adolescence, soaring toward adulthood. It seemed frightening, appealing and sad all at the same time.

The sadness was the emotion most overbearing. Yet again, I was spending another year of my life without my family close by. Though I felt I had achieved little during my teenage years, what few things I did achieve were accomplished without my family nearby. Now I looked at the prospect of my Senior year without any of them. It was my choice, but I could not bear to start my final year of high school in a new place. I wanted to be where there were friends. No matter what I chose, there was emptiness. Had I stayed in Boise, I would have spent most of the year trying to establish myself around people I didn't know. In Ava the school year would be happier. I would be surrounded by friends, yet I had no home or family that was my own.

My senior year would prove to be the best of all. I became good friends with one of my teachers, Julia Roos. She had seen some of my writing and suggested I enter it into state competition. I was completely floored that one of my instructors thought I could write well. To my amazement my narrative poem, *1484* tied for third place in the state poetry contest. It raised within me an ambition to be more serious about my writing and look to a career in that area. Another teacher that I grew to love and respect was Judy Streight, who taught both my brother and me, as well as my son. Everyone described her graded papers as having been bled on by her red pen, "the pen of death," they would say. She was brutal but amazing. If one left her class without knowing how to write a college paper, it was their fault.

During this year, my love of history and literature was magnified, specifically the Medieval period. I had an in-depth style of writing to the extent that the reader would swear it had been written hundreds of years before. I wrote short stories, poetry and even began a historical novel, all of which seemed to absorb the pain from my past and redirect it toward creativity. I dove headlong into choir as well as even venturing forth to take part in a quartet in competition. The sound of harmony reminded me of when I used to sing with my sister at bluegrass parties. There was a sense that I should be doing more vocally but I had no idea in what direction to walk. I would never entertain the idea of singing alone.

I was also feeling the pull to know more about Joseph Smith, Jr. My aunt's house was below the hill from the cabin, which now stood empty. Often I would walk up and go inside. It was my private getaway and there in the study was Grandpa's trunk. Every time I went up to the cabin I would go through the trunk. This was a vital time. I had no one around me, plenty of solitude, and many questions. I wondered about the people in the images. As I set them down, I was aware of the afternoon rays of the sun peering through a window nearby, illuminating the room. I gazed through those rays, reflecting upon our past in amazement, in awe that we had gone through so much but were still sane. Sane as we seemed, I wouldn't say that I endured, overcame and moved forward. I merely took what came and floated along, immersing myself in books, music and writing. I guess that is why people drink, so they won't have to feel the pain. But drinking was not an acceptable option to me. Reading, writing and singing were my addictions and just as one gets lost in a drunken stupor, there is always the time when you have to face things sober. I came to such realizations on those afternoons in the cabin, peering through the sunlight. I also came to realize that, on many an afternoon as I looked through that trunk, the sense of family and yearning to know more was always accompanied by a fear. There was a darkness that seemed always to be lurking nearby. At times, within the confines of complete solitude, there was an awareness of that darkness which caused me to look over my shoulder. Mom had sensed it as well when we lived there before and there was more than one occasion when members of the Temple Lot Church came to bless the house.

All of Grandpa's papers were at the cabin. I began to read them to see what I could learn of the history but many of the papers I read through consisted of his account of lawsuits and struggles within The Temple Lot Church. There was often friction between the brethren in the Temple Lot Church, and Grandpa, as secretary and apostle, seemed always to be caught in the middle. It was sad. The only conveyance of joy I found was in his journals where he touched upon the missions he served, particularly in Wales. At length I stopped reading, until one day I found a pamphlet titled, *Joseph Smith Tells His Own Story.*

Chapter Nine

"I Was Born in the Year of Our Lord...."

It was early spring on a Saturday afternoon. The cabin was freezing but I stayed throughout the afternoon because when the sun peered through the window at one point there was a nice warm place in the corner to sit. The pamphlet, printed by the Reorganized Church of Jesus Christ of Latter Day Saints, was quite small and very old. I would later learn that the text was drawn from volumes three and four of The Times and Seasons. Finally, I did not have to hear the perspectives of others or be exposed to contention and bitterness. There in my little corner, for the first time I would read the account of my great-great-grandfather's experiences from his own hand. As I began to read the whole room filled with warmth and I felt a presence that was both sweet and jolly; filled with love.

"I was born in the year of our Lord one thousand eight hundred and five, on the twenty-third day of December, in the town of Sharon, Windsor County, state of Vermont. My father, Joseph Smith, senior, left the state of Vermont, and moved to Palmyra, Ontario now Wayne County, in the state of New York, when I was in my tenth year." (1)

As the words passed before me there was a sense of calm in the room. For a few brief moments all of the turmoil which had surrounded my father's family when they spoke about anything to do with Mormons washed away from memory. Instead, my mind was filled with words of purity and sincerity, and every word rang true as if the author himself were standing before me bearing witness. I read on until I had reached the point where Joseph was about to go into the woods and pray. By then the evening had set in and I could barely see. I longed to take the pamphlet with me but I did not want my aunt to know I had it. Placing it carefully in the trunk, I walked back down the hill with a renewed desire to know of my heritage. I still did not understand why there were different churches. I did not want to know. My whole desire was fixed on knowing Joseph's story. I promised myself to go every chance I could in order to finish reading the pamphlet. The next day I went with grandma and Aunt Marie to a Temple Lot gathering and did not get back until late.

On Monday, I was called into the counselor's office and was told that as they were calculating the senior student's credits to make sure everyone met the requirements, they noticed that I fell short two credit hours. With all of our moves no one had examined my records close enough to see that some of the schools I had attended did not require as many credits as Ava's school district. There was not enough time to make those credits up and my heart sank. The counselor told me that I could walk with the class at graduation but my diploma would not be in the holder. She suggested that I take summer school and earn the credits, after which I would receive my diploma. I agreed, knowing full well that I would not be able to for I was to go to Idaho directly after graduation.

The incident knocked me for such a loop that I lost all interest in everything. I was planning on applying to colleges for writing but I felt defeated in that as well. I still had little confidence in myself and saw no way for me to achieve anything. During that time, Tim had moved back to Ava and married. I moved in with them until school was over. The rest of my senior year was spent in depression. Once again I resorted to my room. Graduation came and went with my classmates surrounded by all of their families.

Chapter Nine

Soon I would be bound to Idaho for the summer. I hated it there. It wasn't the state or the people but the situation we were in. Anytime I had to go to Idaho I was leaving a place that I loved. After graduation, I left everything behind as I headed west, including the trunk that I had never had a chance to revisit after reading the first part of Joseph's story. What little I did read had clung to me in waves of belonging. Even though I felt lost and unattached to anything solid, something had begun to take shape. An understanding had started to develop within me that the connection I felt to Joseph and Emma extended beyond lineage. With all that had happened since the last trip to the cabin, I had allowed the trials of life to pull me away for a season, but in retrospect I have to wonder if it was not yet time to know the whole story.

Candy, Tim and me, 1980

Chapter Ten

"If we have no peace, it is because we have forgotten that we belong to each other."

—Mother Theresa

The summer of 1980 was one of my most miserable in many ways. It was the hottest on record and I was in a small barren town with no trees called Horseshoe Bend, Idaho. Dad would work in the timber during the week and come down on the weekend. During my time there, I cared for the children of some friends of ours. On days off, I would read and every now and then we would go to Boise and I would see a movie. Still, much of my time was spent in my room lost in music. I was restless. I wanted to be on my own heading in any direction but where I was. When my sister said she was going to Missouri for a while, I asked if I could ride along. I had planned on staying with Grandma Smith until I could find employment.

I was not looking forward to the long drive back to Missouri. The heat index at times was over 100 degrees and Candy's air conditioner did not work. I was already nervous about the ride for Candy was in the habit of picking up hitchhikers and I made her swear not to or I was not going with her. We had very little money, enough for gas and very little for food. The decision was made that we would sleep in the car on the way to save money.

Chapter Ten

As we headed down the road, I noted one of the road signs gave the distance to Salt Lake City. A dreaded fear ran through me. I had heard horror stories about that place. When I asked if we were going through Salt Lake and she said yes, I was mortified. I didn't say a word. As we came close to the city it was early afternoon and I sank low down in my seat so I could not be seen. I didn't want to see anything either. I just thought to myself, if I pray that we pass through safely it will be over soon, but then Candy did the unthinkable. She pulled off on an exit. Something was wrong with the car and she needed to get it looked at. I was in shock! Stop? In downtown Salt Lake City? Was she crazy? I mumbled a hesitant agreement but I refused to get out of the car.

It turned out that it was an easy fix and we soon got back on the road. As soon as we started through the canyon I sat back up in my seat. As it came close to nightfall we pulled over for some food. I told Candy what I wanted and she said I could get out and order for myself. What she didn't realize is that I was still so frozen about doing public things, I didn't feel comfortable ordering my food. It was different when I was in choir or pom-pon. In those moments I was someone else doing something with a group. Whenever I was faced with doing something on my own, I could see the person before me boring into every part of me, laughing, scorning, disgusted by what they saw. I was told I could order or go hungry, so I chose to go hungry. At length she gave in and ordered a hot dog for me.

A few weeks after arriving in Missouri, I got a job with Emerson Electric. My job was inserting all of the wires into a casing, dropping the rotor into a ceiling fan motor, putting the

Hills & Valleys

in shield on and screwing it down. This was all done on an assembly line. It was hard work but it was a paycheck and at that point any chance I had of going to college seemed lost as well as my dreams of being a writer. I didn't believe in myself enough and no one in my midst knew of my desires. Within a month of starting work, I received news that my Pappaw was dying and I was devastated that I could not leave and be with my family in Tennessee, but I had just started work and it was impossible.

It bears significance here to examine a period of my Pappaw's life between two illnesses; one in which he was healed, and the other which would claim his life. In 1962, the year I was born, Pappaw was diagnosed with Leukemia and given three weeks to live. One day the hospital sent him home and told him to come back in a few days for more tests to see how far the disease had advanced. While at home, Pappaw had a vision. In this vision Moses took him to a high mountain. Across from where they were standing was another mountain and Pappaw could see all of his people who had passed on. Moses looked at him and said that it was not yet time for him to be with his people. After coming around, Pappaw wondered at what the vision meant. Upon his next hospital visit, the doctors ran all of the necessary tests and walked into Pappaw's room amazed, telling him that there was no more cancer in his body. He would live another sixteen years when pancreatic cancer would take his life.

When Pappaw was diagnosed with cancer for the second time, Mom went to spend time with him. At the time she had already been baptized into the Temple Lot Church. She did not understand why the Lord prompted her to be

Chapter Ten

baptized into that church, for she had always felt ill at ease with the contention among some of the members. Because of that contention, she did not feel the spirit as she had so often in her life. But she moved in the direction she had been given.

While she was visiting Pappaw she gave him a Book of Mormon, for he had always been searching for more. Pappaw had been reading it for some time when Mom went to see him one day in his hospital room. He told her that he didn't see anything in the world wrong with that book and he asked if she was happy in the decision she had made. She replied that she had done what the Lord led her to do. He then said something that truly stands out to me today, he said, "If the Lord leads you into another church someday will you go?" And she said that she would. That promise would hold special meaning in later years. Pappaw died in September 1980. There followed the most horrible actions of specific family members, especially one, whose jealousy of Mom had festered so over the years that she made sure that Mom got very little of her father's belongings. By such action, Mom was denied things which he had promised her. Devastated and hurt, she came to peaceful terms with it all, cherishing the most special thing that she shared with her father that no one could take away; the pure and loving relationship they had.

Mammaw seemed to spiral downward after Pappaw died, causing Mom and Dad to go stay with her for a while. There in her mother's home, Mom took care of the woman who had been cruel to her for so many years. Mom loved her mother but she still had not reconciled herself to the cruelty of an abusive childhood. She had forgiven her mother, but there was still the question of "why?" Why did she hate her own daughter so?

One night Mammaw asked Mom if she would sleep with her. It was as if a frightened child had asked her, too afraid to sleep alone. Mom was an adult now with one grandchild and still she was terrified of her mother. Though she resisted, Mom felt sorry for Mammaw and told her that she would sleep in the guest room with her but not in Pappaw's bed. That night Mammaw put her arm around Mom's waist and through the night cried periodically for the Lord to help her. For Mom it was a night of complete unrest as she felt Mammaw struggle with a torment that she had no way of understanding, or helping. After a week Mom and Dad returned to Missouri, leaving the care of Mammaw in the hands of siblings who lived close by.

New Life, New Direction

I worked at Emerson Electric until the summer of 1982 when I quit in preparation for my wedding in September. At the firesides I do today, many ask of my husband and I choose to remain silent. Here I will only allude to certain events which increased my faith as I walked toward the fullness of the gospel. Suffice it to say, I followed in my mother's footsteps and married too soon. I was so much in love that I didn't notice he wasn't. Like my father, he thought he was ready to get married but soon found himself in a situation that was not what he had hoped.

Both of us were raised to believe that once you marry you stay married. Unfortunately, the hollowness of our marriage brought out the worst in both of us: with him, the

Chapter Ten

magnification of an already violent temper, with me, even more depression. I withdrew from nearly everyone as the years passed except my children. Somewhere in my hopes of some kind of future, I entertained the idea of going through correspondence courses to finish the credits I lacked in high school to graduate. It was my intention to go to college for writing. When I mentioned it to my fiancé he flatly said we could not make a living off of my writing. He had never read anything I had written, but I felt as if I was not good enough to try after he said those words.

As in the case of my mother, I focused on raising my children to have sound morals and to know what the pure love of Christ is. I did not suffer physical abuse, but there are scars that cut much deeper than physical abuse and I already had an abundance of those before I got married. The unhappiness of our marriage caused me to eat even more and like myself even less. There were clearly issues and addictions that my husband needed to overcome as well which were dark and damaging to one's spirit. To say more about my husband's character while we were married would be an ill thing indeed, for though there were problems that were traumatic for me, he was generally a good man who had just become stuck in a situation that made him unhappy. He has since remarried and is a different person, having learned from his errors and changed in many ways. I feel if I were to air all of our dirty laundry it would just open old wounds that are now healed, altering his progress toward change. Having moved forward, we are better friends today than when we were married. It is enough to say just that and go on with my story.

The first four years of our marriage I spent much time trying to find out about family history. I was settled for the first time in my life, had my own home and finally felt as if I could relax and truly find out just what my lineage was on both sides of the family. There were not many avenues to take in the small town of Ava. One day, I remembered the trunk at the cabin. It was still there even though we had not lived there for years. I drove out one fall day in 1984 and retrieved the trunk, delivering it to its new home in town.

Any time I spent pouring through all of those pictures caused the old aching feeling to return. Who were they? What did they have to do with me? They seemed to call out to me and I was frustrated to no end that I did not know who they were. I thought surely some of my aunts in town could tell me who they were but as I showed them they had no idea. I wondered to myself what was wrong with my father's people, especially the generation above me. Why were they unable to tell me who these people were?

Mom and Dad were still living in Idaho so I could not ask him. Once again I put the pictures in the trunk but try as I might I could not find the pamphlet where Joseph told his own story. I was greatly saddened, for that is the main reason I went back to get the trunk.

My husband actually had a friend who was LDS and he would come by every now and then with the sister missionaries. They were very sweet but I had my guard up and would not discuss church with them in depth. After some time, they were told they had to cut us loose as prospective investigators because we were not receptive. It is interesting because I could feel that they had the Spirit but had convinced myself that they were spreading lies and trying to entrap me so I did not allow myself to open up to them very much. I talked to them about the Temple Lot Church but asked that they refrain from talking about their church. In 1985 I learned I was expecting our first child. I was so excited! As the day grew closer for delivery I found myself being more and more impressed with the necessity of learning my genealogy.

Mom and Dad had moved back to Ava when I was about eight months along so Mom was there to take me to the hospital when I went into labor. I only dilated part way and then the labor stopped. They sent me home and three days later I went into labor again but only went so far and then stopped again. As the doctor examined me he discovered that my pelvis was tilted. Oddly, it was similar to Mom's pelvis being tilted into the birth canal, though I had never received an injury to cause such a distortion. I still remember what the doctor called it; Cephalopelvic Disproportion. My son was big and my pelvis was so tilted that he would get so far then stop because he could not progress. An emergency C-section was performed and when I woke up I had a beautiful 9lb 3oz baby boy. We named him Bryan Dale Davis.

Bryan was a child of light to me, always laughing, gentle natured, and content. He filled a part of my life that had been missing. As he grew into his first year, I became increasingly aware of the importance of family. Often times as I looked into his blue eyes I would reflect upon the blue eyes in the portrait, which had given me the desire to know who my ancestors were. The feeling within me was strong to know them and become acquainted with their stories. Maybe as I did so, the answers to why I felt such a connection to a history I did not fully know or understand would surface.

Genealogy: The Door to My Past

Ava's library was small and they had some reference books pertaining to genealogy, but not a lot and I didn't even know where to start. I had only four generations back to Joseph and Emma on Dad's side and two generations back on Mom's. Upon one visit to the library I found myself in the reference room where another woman was cataloguing books. I thought she worked there so I approached her and asked the best process in doing genealogy. She told me that there were a few good sources there but the best place to go was a Family History Center, which made perfect sense to me. So I asked where to find one and was told it was sixty miles away in Springfield, Missouri at the LDS Church. "What is that?" I asked, eager to find this wonderful place where I might do research. "The Mormon Church," She replied.

The woman may as well have run a knife through me. Imagine my feelings, my hopes dashed in one fell swoop. There was no way I was setting foot into that building! My father warned me about Mormons, missionaries in particular; how they are well trained, and if you are not careful you could be easily snookered! I left feeling defeated and almost fuming as I sat in the car. Then the spirit whispered to me it was more important to get the information no matter where it came from. So I decided to take my tablet with the four generations to this Family History Center and act like I knew what I was

Chapter Ten

doing. Then I would not have to talk to anyone for fear of getting snookered. But I didn't know then that such a plan is not well laid, for sometimes there are missionaries in a Family History Center and I would soon learn that missionaries have a sort of beacon that can spot a nonmember fifty miles off!

As I walked into the Family History Center, I was greeted by a kind lady wearing a black tag; a missionary. She asked if I was there to do family research. I nodded and then she asked if I was familiar with the computers. I lied and told her I knew how to use them. Then she said if I needed anything to let her or her husband know. I then knew I had it made; I would simply sit down and figure everything out for myself. I would not need to ask for any assistance, but after I clicked on "enter here," on the computer screen, everything went downhill.

I tried several avenues but did not know what I was doing. I was not about to announce, "I need help," five minutes after I sat down. This is when I learned that missionaries work in teams. I did not realize that the Elder had been eyeing my progress, or lack thereof. Just as I formed a brilliant plan of how to make a successful exit, the Elder came over, sat down beside me and asked if I needed any help.

"Sure," I replied with a smile, feeling thoroughly defeated inside

"Well, I'll tell you what," He responded, "let's take a name through and I will show you how it is done. What is the farthest name back that you have?"

I thought to myself, "What? I can't tell him that!" I was afraid to tell anyone I was Joseph Smith's descendant. "I need

185

Hills & Valleys

a surname," He said. "Smith," I answered hesitantly. And as he typed it in I began to think that maybe it would not hurt to give that much information out. Smith is a common name after all and what could happen here in this little room with these two missionaries?

"Okay," he said, "I need the given name." I paused for a moment looking down at my tablet. It was a moment I will never forget; all manner of thoughts passed through my mind. Then I thought, "Maybe he won't notice!" After all, Joseph is a common name too and no one at home ever talked about him, so maybe these people would not realize who I was talking about.

"Joseph," I said quietly. There was no reaction. I was so relieved that I sat back against my chair and let out a breath.

"Birth date?" That was an easy one. "December 23, 1805," I responded, almost jubilant at my success in eluding attention. The Elder turned and looked at me suddenly, "Really, now! Would that be Joseph the Prophet?" He smiled.

I would have been upset that my attempts at anonymity failed were it not for his excited behavior. I thought saying such a thing would bring harm to me. He called his wife over and they began asking a barrage of questions about me and my history; questions I could not answer. I left feeling very ignorant about myself, convinced that once and for all I should find out the history behind my ancestry.

There were two things I noticed about those missionaries. They were very kind, and they had the Holy Ghost with them. I knew it because of how my mother taught me. But it contradicted everything my father had said about

Chapter Ten

these people, and I was not sure how to handle the experience. I did feel comfortable enough to keep going back, and it was during those visits that I learned about a town named Nauvoo. From the time my eyes fell upon the word, I knew I had to go there. The trip would have to wait until another time, but I later found out that there was a Family History Center at the LDS Church in Ava and I began to go there instead of Springfield. During the winter of 1988 I would spend hours there. On one visit I learned I could order a microfilm of a book that was written by my first cousin two times removed, Audentia Smith Anderson. Audentia was one of Joseph Smith III's daughters.

Throughout January of 1989 I partially learned the in-depth history of my lineage. Oddly enough, I skipped over Joseph's biography and went to the generation above him then back from that point. I would begin to read his, but then felt compelled to learn of the earlier generations first. These biographies quenched my thirsty imagination, linking to kings and queens of England and other historical figures in European and American history. I was both amazed and delighted for I began to discover the reasons behind my love of certain periods of history and why I was drawn to certain cultures, such as Celtic.

When I learned the microfilm could be copied, I began to do just that with each visit, compiling one chapter here and one chapter there. I had to do it slowly because it was expensive. After about a month, I became engulfed in problems at home, putting a halt to the reading. I never could read during stressful times. I found myself in survival mode most of the time, trying to figure out how to make things work. Spring arrived as I found I was expecting another child and as the freshness of the seasonal change ushered out the staleness of winter, I became even more anxious to break free and head to Nauvoo. Summer could not arrive fast enough.

When I mentioned to my dad that we were going to Nauvoo, he did not seem very enthusiastic. He began telling me how Nauvoo was a mistake and never should have happened, that the Saints had erred and that is why the temple was destroyed. There I was listening to all of the negativity, excited to go yet at the same time feeling pained by the stinging words. Something within me cried out urging me not to listen as if to say, "Wait a minute, you must hear our side." I was darkened by what my father had said. I felt like something was off-kilter, as if someone had painted a picture but used the wrong scale with inappropriate colors. The canvas was sorely misused and I knew there was a better form of art out there. I just needed to find it. Why accept the distortion of Picasso when I could have the wholeness of Raphael?

It fell to me to find out on my own why there was such bitterness in the family toward the Mormon Church and why all of my Smith relatives refused to talk about Joseph. I knew it would be a long and arduous task. Even thinking about it seemed to almost smother me, for I was surrounded by so much negativity within my father's family. One thing I knew for sure, that there was a place called Nauvoo, and I needed to go there before I did anything else because the yearning was so strong.

When June arrived, I got out the atlas and turned to the Illinois page, scanning over the entire state. I had no idea

Chapter Ten

where Nauvoo was supposed to be. After a while I found the little town and saw that it was merely 367.56 miles, not very far at all for me to drive. We had traveled most of our lives all over the United States and a six-hour drive felt like nothing to me. I was happy, excited and a little scared at the same time. I didn't know what lay ahead.

A Winding Road by the Rivers Edge

Family trips have always been fun for me. When I was growing up it was not necessarily a trip we were going on, we were merely moving once again, for the one hundred thousandth time! This in turn had become another adventure, something new and undiscovered. As I loaded the car and took off down the road toward Nauvoo, I could not shake the excitement that welled inside of me. I had decided to ask my Aunt Lorraine, my cousin Christy, and my own sister, Candy to come with me and my son on this first trip to Nauvoo. Many thoughts went through my mind as we traveled. Truly I did not know what to expect. There had been so many years that I had heard my father's family speak ill of the LDS Church and in the background, buried deep within, was the belief that Brigham Young had Joseph, Hyrum, and Samuel murdered. Part of me wanted to turn around and forget the whole trip, yet I could not deny the pull to keep going forward.

As we came closer to our destination, we drove into a town called Hannibal, a name that I was very familiar with having spent my childhood hours with the colorful and adventurous stories penned by Mark Twain. I could not resist spending a couple of hours looking over his boyhood hometown. The side trip only fueled my anxiousness for I have such a deep love for historical things, and to see the Mississippi roaring in front of me made *The Adventures of Tom Sawyer* come alive. It was a fun place to stop with my son and we enjoyed the time there before we took off yet again toward Nauvoo.

Nauvoo is approximately 71 miles from Hannibal so I had ample time to further reflect about my father's family and their outlook on Mormonism, the yearning to know more about Joseph Smith, and the scant information that I had researched up to that point. I wondered how my aunt was feeling about the whole trip; after all, she had never been to Nauvoo. When I asked her what she knew about it, she could not offer any words of wisdom upon the subject.

At one point during all of this reflection, I came to a sign that said Historic Nauvoo. There was a picture of a wagon being pulled by oxen. It was the first time that I had ever seen anything positive concerning Mormon history. I could not help smiling, like a child who waited to get on that one ride for the first time at an amusement park; excited, happy, nervous, and scared all at the same time. With all of the anxious feelings that were coursing through me, there was one emotion that stood out, a feeling of positive and spiritual awareness that could not be named. It prompted me to know that everything was alright and that I was doing something worthwhile.

When we crossed the bridge in Keokuk, Iowa and as we veered to the left we were rewarded with the beauty of a twelve-mile drive along the Mississippi River. I felt a connection to the scene before me. The glorious beauty of a raging river that ran for miles on the left, and on the right, plush hills adorned by trees whose branches arched over the highway as if to reach the water that gave them life.

I do not remember much in the way of discussion. I believe we were all fairly deep in thought and I wondered to myself what my ancestors might have been thinking as they ventured into this area so many years before. For some reason, Emma came to my mind. At the time, I was unaware of the harsh situations she had endured, that she had crossed the frozen Mississippi as she fled a bloodthirsty mob in Missouri, her two babes in arms, and other children clinging to her skirts. One of those children who nestled in the crook of one arm was my great-grandfather, Alexander. Being unaware of the full details of those times, I could not describe accurately the feelings that welled inside of me, except to say there was a kind of melancholy that swept over me, bringing tears.

I still had very limited knowledge of the history. To that point, I had only partially learned the First Vision account and the places the Saints had moved to from 1830 to 1832. The information concerning why they had moved and the circumstances they had lived under were still a mystery to me. Liberty jail was a topic I knew nothing whatsoever about and I had no idea about the manner in which Joseph and Hyrum had met their deaths. I was determined to learn what I could while in Nauvoo, yet remained cautious of the Mormons and their practice of ensnaring poor unsuspecting descendants, thrusting them into a cult made of iron gates in which there could be no escape or chance of leading an independent life, or so I was led to imagine.

Whatever apprehensions I had melted away as we drove around a curve which straightened and led us into

Nauvoo, passing a sign that said Joseph Smith Historic Site. To see a sign with Joseph's name in such a large print surprised me. Apparently, he was well-loved and thought of to merit such honor and recognition. As I turned down the road that led to the Smith homes, I wondered to myself why there had been such a need to keep the topic of Joseph silent in my family. What was it that he had done that was so bad that there was no discussion of his life? What lay inside of me was split in two halves; one half viewed Joseph as a dark figure who had committed wrongs that were so great that his name became unspeakable, the other half held the memory of the blue eyes in the portrait, where goodness spoke to my heart of spiritual matters. It was that goodness which moved me forward. It was a joy I had never known before and I trusted it because I knew it to be of the Holy Ghost.

The first thing that caught my eye as we headed toward the Smith homes was a large weeping willow tree located behind the Riverside Mansion. I was immediately drawn to it and felt as if I had seen it before. It seems odd to say that a tree seemed familiar to me, but that is how it felt and at that time in my life I did not know how to reason many of the things that I had experienced from my youth throughout adulthood. I just felt different than others and thought myself quite strange.

There was a log cabin that we came to and I pulled over. The sign on the corner of the property said, "Joseph Smith Homestead," and as I put the car in park and sat back in my seat I said softly aloud, "So this is it." My eyes scanned a view that brought instant tears from a time and place that was long since passed, a time and place I knew little about, yet

Chapter Ten

could feel intimately. As I walked down a sidewalk which led to the graves of my ancestors I felt a shift. With every step there was heaviness and I became very emotional.

I kept looking for the grave marker that had been Emma's. I saw it in a picture with my very young grandfather sitting on top of it but upon entrance to the cemetery, I saw that there was one huge stone that encased three graves, the top of the stone angled upwards as if they were reclined halfway back; resting, yet keeping an eye on the goings-on around them. Beneath this stone monument lay Hyrum, Joseph and Emma Smith. Still ignorant of the bond that these three individuals shared and the depth of their history, I became curious as to why the three were lying side by side. There was so much emotion swirling within me I could not hold back the tears.

As I looked at the river, the Nauvoo House, Homestead and in the distance the Mansion House I became a little upset, for I could not reason why knowledge of this place had been kept from us. Putting religion aside, this was our ancestor's home and all of their descendants should know of it. Within thirty minutes of standing on ancestral ground, the desire to know my heritage blew wide open, but I would have to be satisfied with the small glimpse of my heritage that those few moments by the graves brought. The sites were already closed and night was soon upon us, reminding me that we needed to check into the bed & breakfast. I was looking forward to a good night's sleep, anticipating what the next day would bring.

Hills & Valleys

Bryan at three years

Chapter Eleven

A Voice From the Dust

  Ralph Waldo Emerson once said, "All I have seen teaches me to trust the Creator for all I have not seen." I could not think of a better description for what has been my direction in life. All of the years I spent growing up and listening to so much anti-Mormon banter taught me to fear the LDS church and in some ways become bitter towards it. Yet, there was something inside of me that held a space of fair judgment concerning the matter; a door that refused to become locked by the persuasion of others even though I was swayed by fear at times.

  The next morning came, awarding us with the beauty of a clear day. The first thing on my agenda was to tour the Smith homes. As I walked toward the car I took in the soft air tinged with dew. Shards of light reflected brilliantly upon spring moistened grass and I could hear a society of geese in the distance. The mixture of nature's bliss swirled in my mind with a ring of familiarity. As I walked with my head down, deep in thought, there was a knowing in me that this day would bring many changes. Part of me resisted the pull that I was feeling inside. Another part of me smiled.

  I did not know what to expect upon entering the Reorganized Church of Jesus Christ of Latter Day Saints Visitors Center. I had some reservations, as I had heard negative things about this particular church as well through members of the Temple Lot church, including some of Dad's family. According to them, all churches were going to hell except for The Church of Christ Temple Lot, and the many Mormon sects that had in their eyes broken away from the original church organized in 1830, would fall under the greatest damnation.

We were helped by a genuinely nice woman who showed us a film about the history of how Nauvoo came to be. I remember sitting in the chair watching the scenes before me and I felt ill at ease. I could not reason why, but I felt as if the message contained within the film was hollow, like a picture that is only partially exposed. Still, it was the most I had ever seen covering the history of Nauvoo and I walked out knowing somewhat more than I had before. My focus fell toward the Smith homes as we greeted the spring air once again. It was a great day for walking and that is how the tour started after the film; a walk to where the stables had been and then to each home.

There is a winding path that leads around the Riverside mansion and as we walked toward the river I looked to my left and beheld the willow tree that I had seen the day before when we arrived. I could not quit looking at it as I walked, glancing back at intervals until we reached the Riverside Mansion. At the time, I was not aware of the age of the tree and I thought to ask but kept silent. The willow seemed like an old friend I had not seen in years and longed to embrace.

As the guide spoke about the Riverside Mansion, I could not help but gaze upon the beauty of the river. My ears were hanging on every word the lady said, yet my eyes were taking in the expanse of the river and the wildlife that decorated it. I could not help but feel as if I were looking through someone else's eyes. These feelings would all make sense in the years to come, but for the time being I could only absorb their unique family essence.

I was disappointed to learn we could not go into the Riverside Mansion but somehow I felt that one day I would be able to see the inside. The guide walked us around to the graves by the Homestead and began to tell us a little about Joseph and Hyrum, where the bodies had been buried before, and how they had been moved when the Keokuk dam was built. Once again I had questions but seemed held back from asking. Why did Emma hide the bodies and move them? Why was it so secretive, and what had Joseph and Hyrum done that was so bad that others sought their lives? These were all questions that surfaced in my mind, prompting me to learn even more. My head was down, still deep in thought as we walked up the steps and into the front door of the Homestead.

As my eyes adjusted, I looked up and breathed in sharply. It was one of those moments that people identify with déjà vu. I felt as if I had been there before, yet realized as I struggled with the emotions that coursed through me that it was more. It was as if I was having a memory that was not my own. As I breathed in, thoughts and feelings about Joseph and Emma filled my heart. I would in later years come to identify this moment in my life as the clarion call, the instant where I was called from within by my ancestors. At the time, I did not know what the call meant. I only knew to follow it. Tears summarily fell down my face and I lagged behind the others so that I might absorb as much as possible.

Chapter Eleven

I had dealt with feelings similar to these before, but not so deep and personal. This was profound, intimate, filled with sorrow, yet held together with joy; a precious gift that seemed broken. I walked out of the Homestead with an assignment that came from whispers, like when a friend is standing beside you urging you to read a particular book or visit a certain place because it is so rewarding, only I could not see who was whispering to my heart. I only knew that there was a host of what felt like family and friends about me and an unmistakable presence like a guardian angel that I had felt from childhood, a familiarity that had no name until that day: Joseph.

As hard as it was for me to leave the Smith homes and property, I was overcome with curiosity about the rest of Nauvoo; the various old buildings that I saw in the distance and the history behind them. Standing by a large tree at the entrance of the Mansion House I looked at the buildings that dotted Main Street and drew a long sigh. Someone at some time had experienced a strong emotional moment, looking down the length of that same street. I could feel it. It was a knowledge that could not be ignored and the grief that accompanied the flow of feelings engulfed my spirit. A part of me struggled with the feelings, arguing that those buildings were owned by the Mormon Church and should be avoided.

The guide who had taken us through the Smith homes told us that there were many historic homes on the flats that belonged to the LDS church and that the missionaries gave good tours. Missionaries? Again? I had done my best to avoid them since the Family History Center in Springfield. They were nice and I could tell they had the spirit, but the fear of getting hooked caused me to want to avoid them at all cost. My love for history and a stronger sense persuaded me otherwise and we all climbed into the car and drove down Main Street. I was determined to walk in every door with full armor, unwilling to be charmed in any way shape or form. Those Mormons would not find me an easy target.

After driving around all over the flats, glimpsing historic images, I parked at the Heber C. Kimball home. We were warmly greeted by a sister missionary as we walked into the small foyer just by a stairway, which led to two more levels. By the time she took us through the home I loved her so much she could have been my grandmother. At the end of the tour she began to bear her testimony of Nauvoo, the Book of Mormon, Joseph and the Savior. As she did so I kept thinking of things I had heard growing up, that the Mormons worshipped Joseph Smith, so as she was testifying I thought, "Here we go, always about Joseph, nothing about the Savior."

It wasn't that I did not love Joseph, but I found it offensive when it came to testimony if anything at all was placed before the Savior. I had been taught that Mormons put more value on Joseph and the Book of Mormon because that is all they talked about, that they actually worship Joseph Smith, Jr. What I did not know was that they do indeed believe in the Savior, and it had not been made clear to me early on that my great-great-grandfather was at the root of restoring the full gospel of Jesus Christ. I would come to understand that the emphasis placed upon Joseph and the history of his life is of great importance. Joseph is the example of what is required to serve the Lord in the building up of the kingdom of heaven. Through him came the restoration of precious truths which

Chapter Eleven

had been lost after the time of Christ's ministry on earth. He taught that above all things, we should know and implement the Savior and His teachings in all aspects of our lives.

Just as I was convincing myself of this sister's error, she began to bear her testimony of the Savior and the darkness which had invaded my thoughts melted away, enabling me to feel the richness of the Spirit which had filled the room. Once again, I was given witness that a member of the Mormon Church had the Holy Ghost. It is something I have come to appreciate greatly for there are many who believe that Mormons do not believe in Jesus Christ. Had that sister not mentioned the Savior as she testified, I would have continued thinking she worshipped Joseph. Instead, I learned that she was grateful to Joseph for bringing to her heart and mind a greater understanding of Jesus Christ.

I was trying to process what had just happened as I walked to the car. Everything I felt in the Heber C. Kimball home seemed to contradict things I had heard growing up and a wave of doubt ran through me. After all, I had been told how well the missionaries are trained in hooking people. Sinking down into the driver's seat I thought, "Oh my goodness, she is good! She came so close to getting me!" Convinced that I almost got snookered, I promised myself that I would not be swayed by any further testimonies no matter how it felt. But I could not deny the feelings of the Holy Ghost either, the one voice my mom taught that would never lie. It was an excruciating game of tug o' war that the adversary was playing against a pureness of spirit which seemed to surround my ancestry. I put the car in drive and moved on.

Hills & Valleys

Down Main Street I saw a neat building that was called the Cultural Hall, so I pulled over and we walked up to the steps. I was a basket of nerves, my stomach ached, and I wondered to myself whether or not I was getting mixed up in something that was over my head. After all, this was a people that I had been told were very cunning and cruel if one crossed them, cruel to the point of casting the women off from the top of the Salt Lake Temple and into the Salt Lake if they tried to leave the Church. I hesitated by the steps and looked upward to the windows of the top floor and once again the fears were washed away. Something told me not to worry and as I looked toward the entrance doors I felt a sense of peace. It was the only thing that I needed to feel safe in proceeding, that measure of peace settling into my heart and mind.

The majority of that first day in Nauvoo was filled with similar moments; a little fear, hesitation, suspicion, and then a moment of peace before entering each building. I kept looking for those horrible missionaries who were so adept in snaring unsuspecting, innocent people into their web of lies, yet I found only sweet and precious souls whose testimony of faith streamed from their countenance like a glowing lantern in the night. Try as I might, it was hard to dislike them, but I knew they were wrong, no matter how sweet they were. At least I had learned that they were not actually monsters and I could hold a conversation with them without fear.

There were times during the tour of the homes that I felt prompted to tell them who we were, of our lineage, but I held back because I was not sure what kind of a reaction it would bring. Would it promulgate an atmosphere that would put us in harm's way, or would the missionaries treat us kindly? At any rate, I held my peace until we got to the Joseph Noble home, which is where my third great-grandmother Lucy Mack had lived at one time. When we first walked in, I was utterly charmed by the quaint little house. Two sister missionaries came and welcomed us in, asking where we were from and if this was our first time in Nauvoo. Then one of the sisters began to talk about Lucy Mack and how she was a small lady, standing only four foot and nine inches tall. I remember thinking silently to myself that now I knew who to thank for my shortness.

As we walked through a small hallway that led to some stairs, I glanced to my right and saw an image upon the wall that reached out to me. It was a painting of Joseph Smith at a young age, eighteen or maybe twenty. There were those blue eyes once again. I felt I could not move and told the guides that I preferred to stay down stairs. One of them stayed behind with me and offered me a chair. I obliged, feeling a little exhausted from all of the walking.

It is interesting what fear can do to a person. It is a predator that far outweighs any carnivore in the art of attacking and consuming, for it is very subtle and deceiving. The fear that I had felt for so many years toward the LDS church began from something as small as a few words uttered by my father's family; "they corrupted what Joseph had built," or "Brigham Young was behind the deaths of Joseph and Hyrum." The sting of such conversation mingled with others throughout the years snowballed into contempt and fear toward a church and a history I did not even understand. Now I found myself in a small room with one of those wolves in sheep's clothing and I gathered all of the strength inside that I could muster to counter whatever she was about to say.

"That's an interesting picture isn't it?" She said, and I looked upward and smiled softly at the blue eyes. "Yes," I answered. Something in the face softened my fears, and then in the time it takes for the heart to beat once I said, "He's my great-great-grandfather."

"Really? Now where did you say you were from?" Something pulled me back into defense mode. "Uh oh", I thought to myself, "She is asking me personal questions. I have to be careful."

"We're from Missouri." That's right. Don't be too telling about yourself, just generalities.

"Have you signed the descendant book?" I had no idea what she was talking about but as she reached to get the book I felt a little more at ease. This missionary was extremely nice and seemed excited that a descendant of Joseph was there which threw me off guard. I fell into pleasant conversation with the missionary but felt completely ignorant because she was asking me all of these questions and the answers were not there for me to give her; "Tell me about Emma, why did she stay behind?" I could only tell her that I knew very little.

She asked me what church I grew up in and I told her that I had attended many churches but my father was a minister in The Temple Lot Church, the Hedrickites. The woman shook her head in question and said she had never heard of that one. I told her that it was based in Independence but that is all I could say because I knew very little about it. About that time the other missionary came down with the rest of my family and her companion told her with excitement who we were.

"Oh," she said, "that's wonderful. Which wife do you come through?" Now if she had not sounded so sincere and sweet when she said it I might have been verbal with my thoughts. I dare say that my jaw was clenching. I may not have known much about the history yet but I did remember how often Grandma Smith and her children, my father included, used to voice angered opinions about the Mormons and their connection to polygamy; how they lied and placed the origins of the practice in the nineteenth century on Joseph to justify it. It is what I had been taught and I had adapted the same bitterness toward The LDS Church and the topic of polygamy. I was torn. As a rule I hate any kind of contention, yet a part of me resented what the missionary had said and I felt wounded. I kindly replied that I came through Emma. We decided that we had seen enough of the historic area and drove up to Mulholland Street.

A Precious Spot on a Lonely Hill

Nauvoo has a charm all of its own. There is a calm and serene blanket of wooded parks and old homes bordered by tranquil streams that wind their way through untouched wilderness on their journey to join the Mississippi in her endless voyage. All of this timeless beauty is matched by a marked impression of trials and sacrifices that many pioneers of the early restoration endured. The mingling of love and sorrow is etched in the trees which still remain.

The geese, ducks, cranes, and other wildlife were enthralling and I mused at their camaraderie as we drove down Parley Street toward the Mississippi. It was the wrong way to go, town was in the opposite direction, but I wanted to see where the Saints had taken off on their trek to the West. Though ignorant of information, I had an inner desire to see certain places that I had heard the individual guides speak about during the tours, and the Trail of Hope was one of them. I did not know what to expect as we drove down the road but as we approached the river I turned the car so that the driver's side was facing the water.

    For some reason I preferred to sit and look out upon the water from my seat. I rolled the window down and took in the breeze, looking out upon the great river and contemplating what might have been on the hearts and minds of those early pioneers, for as I looked upon the scene I put myself in their place and thought "what lies ahead?" I wondered with awe at what that moment might have been like; facing a river, unsure of their future yet trusting that they had one, placing their faith and hopes in the hands of their leader, Brigham Young. I wrestled with those thoughts, admiring their strength and faith, while at the same time shaking my head at them for following such a man blindly. I was still carrying bitterness toward Brigham Young at the time and could not reason how he had snookered so many people!

    Still deep in thought I turned around and headed for the hill where all of the shops were, the majority of which were in buildings that dated back to the early Nauvoo period. I was entranced by it all, loving history the way that I do. It was all so enthralling that I failed to notice at first that the bare spot of land just west of the Nauvoo State Bank was no ordinary landscape. At one point while we were walking, I

Chapter Eleven

became aware of a small model that was surrounded by a three wall monument. The lot area sloped on all sides toward the middle causing it to appear is if there had been a pond there at one time. As soon as I started walking toward the model I began to feel strange inside. Once again the tears were spilling over my cheeks and I walked ahead of everyone, not wanting them to see my emotions. How could I? The feelings that were surging were a mystery to me so I could in no way explain them to anyone else, and those feelings seemed too personal to share. I seemed to know inside that the stirring I was feeling was for me and me alone.

    As I approached the model of the building, I was filled with a mixture of joy and sadness. I have always been drawn to large, spacious buildings, grand architecture and particularly things designed with marble. I never knew growing up what attracted me to such things but as I grew older I realized that it was not an attraction to wealth or prestige that called out to me. Instead, I believe that such buildings remind me of holy places.

    Walking around the model, my eyes caught one of the memorial pillars and I began to read for the first time the revelation that Joseph received to build the temple in Nauvoo. It was the first time that my eyes had ever beheld the words from the beginning unto the end and I knew it to be of the Lord. I was more overcome with feelings of confusion. Why did my father and his family hide things from us? Why did they feel it necessary to keep our history and ancestry so buried and hidden? Everything that I was seeing and feeling in Nauvoo contrasted with what I had been led to believe. Everything in Nauvoo felt good, and spiritual. The emotions I had been carrying from the time I set foot in the homes of my ancestors pulled a curtain of inhibition away, and a people who I once saw as something to be feared found a place in my heart even though I still felt the need to be cautious.

When I finished reading the monuments, I watched my Aunt Lorraine looking for some sign that she was experiencing the same things that I had, but I could see no hint of expression or tears. Mouth set tight, she walked around for a bit with folded arms and then made her way back to the car. Seeking a few moments of solitude, I told my sister I would meet them later and took my son by the hand as we walked the grounds.

At the setting of the sun, on a warm spring day, my son and I walked to the western edge of the lot where the temple had once stood facing the Mississippi. I inhaled deeply as a soft breeze carried past me. Closing my eyes, I felt a rush of something that seemed almost like joy, yet there was a sense of unfinished business. I came to realize at that moment the sacredness of the land where I was standing, that precious spot on a lonely hill. It marked the first time that I had felt Joseph so strongly, knowing that it was him, feeling his presence, and recognizing the ushering in of a new era in my life. Though I did not understand what those feelings alluded to concerning the future, I knew with a surety that it involved me and my children.

I placed my hand gently over my stomach wondering if the child I was carrying was experiencing the emotions with me. I was very aware that there was significance in what I had experienced on that hill even though I did not know what it all meant. From that moment I vowed to visit Nauvoo often and hoped that in time I would come to an understanding of why I felt so connected.

Mannequins, Jail, and Blood on the Floor

Carthage. The name implies something Greek in its connotation, a faraway place where historic things happened long ago. I did not know what to expect as we drove toward the town where Joseph and Hyrum were killed. Nothing much had ever been said to us about their deaths; I only knew that they had been murdered. There is a view from some of the family that their deaths were brought on as consequences of Joseph's becoming a fallen prophet, that because they had leaned on the arm of flesh instead of heeding the word of God they were allowed to be taken and the work halted until someone worthy was chosen to finish the work. Somehow that perspective did not seem right to me, especially after the things I had experienced in Nauvoo.

As we drove into the city limits, I saw a sign that said Historic Carthage Jail. The realization of what we were about to see moved upon me as I parked the car and walked toward the brick building. I remember thinking, "Oh no, I'm not going to start crying again am I?" Try as I might I could not hold back the emotions that once again flooded over me. As we climbed the stairs to the martyrdom room, I knew that my efforts to learn more about Joseph had to be redoubled because the yearning inside of me was so strong.

Though not many in number, they were the longest stairs that I ever climbed. I could not help but take my time, my right hand sliding ever so slow up the railing, wondering, absorbing, sensing trauma. The steps seemed to become transparent as my thoughts meandered to reflection upon a time that I knew little about, yet I felt that there were those around me who were giving me a sense of the depth concerning what had happened there. While in Carthage, I came to know for a fact that our ancestors who have gone before surround us while we are here on earth, and if we are close to the spirit and listening, we can feel and hear them. No one could ever convince me otherwise.

As we approached the door to the martyrdom room we walked forward into a darker room called the dungeon, and rightly so, for it was surrounded by stone walls, with two cells, and a small slit on one side of a wall for a window. I would have liked to have heard everything the woman said but I was standing by the door which was located at the top of the stairs we had just climbed and I situated myself half in and half out of the room. My full attention was on the door to the martyrdom room which seemed looming with its plain design and old black doorknob, a hole situated just above it; a small ray of light streaming through. I left the room while the guide was still speaking and walked slowly over to the door, placing my right palm against the cool surface. Moving my hand slowly downward I made contact with the hole in the door and drew a breath inward. Common sense told me that it was a bullet hole but my mind did not want to accept. Tears fell freely down my face.

As I heard the guide speaking louder, I moved back from the door, sensing that they were coming out from the dungeon room. She smiled kindly at me and laid a hand on my shoulder, patting it lightly as she reached for the door knob. In retrospect I believe she knew that I was feeling something. Since I had been standing at the door I was the first one to enter and at first did not look directly into the room. I simply looked downward as I walked in and moved to the corner to make room for everyone. I caught a glimpse of some figures in the room as I was walking in but did not get a good look at them until I leaned against the wall and looked forward. There was a chair nearby and I was compelled to sit down because I was so overcome with what was before me. There were mannequins: one standing, one sitting, and the one sitting looked exactly like my brother in every way, right down to the cleft in his chin.

The guide began to explain that this was the room where Joseph and Hyrum had been murdered and that the mannequins were placed there to portray as nearly as possible where they were before the mob rushed up the stairs. She went on to say that the faces of the mannequins were made from the death masks of both Hyrum and Joseph. I could only gaze deeply into those faces as she continued talking.

In that first visit I can honestly say that I did not hear everything the missionary said because I was too absorbed with the personal, sacred connections I was feeling. I do recall at one point that she said something about there still being blood on the floor, though it had reportedly been removed years before. Visible or not, in my mind's eye there was blood everywhere; the same blood that coursed through my veins. As we silently walked back to the car to head home, I realized that I had passed through a door. I could have chosen to leave it locked like the rest of the family but the things I had experienced while visiting Nauvoo and Carthage moved me to turn the key and walk through, and I knew that upon entering I would never turn back.

I felt that I was in unknown territory, aware that I should move forward, yet still a little afraid of what I had absorbed from the family for so many years. The most frightful thing to me that my father ever said was that if we ever left the Temple Lot Church we would be denying the Holy Ghost. I knew that to be an unforgivable sin. But Nauvoo and Carthage bore witness to me. Voices from the past whispered to my heart, and my great-great-grandfather, Joseph, testified to my spirit.

I could not help but move forward. The thought of refusing to do so brought a sense of pain silently voiced by many who had long since passed from this mortal estate. We left Carthage Jail and headed back to Missouri, where we ran into severe weather. The symbolism of the storm could not have been more perfect as I thought about how I would begin to learn more about Joseph Smith and his life. I could already feel the clouds of opposition gather.

Chapter Twelve

Every Little Thing

It is amazing how often we as human beings are exposed to reality and truth, yet at the moment our attention is turned away, we let doubts or fear creep in. I was not in Missouri for more than a week before I began to deviate from the things I had seen and felt. Had I been deceived? According to my father, Satan is very cunning in his ways of persuasion. I had only to mention how wonderful the trip was and how great the people were and it opened the door to all manner of negativity. I was cautioned to beware the ways of the Mormons. Their main goal is to take people in with their good ways and kindness, hiding the dark side of their history which had caused the LDS Church foundation to be built upon lies, secrecy, and deceitfulness.

The more Dad talked, the more I pulled back from what I had experienced, deciding to put my yearnings aside and just go through life as I had done before. I had somehow convinced myself that what I had felt in Nauvoo must have been from the adversary to trick me into getting close to the LDS Church. Even though I told myself this, there was something undeniable moving within me that could not be silenced. For three more years, I kept it pushed back for fear of moving in the wrong direction. Looking back, I can't believe that I let so much time pass by without heeding the voices that whispered to my heart, but when there are generations of

Chapter Twelve

feelings weighing in on the conversation, it is easy to feel cornered.

One of the things that I love about Heavenly Father is His way of putting things into place for a purpose. It is like when you go through a maze and finally make it through successfully: afterwards it is neat to look at the maze from start to finish seeing how it was all laid out. One turn might be placed to make a better way or smoother passage, while another is ingeniously placed tight and narrow with thistles and branches, yet if you have knowledge of how to deal with those things you can make it through okay. At times you might stop in the maze to search out your heart because you are unsure. That is how I felt. I think we are all in that maze many times in our lives. How we make it through depends on our preparation and not just listening to the promptings of the spirit but following with faith. If one knows it is from Father in Heaven there is no reason to question. Just trust and go forward, knowing that the end result will be good and true. With every little thing, I was beginning to learn to walk without questioning, but it was slow going at first. I feel that the trip to Nauvoo was the first nudge even though I stepped back after returning home.

As the summer edged toward an end I found myself being swept up in home life. I was in wonder of my son who was the most pleasant child I had ever seen. He was a three-year-old whose maturity surpassed his age in great measure. With enthusiasm, I looked forward to the birth of the child who by then I knew would be our daughter. As October grew closer, I began to anticipate her arrival even more. Family had come to mean everything to me. Even though there was a great sadness in our home because of the lack of harmony and love, I managed to pour everything I had been taught by my mother into my son in an attempt to create a loving atmosphere as both the mother and father figure.

Just after September 11, I began to feel ill. Part of the agony of our marriage was that my husband never showed compassion toward me. If illness was ever an issue, I learned not to let on how much pain I was in. So anytime I did say something, it would have to be bad. Still, it evoked little response from him and I was always hesitant to suggest a doctor because he complained that it cost money. Days came and went and the illness grew worse until I was dealing with unbearable pain. It was not labor pain, I knew what that felt like. After a week, I was reduced to spending 24 hours a day in a recliner, needing help if I had to get up and sit down. Then the pain became utterly seizing. Not once did my husband offer to take me to the hospital. I knew something was wrong and should have called someone to take me, but I wanted him to react. It wasn't until some friends came to visit that he responded. They took one look at me and told my husband to get me to the emergency room. I was very scared for it was a month too early.

As a nurse worked with me a sharp pain went through my side and she said in an almost patronizing manner, "Now, it's fine, you're just having a contraction." I immediately grabbed her arm and said, "Ma'am, get me some help, something isn't right." When I told her I had been in pain for a week she went for a doctor and they ordered blood work. They took one look at the results and before I knew it I was being rushed to an operating room. As soon as I was under anesthesia they had my daughter out, cleaned her, charted her weight at 5lb 4oz and rushed her to ICU. I had no idea how close to death we had both come. The doctor told me that another six hours and both of us would have been gone.

It was the unthinkable, yet one of the things I had feared most of my life when it came to pregnancy. I remember being very young thinking how horrifying it would be to have an appendicitis attack while pregnant. For it to happen at such a time was rare. I remember my brother having his appendix out when he was young. I knew that once it bursts there is very little time to save the patient. But mine didn't burst; it slowly leaked during that week I was in pain. As Leah grew in the womb, somehow my appendix became stretched over her from the right side over the top of the womb to the left. As a result, it began to leak toxins into my body, which spread throughout causing parts of my intestinal lining to become gangrenous. When all was said and done, I was jaundiced and had to have part of the intestinal lining removed and Leah had to spend two weeks in ICU to clear her body from the infections she had contracted.

I have a great threshold for pain, but what followed was weeks of some of the most tremendous pain I had ever experienced. At times it was so great I slept on the couch and shoved a pillow in my mouth to silence the loud cries so I would not disturb anyone. There were many nights I poured my heart out to the Lord for I felt He was the only one there for me. The pain didn't lessen, but I knew He was there. There was an awareness that if I could endure this and overcome then everything would be fine. I had to stay strong. It was like having an adult with me with their hand on my shoulder saying, "You can do this, just get through it, then it will be over and all will be well." I remember several times nodding my head and saying, "Okay."

After about a month, I was getting around easier and the pain was gone. Leah was having problems sleeping and it would be four years before she would sleep all night. The traumatic premature birth had caused some neurological damage, nothing severe, but just enough to cause problems. As she grew she would be diagnosed with a mild form of Tourette Syndrome. Doctors tried to prescribe medicines for her but I felt that if she could work through some of her challenges she could overcome them. She mainly suffered from mild vocal and physical tics, most of which she learned to control and for the most part overcome throughout her childhood.

When I went for a checkup three months later, my doctor sat me down and told me that due to the nature of my distorted pelvis and the high risk deliveries I had experienced, there should be no more children. I had already come to the conclusion that there would be no more. My husband was reluctant to have any at all at first. After two he was finished. I do not want to leave an impression he does not love his kids. He does. But at the time, things were different.

When I told him of the doctor's advice he refused to have anything done and left it in my corner. It was a devastating decision for I had always wanted a lot of children, but I told the doctor I would have surgery, with a request that he perform the kind that can be reversed. I found myself in the same place my mother did years before. I could not risk death and leave my children in an atmosphere I did not approve of, yet I was not sure what the future held for me. That is why I asked for the surgery which could be reversed. I felt horrible.

Dodging A Bullet

When Leah started pre-school ,I began working for the Headstart program. It was the perfect job because it had the same hours as school and I had vowed I would never work a job that took me away from my kids. I love both of my kids and have always been deeply bonded to them. Our summers and off time were spent together. We took a yearly trip to Tennessee and I always tried to make sure there was a combination of fun, laughter, music, and movies. I passed a generous portion of those aspects to both of my kids. I made sure they watched quality shows that I grew up on. Abbot & Costello, Leave it to Beaver, Mr. Ed and Loony Toons were staples in our home. I was in awe of Bryan's maturity and Leah's wisdom and artistic capabilities. Throughout those years, in the back of my mind was the man in the portrait, but I was so busy with life I kept telling myself I would get to it. We tried our best to visit Nauvoo once a year but in time it turned into every other year.

One day in 1993, I found some time to work on a novel I had been writing but my thoughts went to Grandpa's old trunk. Once again, I pulled everything out and laid it before me. The house was quiet that day because the kids had gone to Mom's for a visit. In the background, there was mountain music playing, stirring the other side of my heritage within me and I began to cry. Everything had been scattered to the wind for so long: my lineage, Mom's life, our years growing up and now my adult life. Inside, I just wanted to pull it all together. It was a source of great pain to me that all of these sides of me were not bonded together. I knew that my Heavenly Father wanted things united. I knew of the Savior's pure love and as I reflected upon the generational environment on both sides of my family, the weight of what needed to be done sank in.

But what could I do? I felt inadequate to do anything. I couldn't manage to make my own home a united one. It was just me and my kids most of the time. Inadequate or not, I felt an overwhelming sense that I needed to do something, yet I did not know what. The phone rang and pulled me out of my thoughts. After I hung up, I noticed something had fallen from the papers as I pulled them from the trunk. It was the small pamphlet I had found years before while at the cabin, the one in which Joseph tells his story. I broke into a wide smile and became excited. I had forgotten all about it but I didn't have time to read it at the time. I left it out from among the other items so I could read it later.

As I left to go pick up my kids, something came to my mind. I remembered seeing a VHS tape at the Family History Library about Joseph when I had been copying microfilm. It had been nearly four years but for some reason I remembered it that day. I promised myself when I had the chance I would go check it out. As usual, I let life take control of me and I did not get around to it. It was around this time I heard that the Osmonds had started to perform in Branson and I was in hopes that there would be an opportunity to see their show in the future.

Summer to me and the kids was a fun time. It meant a trip to Tennessee and other excursions. It also meant it was time for my yearly physical which was required to work in the

Chapter Twelve

Headstart program. We had a good friend in Ava who was a doctor so I got an appointment to see him. It is amazing to me how the Lord speaks to us in quiet ways. As I sat awaiting my turn, something my mom had told me years before just popped into my head.

 Mom had a father and eleven uncles and aunts who had passed away from some form of cancer. Pappaw's doctor told Mom and her siblings that due to the high risk of cancer in the family they should have yearly blood work done. As I was remembering the advice Pappaw's doctor had given Mom, it brought to the surface a concern which had been occupying my mind. Two months previous to the appointment for my physical, my menstrual cycle had come to an abrupt halt and I knew I was not pregnant. I felt prompted to convey all of this information to my doctor. When I explained my reasons for the blood work, the doctor agreed and ordered a series of tests focused on female cancers, primarily uterine, ovarian, and cervical.

 With the worry which comes with waiting, I lost all thought of family research. Four days later I got a call. I sat in the doctor's office, numb as our doctor explained that a normal CA125 count is 35 and below. Mine was double. I had no idea what he meant until explained that the CA125 is performed to screen certain cancers of the female organs. I sat in a haze as he made a call to schedule an appointment in Springfield to get more blood work done. I could only think of one thing, my children. My heart whispered, "No. No Heavenly Father, not now, not yet." Dr. Hennan assured me that whatever it was, it had been caught early and could turn out to be nothing, just a spike in the levels for reasons other than cancer. A week passed and the second results showed that the numbers had tripled. I was immediately scheduled for exploratory surgery.

At the time I had my exploratory surgery, technology had advanced to such a degree that I had fresh glossies of my internal organs instead of the graphic black and white. It was as if someone took a Polaroid and handed it to me. The doctors were stumped. They found nothing suggesting such a rise in the CA125 levels. I was sent home with instructions to return in two weeks for more blood work which would present levels numbering over 800. I was unsettled by a range of "what could it be." There was something there the doctors were missing and it was growing rapidly.

I tried to focus my mind on other things but when it came down to it, music was the only escape that took away the concern of the secretive villain which was spreading undetected throughout my body. When I wasn't with my children, I had my Walkman by my side. I had many conversations of pleading, repenting, and love with the Lord. He was in my thoughts at all times. There was also a sense that I had family surrounding me. One presence in particular seemed ever-constant. I was given assurance that I would get through the trial in good measure. Still, it was hard to pass through time playing the waiting game.

My next appointment consisted of an ultrasound to check for gall stones, for the presence of stones apparently causes a spike in CA125 levels. Sure enough, they found enough to warrant concern. I was sent home to consider options. I could try to get rid of them naturally, which is the route I like to take. I never bought the idea that one can do

Chapter Twelve

without certain organs of the body because they have no real function, which is what some doctors will say. If they serve no real purpose, then why were we equipped with them? Something just did not seem right about the reasoning of it but I had been deathly ill for a long time, trying to get through work every day and juggle things at home. I had people on one side saying get the surgery and others saying not to because it would affect the balance of my health in the future. I was tired and I was tired of not having someone beside me who could be a support to me. After much prayer I was prompted to do what the doctors suggested and I reluctantly called and made the appointment.

Gall bladder surgery used to be a major procedure but when I had mine they were able to do it as an outpatient using the laparoscopic method for removal. I was home in a day and recovered by the end of the week. My doctor suggested that another panel of blood work be done in a month just to make sure that the levels were down. If so, I would be given an all clear. One month? What is it with people having serious health issues being told they have to wait long periods for further testing? I mean, surely those with more scientific minds are aware that during those long stretches of time the internal culprit is planning more serious attacks, enlarging its forces as it aims for victory. The victims of those silent assaults are left to wonder, grieve, and stress.

One month later I went for my blood work. Although the illness I had been feeling in my gut had been relieved, I still did not feel well and throughout all of the time which had stretched out into several months, I still had not had a period. Three days later, I was called into my doctor in Springfield.

His name was Dr. Wyrsch and he had been my gynecologist since I had become pregnant with Bryan. I could tell as soon as I sat down before his desk that the news was not good. He seemed very perplexed as he explained to me that the levels were now at 2000. My mouth dropped open.

"We have no other choice than to do a complete hysterectomy." he said shaking his head. "There is something in there that we are not seeing." I was devastated. He went on to say that he had consulted with members of the board of the AMA before the gall bladder surgery and that my situation had become a nationwide case study. The humorous side of me kicked in as I thought to myself how all of my life I have just wanted to be loved for me, but it was appearing I would have to settle for hundreds, maybe even thousands taking an interest in me for my CA125 levels. "Well," I thought to myself, "it is something."

Dr. Wyrsch shook his head in wonder and told me that first it was my tilted pelvis, then the rare leaking appendix episode, and now this. He told me this latest trial was the best challenge he had ever had as a doctor and that my hysterectomy would be his last for he was retiring. Basically he was saying thanks for letting him go out with a bang. As a medical doctor, he was desirous to see this case to the end. He wanted to be there to see what was causing all of the problems. But for me, it was my life. I just wanted to get past it and move forward.

At the time this medical nightmare was unfolding, I was aware of the existence of priesthood blessings, but it was not something I had often seen. I knew that Dad gave blessings and if I needed one at any time in my life it was before that surgery. It wasn't a thought to me whether or not he had the fullness of the Priesthood; I only knew I needed a blessing and he was the only one I knew who gave them. It is my belief that blessings are received by the faith of the person asking. I knew that if I asked for a blessing, the Lord would hear the desires of my heart. The day before surgery, Dad gave me a blessing in his home. The next day I entered the hospital.

I remember well the anesthesiologist telling me as he put the mask over my face to count backward from ten. I was out after I said ten. The next thing I knew, I was being rolled down a hall to recovery. I could hear people talking and my body was enraged by raw pain. One of them said, "She's coming around too soon. Hurry." I had awakened early and they did not have me hooked up to the machine that administers the pain-killing drugs. For the first time in my life, I did not, could not hold back. I was screaming from the searing, burning pain.

The staff was trying to work as fast as they could and as they moved me from the stretcher to another bed I cried out even louder. My sister, who was waiting in the hall with my parents and husband, threatened to go in and take over because they were not doing enough for me. Mom calmed her down and told her to sit in the waiting room. Before too long I was out, floating on a river of pain killers.

The next day Dr. Wyrsch came to see me. He had a baffled look upon his face. He explained that only after they removed all of my female organs and thorough dissection did they find the culprit. Four cancerous tumors lay embedded unseen where the fallopian tube connects to the ovary. He told me that if I had not requested the screening months before and come to see them about my periods stopping, they would have prescribed something to start my period monthly. Ten years down the road I would have had full blown ovarian cancer. Because it was caught extremely early, the cells had not spread.

I had been taught to always follow promptings, or those thoughts that seem to fall into one's head out of the blue. But the experience I had endured taught me the value of listening and acting upon that small voice. I had barely escaped a nightmare that many women have had to endure. After that experience my gratitude toward Heavenly Father knew no bounds.

Leahna Sue Davis

Chapter Thirteen

"Closure is a door best passed through
Only when the heart is meek."

—*Kimberly Jo Smith*

While I was recovering from surgery, there was much time to read and write. One day while the kids were in school the thought of the pamphlet came to me and I went into my bedroom to find it. There, alone in the house surrounded by feelings of gratefulness for my life, I began once again to read Joseph's story. It was the perfect time. The medical scare I had just experienced taught me that time is short and the monsters in our lives are only as big as we allow them to be. From the time of the molestation, I had let myself believe every dark thing that had been said to me, both by human and adversarial means. Whether it was ridicule from those who didn't know any better, effects of abuse, the bitterness in my father's family, or the unstable environment which surrounded our childhood, I had bought into it all.

As I read Joseph's testimony, something awakened within me. I had felt a glimmer of it before when I first found the pamphlet. Upon reading further, the awareness grew and I knew the words that I was reading were genuine and sincere. They truly came from him. Feelings inside of me surged and became alive as if they had been sleeping for a very long time. Tears fell yet I was smiling and as I read, there was an

Chapter Thirteen

awareness that I should write of him. But how? I still knew very little, yet what I had read flooded my senses and I could not sit still and do nothing.

The love I had felt so long ago when I first saw the portraits had become magnified to such a degree that I felt I had to express it somehow or burst from the desire of it. I grabbed my tablet and began to write, then came silence in my mind as if I had hit a wall.

There before me on the tablet fell nothing but scribbles. I asked my Father in Heaven to help me, for I deeply wanted to write something. It lay just beneath the surface struggling to get out but was obstructed by something. As I stared into nothingness, absorbing what I had just read, I began to relax. Those words, those beautiful words which had just filled my senses. I knew them. I had never read them before but in my heart I knew them. They were a part of me and the author was as someone who was incredibly dear, like someone I felt bonded to yet had not seen for a very long time: an old, dear friend.

With these thoughts wafting through my heart, I went to my computer and turned it on. When I pulled the word processing program up I began to write without hesitation. Within twenty five minutes I had poured onto the screen a lyrical narration of Joseph's first vision. It came so fast that it seemed he was right there dictating his every thought and feeling. After reading it over I moved the mouse to save it but stopped for I heard something behind me. The hair on the back of my neck went up and I had chills running through me. Turning around I caught sight of nothing but my bed, but I was aware of something and it did not feel good.

Hills & Valleys

I saved my work and the thoughts came to me that I could not really do anything with what I had written because it would expose me to the public as a descendant. Though I was not ashamed of it, I feared persecution. As I looked at the computer, I sought out the opportunity to do some more research. We had just enabled the internet service in our home and I thought what better time to pull up information. After all, I had searched many years in vain for information but was limited as to access. Now I had the World Wide Web before me, why not? I pulled up a search engine and typed in the name Joseph Smith. Big mistake.

It was bad enough being exposed to the Smith family's anti sentiments. Now with the click of a mouse I had just opened myself up to the whole world's view. Some sites were kind in their rendering of my ancestor's life, others not so. Fear overcame the beautiful moments which had just previously blessed my life. As I bounced from one site to another, there fell before me readings of all manner of darkness. There was such a rumbling of emotion within me: fear of persecution, fear of moving in the wrong direction, yearning to know more, being drawn to Joseph. Exhausted by the whole experience I shut the computer down and put the pamphlet away. As I walked down the hallway I looked up and glimpsed the portraits hanging on my kitchen wall and fell even further into confusion.

A Healing of Hearts

It was during this time that Mammaw Roberts' health began to deteriorate immensely. In 1986 it became necessary to place Mammaw in a nursing home because her dementia had become so serious. While there, it was discovered that she was suffering from Alzheimer's Disease. The tests doctors ran of brain activity also revealed that Mammaw had been born with acute Schizophrenia, which explained the lifelong violent outbursts. Still, my mom felt as if there was something more for it seemed that the severity of the rage was aimed at her. Not long before Mammaw passed away, Mom felt impressed to visit her. By then Mom and Dad had moved to Missouri. As she made the trip, Mom thought of all she would say. Her mother was about to die and she needed answers. She needed to know why her mother hated her, why she could never love her as she did the other children in the home.

When she had arrived at the nursing home and was in the room, she appraised her mother's pitiful state. Mammaw barely knew anyone and at times was non-responsive. Mom had decided that she would tell her how much pain she still felt from the past, and then she would ask her why she had hated her so. But as she started she heard a quiet voice say, "No, tell her that you love her." Mom thought to herself, "I can't just tell her that," for she needed answers. The voice repeated, "Tell her that you love her." And Mom knew that the Lord was directing her, that she must look past her own needs. She then sat in a chair beside her mother's bed and looked upon the woman she had feared for so long lying helpless in a fetal position. As she placed her hand on her mother's cheek she said in uncontrollable tears, "Mother, I am so sorry if I ever did anything that would cause you to hate me. I love you and forgive you." Within seconds, she saw tears rolling down Mammaw's cheek and she knew she had heard her.

Mammaw passed away in 1995 and the same family members who had stolen Pappaw's belongings went through and stole away many of Mammaw's things that would be lost forever to Mom, to all of us. But again Mom had something much more precious: peace. For me it was the winding up of my childhood because all of my grandparents were now gone. The loss brought from within me an extreme sadness, yet reawakened my desire to know more of their early lives and heritage.

Back to School

The years 1996 and 1997 were filled with great change. After the experience of writing the First Vision poem, there was cemented within me a knowledge that I must refine my abilities to write. After finishing correspondence courses, I was given my original high school diploma. I quit work and entered Drury University in Springfield, Missouri. I was so hungry for education that I threw myself into twenty two hours in the second semester. One of the classes was Religion.

Approaching the life of the Savior through an institution of learning was a new adventure for me. Up to then my knowledge had been limited by what I learned from my mother and my own reading of the scriptures. At the university, I was exposed to the perception of scholars both past and present. As I went through the lessons, I met much conflict. There were times when I read certain viewpoints that something felt off. I can usually feel if something I read seems out of sync. It is very much like eating a handful of sweet grapes, smiling as you enjoy the taste then unknowingly popping a sour one in. It is abrupt, unsuspected, and clearly not right. Rather than try and

Chapter Thirteen

swallow, it is always best to spit it out. But in school it is hard to do such a thing and maintain a good grade. So I went along with the curriculum, wrote the necessary papers, got an A and walked away happy with my grade. The experience of the class made me aware of conflicts in society which arose as a result of Christ's ministry. It gave me a broader view on how many factions since the time of Christ have bent scripture one way or another to arrive at specific conclusions

Our world history since the time of the written word has run rampant with religion, forgetting that the laws of God are to be written in our hearts and processed in our actions, not used to build a society of unrighteous dominion and tyrannical rule. I found myself wondering how it had all become so complex. From the time I was little, the life of Christ and His teachings seemed simple. I would come to learn that I was indeed correct. The gospel is very simple; it is man who complicates it.

While attending college, we made several trips to Nauvoo and I learned more and more of our history. I also became friends with several people at the Ava Family History Center, but only a few knew I was a descendant of Joseph. I found myself by that time in a phase where I loved the LDS people. It was a paradox to me that they could be so good and be involved in a church that I thought to be so wrong. What was even stranger to me was how the Spirit could be so strong in that church building. I had always been taught that when confronted with wrong, or things of the adversary, the spirit departs. It was confusing to me for it seemed the spirit sure did spend a lot of time around those people and in that building!

Stress at home had become so overbearing that during some years I could only attend one semester. As the fall of

1997 approached, I was beginning to work on a new novel. I had formed the outline for a creative writing class in school. My professor commented that I should do something with it. Several of my professors told me that I should pursue writing and I was getting the idea that I might actually have some potential. The encouragement caused me to write even more.

Nostalgia's Embracing Arms

One afternoon I was sitting at the computer researching something and I saw a heading that grabbed my attention. "Whatever happened to...." It was an article on celebrities of the past. Having a very deep nostalgic nature I began to wonder what all of those favorite childhood idols of mine were doing in their elder years. As I browsed through biographies, I was saddened that many had endured severe trials, turning to drugs and alcohol as a means of escape. Their lives had been ransacked by poor choices but there were also those who had turned themselves around and were rebuilding their lives. Some unfortunately had committed suicide or died by other means. Then my mind turned to the Osmonds.

I knew that some of the brothers were performing in Branson and that Donny & Marie were doing their own things but I wanted to see how their lives had been throughout the years. I found their family website and began to explore. When I came to Merrill Osmond's page there was a section on beliefs and I proceeded to read it. His testimony of the Church was very loving and he mentioned Joseph Smith in one section. I could tell by his words that he had a deep love for Joseph. I sat back in wonderment thinking, "Imagine that. Here is a family I grew up adoring and now I am reading of

Chapter Thirteen

the love they have for my great-great-grandfather." For several years I promised myself I would go see the brothers perform in Branson, but every summer as we passed their theater on the way to our favorite fun spot, Silver Dollar City, that promise somehow went unfulfilled.

My mind also went to the boy actor who I had felt a connection with, Stewart Peterson. I found very little about him online except that he lived in Cokeville, Wyoming. I had always wondered why I felt drawn to him. There was something about his countenance, something familiar. It was almost like the feeling I had when I saw the portraits but not near as strong. The next month it would all come into focus.

Reading the testimonies of all the Osmonds caused those old feelings of curiosity about the past. Any time I thought of it there was a burning inside to move forward but something always happened to distract me, or I should say I allowed myself to be distracted. Spending the day online had fueled those nostalgic emotions and I remembered the video at the Family History Center that tells the story of Joseph Smith.

One day on the way home from picking the kids up from school, I stopped at the Family History Center and checked out the video. The next day I was alone in the house and took a moment to lay my homework aside so I could watch the movie. It was three o'clock and an autumn wind was stirring as the video started and lo, before my eyes portraying my great-great- grandfather as a boy was Stewart Peterson. I sat bewildered. He was LDS? Is this what I had been feeling during those years when I saw him in movies? That he had some devotion or admiration for Joseph Smith and the Church he started? I picked up the movie case and it was dated about the same years I had watched Stewart's movies. After the video had finished, I turned off the television and stared at my reflection as the screen faded to darkness. There seemed to be a host of awakenings of truth within me but I didn't know where to take those feelings. Time would prove to bring understanding to the familiarity, for years later I would learn that Stewart is actually a double cousin of mine, one link through Joseph and one through Emma. It amazes me how so many influences reach out to us in ways we do not even comprehend as we draw nearer to truth.

The next afternoon my husband called from work and said we had won tickets on the radio for a Branson show. I would find later that it was for the Osmonds. I thought how odd and random that was because I was just thinking about them the day before. We decided to go see their Christmas show. I was excited beyond measure! These were people I had never met, yet felt a common bond to. When I was young I passed it off as the teenage crush all girls get for their favorite group or actor. It was clear there was something deeper. The feelings were of a spiritual nature and I needed to know what they meant.

A few days before we went to the show, Merrill Osmond had a vision. With his permission I share this experience. In the vision, he and Joseph went into a barn where a portion was sectioned off by a curtain. Joseph pulled back the curtain and there before him was a sea of faces. These faces appeared to be miserable and in despair. Turning to Merrill, Joseph said, "This is my posterity. Would you please help them?"

Two days after Merrill's experience, we were sitting in their theater watching the show. It was their last show before

Chapter Thirteen

Christmas break. Toward intermission, Merrill came out to sing and I saw that his countenance was shining. To me it was more than the lighting, for I was being affected spiritually. I felt directed to meet this man for some purpose. But how? Before he finished the song, I made my way to the gift shop and bought a postcard. I thought perhaps if we had the chance I could get them all to sign it and in that moment find out why I was having such feelings.

After the show, all of the brothers came out except Merrill. They were all very gracious, taking time to visit with the people who wanted to meet them. I told my husband to go on ahead and start the car so it could warm up, that we would be out in a moment. I waited in the theater until the cleaning people came out and decided that Merrill would not be greeting admirers that night and turned with my children to walk out. As I got halfway up the aisle, I turned and there behind me was Merrill.

He had gone backstage to change, not intending to greet people that night. They were in a hurry to get to the airport. I wasn't quite sure what I was going to say so I simply walked up, introduced myself and my children, then I told him how much we enjoyed the show. As we talked something kept urging me to tell him who I was. But I was too nervous. Then I remembered what he had said about Joseph on his website. Gathering up all the courage I had, I looked at his smiling but tired face and said, "I saw on your website how much you love Joseph Smith." In that moment the tiredness fled his face and his eyes lit up.

"Yes, I do. Are you a member of the Church?" He asked. *Goodness, the very idea! Good heavens no!*

Hills & Valleys

"No, but your words were very touching and I have a deep love for him myself. He is my great-great-grandfather. It was very nice what you had to say. It isn't often that I hear nice things about him."

To say he was amazed would be putting it lightly. The man standing before me seemed to change and his eyes filled with tears. "Oh," He said in wonder, "I need to talk to you. But we are leaving in just a few hours to fly home for the holidays." He then asked for my contact information. The only thing he had to write on was a receipt in my purse and I wrote my number and email down on it, after which he put it in his pocket and shook my hand conveying once again the importance of getting together to talk. I walked away sensing that something had changed. It contrasted greatly with the mood in the car as I climbed in, being chastised for taking too long. I apologized and remained silent all the way home.

The Discussions

Spring came and went without a word from Merrill. By midsummer, I began to think that he had lost my contact information. I had no idea how to contact him, but one afternoon I took a chance and contacted the theater office in Branson. I was asked to leave a message and contact information. No more than an hour had passed when the phone rang. It was Merrill's publicist. "I am so glad you contacted us," she said, "Merrill lost your number and has been trying to figure out how to get in touch with you!" A meeting was arranged. The children and I went as invited guests to see The Osmonds perform. We arrived with a small box of old pictures and artifacts and were greeted by Merrill's brother, Virl, who invited us to sit and visit for a while before the show started. He then took us to our seats.

It was during the intermission that Merrill told me about the vision he had received before our first meeting. As he spoke, I knew he was telling the truth because of how drawn I was that first meeting to tell him of my ancestry, and how I was directed to meet him. This confirmed to me that someone on the other side wanted us to meet for a reason. I wanted to know what that reason was. During the next two months we went to Branson several times and visited with the family.

Through those visits I came to know the whole Osmond family, meeting Donny briefly when he was visiting Branson and Marie later as I went to visit Mother Osmond in the hospital while we were in Utah. For the first time in my life, I was actually allowing myself to get to know the person behind the Mormon instead of recoiling from any acquaintance at all due to their faith. Clearly this Mormon family was not monsters. I learned many things about the family beyond their faith.

They are human just like us. They have problems both great and small, their lives are filled with fun and laughter, yet they are tried and tested by both extraordinary and everyday issues. In the face of adversity, they lean on their faith and smile despite hidden pain, and from their hearts comes a love for the people who have loved them for many years. They are a family who has devoted their lives to making other people happy through music, carrying with them an unyielding devotion to a faith they are bonded to by firm testimonies. The

Hills & Valleys

light I had seen on their faces at various times was one that came from within. I recognized it and knew its identity.

With such an intimate gaze into their daily lives, the aversion I had felt so long began to dissipate and as I walked out of the door of Merrill's home one day I stopped, biting my lip in indecision, then turned quickly and said to him, "I want to learn more about your church. But I can't do it in Ava; I do not want anyone to know." The fear of relatives finding out was great. Merrill told me to come once a week and take the discussions in his home from the sisters. I agreed and the next week the lessons began.

I will never forget meeting the sisters: Sister Tracy Swift and Sister Sally Schultz. I remember calling them Swifty & Schultz, joking that such a title would be great for a bar & grill. The first few lessons were attended by me, my children and my sister. With more than one Smith in the room, the wit is guaranteed to be doubled and then some. When one of the sisters accidentally turned her water over on the table splashing droplets onto my arm, my sister said that they would do anything to baptize someone and that the Church must be getting desperate.

It was not so much what was contained in the discussions that reached me. I didn't fully comprehend everything at once. What I did realize was that as they were speaking the spirit was bearing witness to me that what they were saying was true. The room seemed to become lighter and there was a warmth and joy which settled within me. There was a voice that resonated to my very core and an old familiar song arose within my heart called The Old, Old Path. This song has always been a favorite in Restoration hymns and had

Chapter Thirteen

been written by Joseph and Emma's granddaughter, Vida. I remember being very young and hearing it for the first time. It brought up feelings in me that I could not explain. Feelings of sadness mingled with a preciousness I could not fully describe.

As an adult, sitting before these sisters, I felt as if there was a choir of old familiar voices of days gone by singing to my heart and spirit. It was then that the burning within me reached a point that I could not deny the source of the yearnings and promptings which had followed me since seeing the portraits the first time. Emma's words, "Go and do," flooded back into memory. During the third lesson it was confirmed to me that I was to be baptized. Such a mingling of joy and jubilance rushed forward as I made that decision, leaving no room for fear of the past, at least not until I arrived home.

I was honestly giddy all the way home from Branson. But that evening reality set in and I saw all of the obstacles. It happened when my husband came home from work. What was I going to tell him? He did not agree whatsoever with the Church and was in fact anti-Mormon. Then there was my family; my father, my cousins. What in the world would they think of me? If that wasn't enough to rattle me, the silence of the evening hours brought up other issues, the old haunts of the past: Brigham Young, polygamy, baptism for the dead, and fear of denying the Holy Ghost because we had been told that's what we would be doing if we ever joined another church.

I stayed up late in the living room alone with generations of warnings swirling in my head. It became such a vicious circle of fear that I had to trace my steps backward to one important thing I had learned from my mother: what to do when the Holy Ghost tells you to move in a direction. There should be no questions. One simply walks forward. It will make sense later. You just have to trust as you walk that all will work out for the best because He is one who will never lie to you or steer you astray. One could not be in better company even if all others abandon you. Where the Holy Ghost is, there you will also find the Father and The Son. As I recalled those teachings the circle of darkness began to fade away and it did not matter anymore to me whether or not the things I had been told for so many years by the family were true. If people of the past behaved in ways they shouldn't, I could not help it. I was responsible for me and my own direction and I must base that direction on the Spirit, not dark periods of the past. I was determined to move forward but it was something I would keep to myself for a short time. I did not want a great opposition arising in my family at such an important time in my life. I wanted things to be done peacefully.

The next week we went to the show in Branson again. During intermission, I sent a note backstage to Merrill which said simply, "I would like for you to baptize me, signed Kimmy." Kimmy was a nickname he had tagged me with and I wanted to make sure he knew who the note came from.

I had seen the show enough to know that he would be doing the first number during the second half of show. When the curtains parted and he emerged, his face was brighter than the first time I had seen him, and the smile went beyond that

Chapter Thirteen

of pleasing a crowd. He spotted us in the center of the theater and gave us a quick wave as he went on singing.

I had to wait until the lessons were complete and I also had to attend the LDS Church for one Sunday. Then there was the interview to make sure that I understood everything and was truly ready. These were interesting times. I have forgotten intricate details but I do recall that regardless of my testimony, I was still very fearful about people finding out what I was about to do.

In 2011 I did a fireside in Ava and one of my friends, Lucinda Higley, came up to me and said, "Do you remember when you first started coming to church?" I told her I remembered some things and asked why. She said "You snuck in and sat in the back beside me and leaned over saying, 'please don't tell anyone I was here.' "I had to laugh when she reminded me. I had forgotten how terrified I was then.

As the baptismal date of June 7, 1998 approached, there came upon our household the greatest amount of opposition I have ever encountered in my life. In those days, I did not understand how things of the spirit worked in that manner. I was fast learning that things become the darkest just before something great and significant is about to happen. Wherever there could be turmoil, it erupted, and it got so bad that I considered postponing the baptism. I thought to myself how stressful things really would be if everyone knew what I was about to do.

Taking my despair to email, I explained to Merrill what was unfolding all around me and he answered telling me that it was the adversary trying to stop my progression. I thought about how far I had come since seeing those portraits when I was twelve and it had become evident to me that there was a purpose in my moving forward and that it had something to do with Joseph and our family. Indeed it made sense to me that what I was about to do was stirring up Ol' Scratch to a fever pitch. It was just so before Joseph knelt in the grove and that very thought gave me the strength to keep moving forward.

I had been wondering for some time why the connection with Joseph was so strong and what it meant. Up until that point, I only knew I should gain as much knowledge as possible but now there was an awareness that something deep lay at stake depending on the choices I would make. There was always a desire in me to do right by the Lord, not to disappoint Him. Now I was feeling the same toward my ancestor. Even though I had researched a portion of Joseph's life during the early Restoration, I knew there was much more to learn. With all of the assurances standing guard against darkness to quell the fear, I kept the June 7, 1998 date and waited in anticipation.

Waters of Life

It was a bright Sunday morning. The heat of June was already setting in and I arose from bed quietly and walked into my son's bedroom. My husband, who rarely attended any church at the time, always slept late on Sundays. I shook the sleeping form of my son and as he jerked awake he caught sight of the finger I held against my lip, begging silence. I told him to quietly get dressed, for that very morning I was going to be baptized but I did not want anyone else to know yet. In all

Chapter Thirteen

fairness, nobody had explained to me that I needed my husband's permission to be baptized. Merrill knew my home situation, as did the Bishop, but not at any time did the subject come up. I have thought it over in my mind and concluded that it must have been meant to be, for it slipped everyone's attention and was never brought to mine.

I had told the Bishop that I wanted to keep this baptism as quiet as possible so I was expecting everything to be very low-key. But there is nothing low-key at all when it comes to Latter-day Saints and baptisms. Quietly, on that bright morning, we slipped away in our little red van and as I walked into the church building a new door was open with many possibilities. I went into the dressing room and changed then walked into the room to be seated, shocked and amazed to see that it was filled with people! *This is low-key?* I thought to myself.

I would love to say that I recall every word which was said during the talks that day. But it seemed that my mind was taken to another time. Two faces in portraits: the man, for whom my middle name Jo was given, whose blue eyes twinkled in a memory of long ago and the woman, whose brown eyes spoke of a monumental life. In that atmosphere, I looked at my son sitting beside me and realized that I was not just opening a door for me, but for him and my daughter as well. It had never been so apparent to me until then how the likeness of the man in the portrait, had been inlaid upon the countenance of the boy before me.

A Moment of Truth

I had felt close to Joseph for many years, but on that day it was as if he was in attendance and there was rejoicing in our family who had passed generations before me. I had no way of knowing what the next step was, nor where it would take me. I only knew that I was supposed to walk that way. It was one of the most precious moments of my life, yet in the preciousness was a feeling that my life would never be the same again.

As I came up out of the water, the first thing I saw were the tears in my twelve-year-old son's eyes and the light upon his countenance, as well as an unmistakable presence of one close by. After I changed clothes and re-entered the room, I was confirmed a member of the Church and received the Holy Ghost. It was then that the fear of denying the Holy Ghost completely went away, for until that time, I had not ever had the fullness of it. But as hands were laid upon my head I became aware of the marked difference between having the Holy Ghost near or with you and having the gift of the Holy Ghost. It was as if for all of those years I had access to 60 watts of light but now I had 100 watts; a fullness of light, guidance and comfort.

I had weathered those days trying to achieve what had become a pivotal moment in my life without my husband or family finding out. The excitement was balanced by an equal amount of fear and I still had not really dealt with the major issues that I had pushed aside. Though I understood baptism for the dead, there was still a fear of it stemming from what I had been raised believing, and somewhere in the shadows loomed a seemingly dark and lowly figure named Brigham Young, whose name still sent a rush of discontent throughout my whole being. I knew somewhere down the line I would have to walk through these issues and deal with them

Chapter Thirteen

accordingly in order to bring about the proper state of healing. The process would have to come at some point, for ill will cannot reside in the same place with the Holy Ghost. So I was determined to work through all of my concerns, but I felt those concerns were somewhere down the road, like some out-of-the-way place I would like to visit but never seem to get to. At this point in my life, I learned that some things can't be placed on a shelf without the expectation that they may fall off and hit you when you least expect it.

The first few Sundays, I was unable to attend church because there were problems at home. My husband had decided he wanted to start attending the Nazarene Church regularly and it seemed as if every Sabbath was filled with strain and contention. I agreed to go with him but it felt awful because I felt nothing there. The people were for the most part kind and there was a kindly spirit there but so much was lackin., It felt hollow to me and I had finished that course of my life. I had already been guided to a place that held more knowledge and spirit. It was as if I had already attended elementary school then was shown high school and college, but someone was trying to make me go to grade school again.

Two months after my baptism, I decided that it was time to tell everyone. I remember the day quite clearly because I had never felt so anxious in my life. Figuring on making an easy approach with the subject, I felt to tell my mother first, after all, she is the one who had made the most impression upon me about following the spirit in all things. I gathered all the courage I had and prepared to make the announcement.

My children and I had spent the night at my parents' apartment and my mother and I were running errands the next day. It was pouring rain and we were sitting at an intersection waiting for the light to change from red to green. I remember looking at the light through the rain and how the colors seemed to blend with the water and flow like trails down the windshield. It seemed ominous, like trails of blood. I almost laughed at the image and thought for a moment that maybe it was not the right time, but then there would never be a good setting to bring the topic up. As the light turned green we proceeded forward and I looked upon the moment favorably. The trails of blood that seemed to flow were now running clear. I turned to my mother and simply said, "Mom, I have to tell you something."

Anytime a child says to their parent, "Mom, I need to tell you something," the parent braces for impact. If it was good news the child would be saying exuberantly, "MOM, GUESS WHAT!!!" But the silent tone of what I had just uttered was like an alarm going off. The long pause gave me time to consider how ridiculous it was that generations of contention in Dad's family had instilled so much fear within me to the point I was petrified to utter what should be words of joy and excitement. Instead, I had to do it one person at a time and wait for the fallout. It was good to have at least one person I knew would love me no matter what.

"Is it something bad?" She asked. *Good grief, what a loaded question*, I thought to myself!

"To some it is bad; to others it is very good." I replied.

"What is it?" She asked. *Say it, Kim, just say it*, I thought. My heart rate was going crazy and I couldn't even look at her when I spoke.

Chapter Thirteen

"I was baptized into the LDS Church two months ago." I said looking away at the traffic.

"You what?" She asked, thoroughly dumbfounded.

"I have joined the LDS church." I repeated.

"Well..." she said, pausing, "Do you feel this is where the Lord has led you to go?" She finally asked.

"I know this is where the Lord has led me to go, Mom." I said with pure confidence

"Then you have done the right thing. Now what are you going to tell your dad?"

Well I had really wrestled with that question. I thought of the many ways in which I could tell my father that I had done the unthinkable. How would I cushion the blow for him? He would be facing in his opinion the fact that his daughter had just purchased a one-way ticket to hell. I was probably the first of his father's kin to walk into the forbidden zone and go against three generations of family who had united to quash the validity of the very church I had just joined. If there was a soft way to approach my father about the new step I had taken in my life, I had yet to find it.

As I sat in that van with the rain pouring down, I searched for something to say in answer to her question, a great proposal of what I would say to my father; some good, fearless, strong yet empathetic manner in which to announce what I had done. I had this visual image that whatever I said to my father his face would still turn three or four shades of color and he would point his finger at me without saying a word, disintegrating me right then and there.

As I tossed a measure of scenarios around in my head, I came up with one that avoided as closely as possible a confrontation that could have had severe atmospheric consequences.

"Well," I looked over at my mother, "I thought I would send him an email."

She chuckled softly and I told her I truly did not think I could tell him in person. She would talk to him, an assignment I gladly relinquished to her. I felt some relief but still knew there was much aggression ahead. I thought of how far there was to go in the areas of courage and strength, reflecting upon a young boy many years before and what courage it must have taken to stand before people and say that he had seen the Father and Son. I knew that I too must have that kind of strength if I was going to go forward in a positive way, the strength to open my mouth without being afraid of the reaction of others. Learning to be bold and strong was something I had never accomplished because of incidents in my childhood and I had seen my father's side of the family exhibit boldness and strength but it was in a prideful and hateful manner, characteristics I seemed to naturally repel. I needed to learn how to be strong yet retain the humbleness our mom had raised us with.

When Mom broke the news to Dad, he threw his hands up in the air, loudly exclaiming, "I knew it! Those Osmonds, those Mormons!" He said he wanted nothing more to do with me. I had betrayed the family.

"Wait a minute," Mom said, "What have you ever taught her about your church that would entice her to stay?

Chapter Thirteen

Besides, she is being led by the Spirit. I would not want to stand in the way and be held accountable." There wasn't much that Dad could say. She was right. He had never taught us anything about religion in the home. The first meeting I had with him after she announced the news was cold and stiff but by the time I left he had warmed up to me again. It wasn't that he had forgotten, nor had he forgiven, but we have always been close and as bad as the news was to him, he was still accepting of me as his daughter. Telling my husband had a different outcome altogether.

One morning we were in the bedroom and I told him that we needed to talk. I was petrified. In those days he had a violent temper and I never knew when it would blow. Sometimes it would be the smallest thing and this was no small thing I was about to tell him. I wasn't disappointed. He blew and in a big way. It was his comment to me just before he blew up that shocked me. He said that he was preparing to have us join the Nazarene church as a family. What? This is the man who never seemed to want to go to church, nor did he ever like to talk religion with me. Now he was saying he had planned for us all to join the Nazarene church? I asked him if he even knew what they believed and he didn't. After he calmed down, he said I had betrayed him. In a sense I guess I did. After what had just occurred, I could see why The LDS Church requires the husband's blessing so as not to divide the family. But this family had been divided for years already and as I previously stated, I did not know ahead of time that the husband's permission was needed, so it isn't that I willfully set out to deceive anyone. I was merely doing as I was led to do. The temperature of the home environment had just exceeded the danger zone.

Chapter Fourteen

"Some of the greatest battles will be fought within the silent chambers of your own soul."

— *Ezra Taft Benson*

Most often a conversion story would end after the baptism. But there is still the meat to this story, and then the dessert, for many amazing things followed the events of 1998. I thought that as a new member of the LDS church, I would just settle in and go with the flow, but I have yet to know a convert, let alone a Smith, that has circumstances go that easily. Some of us float upon water expecting to tread the current as it smoothly goes along, then all of a sudden a huge wave casts us forward and we are surged in a direction we did not anticipate.

The first unsuspecting wave I was hit with came upon my introduction to the Relief Society, the women's organization in the church. Although I had attended sacrament meeting just before my baptism, I had not been able to go to Relief Society. I had heard so much about its activities over the years during my visits to the Family History Center in Ava. It all sounded so interesting but I never dared inquire about it, fearing the ever-reaching hooks these Mormons seemed to possess. But the frightening image of those hooks was washed away in the waters of baptism, and as I walked down the hallway after sacrament meeting toward the Relief Society room I was

Chapter Fourteen

beaming. It was an exciting venture for me. I was about to attend a meeting in the organization of which my great-great-grandmother became the first president! Oh, I was alight inside with joy! Many people had stopped me en route to greet me and visit so when I walked into the room filled with sisters, they were in the middle of the opening song.

Right as I walked in, a sister who was sitting at the end row stood and handed me the study manual. I took it, smiling graciously and prepared to advance forward to find a seat but as I glimpsed the image upon the manual my feet froze in their steps. It couldn't be. Had that old nemesis come back to haunt me in this, my happy moment? I looked again to behold the image of Brigham Young. Looking up suddenly, I thanked the sister and excused myself, turning to exit the room. As I walked out the back door, I dropped the manual into the trash, swearing to myself that I would never go back until they were finished with that manual.

I was bewildered as I climbed into the car. I had followed the Spirit and joined this church, but I was not about to have that man's history forced down my throat. I truly believed he murdered a grandfather I dearly loved, one to whom I was very close. I thought that if I pushed the issues I had aside and followed the guidance of the Spirit then I would not have to deal with them anymore. But I would learn in time that it is necessary for us to sort out all issues, forgive and let go, before we can truly progress and heal. The Lord would also appoint a time for me to gain an understanding that our family had been mistaken about Brigham Young, sorely mistaken. Until that time arrived, I would remain tainted by the image of him which had been passed to me. I decided that

I would always go to sacrament meeting, but only occasionally did I go to Relief Society and even then it was because friends in the hallway would ask me earnestly to go. But as I sat in the meeting, I willfully let my mind go elsewhere so that I would not hear what was said.

In the summer and fall of 1999, many special events happened. In August, I became acquainted with a very special cousin. Dad had told me that we had a cousin in Utah who communicated every now and again but he was not interested at the time in forming any kind of relationship. He gave me the email address of Gracia Jones and I emailed her. She responded immediately and invited me to come to the Joseph Smith Sr. family reunion that would be taking place in August of that year. I was so excited! Amazingly, I convinced Mom and Dad to go as well!

Meeting Gracia was something that was much needed. Finally, a family member who was a source of support. We bonded immediately and have since been the best of friends. The reunion opened many doors of understanding for me and we all had a good time. But not all understanding had been reached. There were still issues I had pushed aside that needed to be attended to. Brigham Young waited in the wings on the stage of my quest for clarity and as he came into view, my stage fright re-emerged. In time I would reach a place of understanding, but it would take another year.

The other special event which occurred in 1999 was my patriarchal blessing. It was an exciting moment for me because I was anxious to see my blue print. That is what I like to call it, for actually it is a type of blueprint. The complete design is not there in detail, just a framework that can be built and added to

Chapter Fourteen

if we make the right choices, and an awareness as to where our raw material came from. I was really anxious to see what was said about talents, for often talents are alluded to in these blessings. I had always dreamed of being an author so I was hoping that something about writing would be spoken.

On October 17, 1999, we drove to Harrisonville, Arkansas. Sister Essex, the patriarch's wife greeted us at the door. Merrill Osmond had been gracious enough to attend the blessing and I also had my son with me. After we all sat for a while, Bryan, Merrill, Patriarch Essex and I went upstairs. Owing to the sacredness of a patriarchal blessing I will only share that part which pertains to talents. There was much peace and light in the room as I listened to the beautiful words which were spoken. To my delight, the topic of talents did surface. I braced myself, taking in a deep breath and holding it. Then something I did not expect reached my ears. He said that I was uniquely gifted in music and that I should develop those talents for the work of the Lord to lift and enlighten those around me. Music? I was thoroughly caught off guard. I quickly dismissed my reaction for I truly wanted to stay focused as I heard the rest of my blessing. There was an unmistakable feeling of assurance as I realized that there were more than just the three of us in that room. I was happy, delightfully so. It was the same kind of happiness I felt after my baptism except even more: more light, more love and more knowledge.

There were many questions answered in that afternoon. I came to know more fully of my responsibilities as a descendant of Joseph and Emma, the purpose of why things had been so hard so that I might overcome and be a stronger person. I also realized through that blessing why there was such a bond between myself and my great-great-grandparents, in particular Joseph. This apple didn't fall too far from the tree! But I had no idea how I, who felt like an insignificant nobody, could be an effective tool in building up the kingdom.

The ride home to Missouri was filled with awe and wonder. My thoughts came back around to music. I was still dismayed. What on earth could I offer musically? I loved to sing to myself but only when alone. I had always had a desire to perform but I never allowed myself to even consider that an option in life for I feared ridicule. Mammaw Roberts' talent for making up little ditties, and Dad's musical abilities were deeply engrained within me and I could play a few instruments by ear, but nothing that was nearly professionally adequate. Nothing had been said about being an author, which made me sad indeed. But then I remembered the many poems I had written and how easily I could come up with lyrical patterns at the drop of a hat. Maybe there was something to what the patriarch said; after all writing and music are appendages of the same body. Thoughts filled the miles as we headed to Missouri. It was something I would have to be patient about understanding.

The Great Salt Lake:

A Burial Ground for Fallen Women

As 2000 rolled around, there were countless people waiting for the world to end. It wasn't a fear that preoccupied my mind at all. Instead I began to feel it was time for me to go through the temple to receive my endowment. St. Louis is the temple district for Ava but I did not feel that was where I

Chapter Fourteen

should go. Anytime I considered it, there was something unsettling, not about the St. Louis Temple itself, just concerning where I should go. After pondering for some time, I began to ask some of my friends at church what their favorite temple was. Many names were brought to my attention; L.A., San Diego, Ogden, the names just kept pouring forth with descriptions that formed beautiful images in my mind, yet not one of them clicked. One day I was in the Family History Center and I casually asked one of the sisters who was working in her family line, "What is your favorite temple?"

"Oh," she said with affection burning as she spoke, "that is easy. Manti." Manti. As soon as she said the name everything seemed to lock into place and there was an immediate confirmation that Manti is where I should go to get my endowment.

"Where is Manti?" I asked trying to hide the excitement in my voice.

"In Utah. Oh, it is a beautiful temple...." She kept speaking but my mind was trying to deal with the blow I had just received. Utah? I couldn't go to Utah! I knew it was a dangerous place, especially for descendants. Why, we had known for generations that the people of Utah wanted Joseph's posterity dead. Besides, I had it on good authority that if women in the LDS church ever tried to leave it they were secretly marched up to the spires of the Salt Lake Temple and pushed into the Salt Lake! Didn't I narrowly dodge notice by scrunching down in the seat of the car while my sister and I drove through Salt Lake City in 1980? Now I was being led to go back? I was petrified.

Hills & Valleys

"Why do you ask?" A soft voice penetrated my panic.

"No reason," I said, gazing at the computer screen in an attempt to look absorbed in genealogy.

Later that evening as I fixed supper, I could not help but be lost in thought. I was at yet another crossroad and no matter how terrifying it was for me, I knew what I had to do, for I knew the Holy Ghost would not lie to me. Somewhere inside, scary as it all seemed, something assured me that if I just walked forward I would see that everything would be okay and no harm would come to me.

When I approached my husband, I was met with coldness. But I talked him into going as far as St. George so that we could visit with Gracia Jones and her husband Ivor. My husband rarely went on trips, however, he had become friends with them after they had visited our home in 1999. Part of me hoped that this trip would help him bond better with the kids and soften his heart. Then after a week, he could fly back to Missouri for I would be gone longer than he could miss work.

Any finances that it took to do this trip I had to come up with on my own. So the children and I had several yard sales. I sold an old Victrola that I had cherished for many years. By the end of a month, we had the money we needed to go to Utah and stay for a few weeks. But there was one thing I had not counted on that needed to happen before I took this trip. I had not dealt with my feelings against Brigham Young. He was the farthest thing from my mind at that point. After all, why would I need to think about him before going to the temple? As in all things, it is not what I thought which

Chapter Fourteen

mattered, but what the Lord directed that counted most. Thus, two days before our departure to Utah, the Lord brought to my attention the need to let go of past issues which had blinded me to the stumbling blocks which had been built over time.

Two days before we left for Utah, I was taking the missionaries home from a zone conference. The conversation had been fairly lively as I was used to joking around with the missionaries on road trips. Elder Woods, who was from West Jordan, Utah, sat in the front of the van. I was driving. On part of the trip there was a brief silence, when Elder Woods turned to me and said, "I hear you are going to be in Utah quite a while."

"Yes," I replied. "I am going to get my endowment, and then I plan on meeting family I have out there and doing some research in the archives." By then I had become excited about the trip, despite concerns of safety lurking in the back of my mind.

"Are you going to learn all about Brigham Young?" He said quietly. He couldn't have made a deeper cut through my thoughts had he taken a sword and took off my head. At the mention of the name I stiffened, my hands forging a white knuckled grip on the steering wheel.

"No." I said under a controlled breath. Silence emerged and I was aware of a weight which had settled between me and Elder Woods. Elder Woods was quite an amazing missionary while he was serving in Ava. I had gone with him and his trainer Elder Williams at times when they were teaching new member discussions, or visiting inactive

Hills & Valleys

members. Often I had seen his countenance carry the light of the Spirit when he was bearing testimony. As the silence thickened I looked over at the Elder and beheld a glowing countenance. "Oh, man!" I thought to myself. I knew what was happening. The Lord was working with him. That meant I needed to hear what he had to say. Turning my attention back to the road, I drew in a breath letting out a long but muffled sigh.

"Okay. What is on your mind?" I said in a defeated tone. In that moment, Elder Woods began to testify. With wisdom that can only come from one source, Elder Woods bore his testimony of the Savior first. As he did so the Spirit filled the car and the heaviness that I had felt earlier was replaced by the pure love of Christ. My defenses began to wane as he continued, bearing his testimony of Joseph Smith. Then when he started to testify of Brigham Young, all of my defenses had fled and we had approached a signal light which had turned red. As I pressed the brake pedal down I felt a lightness move within me and within an instant, all of the hardness I had carried against Brigham Young was removed with an energy that caused me to take a breath. The light turned green and I drove forward.

In a matter of minutes, I went over what had just happened in my mind. I had always believed in the healing power of the pure love of Christ, even had witnessed it many times in my life, but never had I experienced it myself. The healing power of His love was manifested in those moments and the Lord, knowing my true character, heart and desires, removed what had for so long blinded me. All of a sudden it did not matter to me what someone so many years ago had

Chapter Fourteen

done. I did not need to know the reasoning behind actions of others. I only knew that the Lord had taken the bitterness away and now I had to replace it with unconditional love without having any explanations of the past. The rest of the drive was spent telling Elder Woods what had just happened and when I dropped him and his companion off at their apartment, I told him that I would learn as much of Brigham as I could, because there was a big empty place where all the bitterness had been and it lay with me to fill it with truth.

The trip to St. George was rifled with opposition. The distance between my husband and me was tense but there were good moments as well. As we drove down a steep hill and entered the St. George area it was nearly ten o'clock in the evening. In the distance, I saw something white and glowing. It resonated with my spirit and I knew instantly that it was the temple. I had never in my life seen one before. If we had passed the Salt lake Temple in 1980 I did not recall it, for I was hiding! I called the kids' attention to the glowing temple in the distance and we all became excited, well, three of us did anyway! Gracia and Ivor's home was located a few blocks down from the temple, and as we reached their residence I asked that we be driven to the temple first. The tension in the car doubled, but he agreed and drove right in front of the St. George Temple. My kids and I gasped in awe simultaneously. "Oh, good grief." My husband exclaimed. "It's just a church." On that note, we headed to Gracia and Ivor's home.

After a few days of sight-seeing, my husband took a bus to Las Vegas and then flew home. Finally I could relax and take in everything I was about to experience. The next morning we all left to head to Manti. Gracia and Ivor went as well, as she would be my escort. It had been arranged for me to stay with Mother and Father Osmond, which was a real treat for me. The fun part about that particular visit was when George Osmond took me to the back yard to an old silver streamliner travel trailer. He called it his museum. Inside were all sorts of memorabilia from the years that their children had performed, such as posters and souvenirs. Some I had seen before in teen magazines, others were more personal such as family gatherings. He took such pride as he walked us through the trailer. For me it was surreal. There I was experiencing the pride of a father toward his children while at the same time remembering the connection to my own childhood. These were people I had grown up adoring, even healing as a result of their music. What made it even more special was that it was those brothers who brought me to the point I was at that very moment.

Olive and I stayed up a little later than everyone else that evening, talking of many things. She wanted to know more about my family, my history and then the talk turned to things more spiritual. We both shared special experiences that we had passed through and I felt to share with her of the closeness I felt with Joseph and how it had kept me searching for so long. I made in that evening a very dear friend in Olive Osmond and I have loved her ever since. Though she is gone now, the things that I learned from her are never far away.

The next day was my day at the temple. I will say very little for it is very special and sacred but I will say that I still had little flitters of fear welling up, but I knew I was doing what I was supposed to.

Chapter Fourteen

As I walked up the steps to enter the temple doors I promised myself that if I saw anything that even resembled what I had been told all of my life, I was booking out of there! Afterwards I had to laugh for I could not believe how far-fetched some of the things we had been told were. Once again I wondered just how many things we had been misled about. When I walked out of the temple and glimpsed the valley and mountains in the distance, there was an awareness of home. Somehow I felt connected to that place, those scenic mountains. I walked on wondering what the next day would bring as we toured Salt Lake City.

There were many things which passed through my mind as we drove up to Salt Lake City. For the first time in my life I felt a sense of peace that was whole. I wasn't sure what to expect about Salt Lake but at least I now knew that there was probably no truth to the story about women being tossed off of the temple and into the lake. I had pictured that lake as a burial ground for fallen women. I should have paid more attention in school during geography. Had I been more knowledgeable of the lay of the land, I would have known that the Salt Lake was nowhere near the temple. But as is usually the case with me, I have to have my ignorance tossed in front of me. I guess the adversary likes shock value. Yes, there we were driving up past the temple and I stretched my neck to look all around but I didn't see any signs of a lake anywhere. I knew better than to ask.. I had already borne the brunt of humiliation years before when I found out that what I thought to be outdoor refrigerators at construction sites were actually portable toilets. I just assumed that once again I had an idiot experience and let it go.

Making Peace With the Lion

     After parking, we took in several sights. The feeling of the temple grounds was amazing and we took in the beauty of the flowers as we made our way to the Beehive House. I love old homes but this one was particularly interesting to me. I wondered how I would feel walking into the home of Brigham Young. My thoughts were those of one who had succumbed to peaceful resolution so I was not fearful of any ill feelings being stirred up. Instead, I walked in and felt the warmth of the home of a man I once hated. I drew in deep breaths as I passed through each doorway, hoping to secure the aroma of the past. When we were finished, we ate in the restaurant on the bottom floor. After a stroll through the past and a nice home-cooked style meal we stepped outside of the Beehive House and encountered the real world, cars passing speedily by, people walking quickly on their way to something important, tourists enjoying their walk among the historic district. It was a melting pot of activity. The sun was blazing down upon the sidewalk, bouncing upward with such an effect that I felt as if I were in a sauna. Everyone complains about the humidity in the Midwest. I would take it in a heartbeat, for though this was a dryer heat, the intensity was more severely felt, pulling almost every bit of energy I had.

     Someone suggested we walk to see some more sites. I had no idea where we were going. I fell behind and was lost in thought as we took in the scenery. Before too long, we were looking at a tombstone which caught my attention for it had a wrought iron gate around it. I walked over and stood on the other side of a plaque that read, "No. 78, grave of Brigham Young." I stood silent for a moment. There I was inches away

Chapter Fourteen

from Brigham Young whose remains lay in silent repose. I searched my feelings. It was a moment that was pure preciousness. Although I had no ill feelings remaining in me against him, I still felt as if something had been left undone. Walking over to the others I told them I wished to remain behind for a few moments. My mind filled with wonderment as I walked back over to the iron gate and ran one palm down the cool surface, settling upon the words upon the plaque.

"Grave of Brigham Young. Prophet-Pioneer-Statesman. Born June 1, 1801 at Whittingham, Vermont. Died August 29, 1877, Salt Lake City, Utah. Brigham Young second president of The Church of Jesus Christ of Latter- day saints succeeded Joseph Smith, founder of the Church who was martyred at Carthage Illinois. He was chosen as leader of the people in 1844 and sustained as President of the Church December 27, 1847. Earlier that year he led the Mormon pioneers from Winter Quarters (Omaha) to the Salt Lake Valley arriving here in July 24. In 1849 he became governor of the provisional state of Deseret and in 1850 he became governor of the territory of Utah. This tablet erected in honor of their beloved leader by the young men's and young women's mutual improvement associations which were organized under his direction."

I knelt before the monument and grave, holding the bars steadily. The love of history and desires of peace which had always been a part of me surfaced in uncontrollable waves. I thought to myself, "Why am I having such feelings to the point that tears are falling down my face? I have asked the Lord to forgive my judgment after the experience with Elder Woods." But a thought occurred to me. I had not asked the man himself to forgive me. I had not thought of it. After all, he

Hills & Valleys

was on the other side of the veil. But something told me that it made no difference and as those thoughts passed through my mind I looked down at his grave and began to pray.

Surrounded by flowers and embraced by raw emotion, I began to pour out my heart to someone I had wronged. I asked Brigham to forgive me and our family for speaking against him for so many generations, for the hatred it had caused and the walls which had been built because of it. I especially asked him to forgive me for I had allowed hate, an emotion which was not part of my nature, to seep into my heart. The adversary had known full well what he was doing. First I was molested, which caused me to hate myself and then he introduced the seed of discontent against Brigham Young, bolstering my ability to hate. I am sure it was his intent to keep fostering such emotions until I became as cold and stiff as some of my family. But there was something he had not counted on. I had been exposed to the power of the Savior's love as a child before I was introduce to the aggression among some of the family. This enabled me to wash away such emotions, even though in some cases it took time. For too long I had accepted without question what some of my dad's family had told me, not even thinking to ask the Lord about it. They were, after all, family and would never lie to me. But they were not lying. They had been misled as well by the traditions of their fathers.

As I continued to pray, I felt a peace come over me, a joy which filled every part of me. As I ended the prayer, I forgave Brigham Young for things he had said and done which hurt the family, because the pain which caused a dividing wall came from both sides, not just one. In that moment, I heard a

Chapter Fourteen

choir singing *Nearer My God to Thee* and I looked around me. I thought how amazing it was that the tabernacle choir must be outdoors somewhere practicing and I could hear them by the grave. But soon I became aware that this was not a choir of human making, but a heavenly choir and it was very audible to me.

Tears fell down my cheeks as the environment grew even more precious. Then my mind was opened and I was given a perspective that I had never stopped to think about. I was given to know that all of our ancestors who lived and toiled together on this earth, partook of love, joys, sorrows and even pain they may have caused one another. They experienced those things, not us. They are on the other side of the veil and have reconciled all offense, basking in the joyous bond of that great work of which they were a part. It was pointed out to me that since we did not experience those events, primarily the hurt which they may have caused one another, then we should have no part of carrying those offenses forward from one generation to the next. Those issues have been reconciled and for us to carry it forward is an offense of our own making against our Father.

It was made very plain to me that we are to look at all parts of our past, even the darkest parts, examine them, forgive and let it go. So it is okay to want to understand why and how things happene;, that is how we come to learn who we are. But what generally happens, is the adversary steps in very subtly and feelings of hurt, contempt, and hate begin to brew. It is necessary for us to view these issues with an open heart, acknowledge how sad it was and then let it go. Then we take all of the good, embrace it, celebrate it, and magnify those good works as we progress forward.

It was then I knew that I had a work to do in speaking to people about healing and uniting. The times we live in call for us to be strong in unity so that we may be able to handle the things which are coming. It is important that we learn to forgive ourselves and one another, love ourselves and one another, and to let go of the issues of the past. We cannot hold on to those issues and the Savior at the same time and it is vital to have the Savior as the central part of our lives for it is through Him that we are able to overcome all things.

The lesson I learned by Brigham's grave was relevant to my life, to the lives of everyone. It does not serve us well to dwell on dark periods of the past to the point that we begin to hate. That is an adversarial agenda. After that day in prayer, I came to learn that it is not necessary for my salvation to understand all of the stories or incidents of the past which had become mired in confusion, accusation and myth. It is merely my duty to look at what is before me today and move forward. I am responsible for myself and my children. If there needs to be an understanding of the past, Heavenly Father will see to it that it comes when it is His will, His timing, not mine and not the world's. The Lord moves us to the right paths if we listen and follow. That is faith and it is the very foundation my mother gave me so long ago.

I stood and lifted my eyes up toward the sky, then to the trees and my surroundings. The emotions which had stirred within me for so long to bring some kind of peace and harmony to the family had never been as strong as they were

Chapter Fourteen

on that day. But what could I do? The answer was not far in coming.

Our next stop on Temple Square was at The Church Office Building for we were to meet another cousin named Elder Russell Ballard. We all sat and visited and I found him to be a very kind and generous man. We then were taken by Elder Watson, secretary to President Hinckley on a tour of the room where the twelve apostles meet every Thursday for prayer. As we walked toward the door which led to that room I looked down to wind the film in my camera and as I crossed through the door, there was an instant awareness of change. The air seemed thick but not heavy and it was very warm. It was then that we were told that room was where the twelve met once a week for prayer and I understood why the Spirit was so strong there.

We were then taken into another room which was President Hinckley's office. I had come to love President Hinckley dearly and I would have loved to have met him but he had just left the building. I saw behind his desk a huge portrait of Brigham Young and I asked Elder Watson if I could sit in President Hinckley's chair for a picture. He allowed it and I was thrilled for there I was captured in the seat of a prophet I loved, with a portrait behind me of a prophet I had come to love.

The whole day was filled with avenues of understanding and miles of peace. Throughout the tour, I thought about how sad it was that so many people had allowed the walls of indifference to become so thick. I so wanted them to breathe the air of understanding I had come to know, for it was fresh and clean. It did not stifle and stir discontent. I became overwhelmed by a desire to get them to a place where they could breathe that air, so pure and sweet, but I was frustrated by thoughts of inadequacy. Once again I mulled over in my heart the question of what I could do and how.

Chapter Fifteen

Out of the Box

    Through my friendship with Merrill, I was introduced to an amazing woman of great courage and faith. Ranelle Wallace had been involved in a plane crash in which she died, but through the blessings of a merciful Father in Heaven was brought back in the hospital emergency room. We had talked many times over the phone and she knew that I would be in Salt Lake City for a few weeks. At the time, we were staying with the parents of Elder Woods who was serving in Ava, Missouri. While there I got a call from Ranelle asking if I would attend a fireside she was doing in Ogden. I immediately said yes.

    "Toward the end of the program I would like for you to share your testimony." She said. My mouth fell open and I was in shock, but something inside of me would not refuse her request. "I would love to." I answered.

    After hanging up the phone, I sat immersed in fear. What could I say? My testimony? How much of such a story did they want? I mean I could speak of many things our family had been through for four generations and it wasn't very pretty. The prospect of standing before a crowd of people whose attention was focused solely on me did not help to boost my enthusiasm. I went downstairs and retrieved a tablet from my suitcase and began to outline what I would say. The pen would not move, but my thoughts were flying. I had fifteen minutes to fill, which at the time seemed like an eternity of volumes. Events of turmoil, trauma, division, and contention all paraded before me until I became physically ill. Putting a tearful face into my hands I poured out my heart unto the Lord, asking Him what I should say.

After a few moments, it was if the clouds had dispersed and the rays of the sun poured through. I knew what I would say and there would be no need for an outline. I was simply to profess my love for the Savior and give an overview of the events from the time I had met Merrill which had led me into this gospel. I would only barely touch upon the adversity I had suffered previous to meeting Merrill. I was also to express the experience of seeing the portraits of Joseph and Emma when I was twelve. Although it was terrifying for me, I knew it was something I needed to do.

As the day of the fireside arrived, I could not sleep. I was not so much concerned about what I would say anymore but how I was going to get through it without passing out. The thought of being in front of people in any measure was so terrifying that when confronted with such an event my heart rate would go so wild that I would nearly faint, so I made it a point never to place myself in any situation which would make me the center of attention. I sat amazed during Ranelle's fireside, but as minutes flew by there was the nagging awareness that my time was fast approaching.

The heart rate began to surge forward, skipping beats and thumping against my chest, even pulsating in my ears. I closed my eyes and told myself that I needed to slow my breathing to regulate the pulse rate. As I concentrated on

Hills & Valleys

breathing my heart began to settle and then I heard my name called.

It was one of the most singular moments in my life as I walked forward to ascend the steps. I was being placed in a position that could affect lives depending on what I said. The weight of responsibility that rested in such a task fell upon my shoulders as I came to the podium and turned to face the crowd. For a few brief seconds I wanted to run, but I remembered the face in the portrait and the pure love of Christ. I could never run from either one of those images, nor could I flee from what I had been asked to do. I could feel my lips quivering from my nerves as I began to speak.

"I am so very pleased to be here with you all today. My name is Kimberly Jo Smith, and I am a great-great-granddaughter of Joseph and Emma..." From that point, it was as if someone took my hand and I sailed through. Before I knew it the fifteen minutes had passed and I was bursting to say even more! As people approached me afterward, I was met with warm smiles and gentle handshakes which spoke of thanksgiving and love. Some even broke into tears and talked of how much I helped strengthen their testimony. What? Me? What did I do that could have strengthened their testimony? I heard a soft voice in my mind say "you opened your mouth, the Lord did the rest." I knew from that point I would be speaking on a regular basis and I had an understanding that it all had very little to do with me, but everything in the world to do with the Lord and healing hearts through His love.

As we were driving away from the chapel, Ranelle remarked that she would like to take me to meet a friend of hers. An hour later, I found myself in the home of Kerri

Guthrie, a talented artist, who upon opening the door caught a glimpse of my son first, and then my daughter. She knew right away that she wanted to include them in a painting she was working on called Generations of Eternal Families. Because she saw a resemblance of Joseph in my son, she wanted to use him to portray Joseph. It was a bit awkward for us as we wanted to make sure people do not perceive that we think we are important or better than others, for we do not. We are just as important to the Lord as anyone else, no more, no less. After she explained about the painting we felt better, for it was portraying the love of family and captured the essence of families being forever. Kerri would become one of my dearest friends, pivotal in the many journeys we would be making in the future.

Dark Places in a Bright New World

Opposition in all things. I had heard the phrase during the discussions I had taken with the sister missionaries in 1997. Lessons in sacrament meeting and the testimonies of others brought to me an awareness of the nature of opposition. I came to realize its pattern and how it had plagued my life and those who passed before me. I was learning the tremendous struggle between good and evil. For much of my life, I was in one place spiritually, never advancing or moving forward in any direction. I had received the basics, the foundational teachings as I grew up but there was not much more than that offered to me. I believe the adversary wants us that way, stalemated in one area. The less knowledge we have the more he is able to deceive. Because I had a close relationship with the Lord growing up, I was given protection and guidance in many ways. Still, because I did not have teachings of the fullness of the Gospel in those days, I was living a half spiritual life.

After my baptism, there was opposition to be sure, simply for the fact that I desired and strove to be closer to the Savior. But it was nothing compared to what I began to encounter after going through the temple. From 1998 to 2000, tensions in my home increased. There was a darkness that settled over my husband which in many ways even seemed to change his countenance. Only through humor and other means was I able to bring some semblance of peace in our home but it never lasted long. When I returned from our trip to Utah, I would find that the more knowledge one seeks, the more the opposition increases, sometimes in a most cruel manner. The stronger the spiritual experience, the harder the opposition.

The drive home from Utah in 2000 became sullen, for we knew what we were going back to. The 12 miles from Mansfield, Missouri to our hometown of Ava was a troubled piece of road. My children and I had experienced so many wonderful things in Utah. Now we knew we had to go back home to an environment that was unpleasant. Still, in my mind I felt somehow I could make this work. I would just have to go through it and try my best to bring out the good I knew was in my husband's heart. It was much like the situation in my mother's marriage when we were children. My father, a good man, jolly and fun-loving in public, found it hard to be those things at home. My husband was not happy and I would not learn for a few years why. I only knew that the misery he was experiencing was tearing him up inside, causing him to be

Chapter Fifteen

closed up to the point that, at times, any little thing would bring an eruption of violent outbursts.

This behavior in turn caused me to want to retract and withhold myself. Instead, I tried to be someone who tried fixing everything, someone who always gave in just to end an argument. I would apologize for things that were my fault, but more so when they were not, anything to appease the situation. But as I did so, I buried myself.

As we approached the sign that said welcome to Ava, I felt a knot forming in my stomach and the atmosphere in the car shifted. All was silent. But instead of facing turmoil when we walked into the house, we were welcomed with enthusiasm. I was in shock, but very happy to have been met with a smile instead of a tight set mouth. But as we began to talk of the excitement of our trip, the countenance grew dark once more. I learned then and there that I would not be able to share spiritual experiences with him, for it stirred anger within him. It was a very sad realization for one always seeks to share things with their companion, but the more I talked of spiritual things the harder it became to exist with him, so I learned to keep silent. He was not a man who placed much stock in spiritual experiences. He believes in God, but as for any incidences passing between humans and those entities he is skeptical, so whenever I had dreams and other sacred experiences I could only share them with my children and my mother.

During the next two years, my mind was flooded with writings of verse as well as the beginning of a historical fiction novel. Many times I wrote stories in verse covering the lives of people and their stories. These writings were not limited to

LDS history, but expanded into world and American history. I recall looking at some old Civil War pictures online and my eyes fell upon a Confederate soldier. As I looked into his eyes, I began to see a story. I cannot say whether or not it was his story, but the story came nonetheless and my heart was flooded with emotion. The sadness and distress of the Civil War pressed upon me as the weight of a mountain. Within thirty minutes I had written the poem *Glory*:

When I was growing up
My mother spoke of glory
And I knew she spoke of truth
With every bible story
I believed that glory
Could only come from God
I learned this in a cabin
That was made of wood and sod
When I had barely turned sixteen
And thought myself a man
I dreamed of finding glory
With a bayonet in hand
My mother shook her head at me
Saying I was wrong
I tried to plead my cause with her
But she broke out into song
Songs of triumph and of glory
How salvation could be won
With unwavering faith in God
But never with a gun

Chapter Fifteen

*Yet deep inside my heart
I felt so duty bound
That I fled away from home that night
Without a scuffle or a sound
I hopped a train in Tennessee
And joined within a week
With a regimental company
To fight at Wilson's Creek
How filled with courage I became
When I saw the soldiers there
Rushing up a sloping hill
Bullets sailing through the air
My eyes beheld the Yankee flag
And I became enraged
Hatred filled my very heart
My thoughts became engaged
In wanting to destroy that flag
And all that it stood for
But I did not know that such a quest
Could cost my life and more
A roaring scream arose in me
From a darkness deep within
And feeling much the patriot
I shot at many men
Then I lost my footing
And fell upon the ground
Beside a wounded enemy
Whose eyes spoke without sound
His pain was greatly evident*

But my instinct was to kill
Yet I could not move a muscle
And I lay there very still
Then he spoke to me
In a raspy, weakened voice
"My leg is sorely wounded
And I have but little choice
Than to lay and bleed to death
Upon this war torn land of strife
I was hoping you would take care
Of this picture of my wife
See she learns I died with honor
As I faced another's gun
And with my death I prayed to God
That glory would be won."
I slowly took the picture
And beheld a lovely face
She was a stunning woman
Dark hair adorned with lace
I paused for just a moment
Amidst artillery fire
And felt the anger ebb away
My spirit lifting higher
Then I told him he would live
To tell his wife he loved her
And I felt a peace within
As I worked to help a brother
I took my holster belt
Securing very tight

Chapter Fifteen

*The badly wounded leg
So the blood loss would be light*

* * *

*I called for stretcher bearers
To help their comrade when
A bullet sailed into my chest
That came from my own men
They cursed my cowardice
For I helped the enemy
But I know in that selfless act
That I had been set free
I walked a few steps down the hill
And slumped against a tree
So I could pen these words
For everyone to see
I do not have much time
To say all the things I feel
As I lean against a willow tree
At the bottom of this hill
Except that I remember now
The meaning of true glory
Just as I did before
When my mother told the story
Of how our Savior died for us
As His blood ran down in trails
Wounded for our sakes
By the Roman's piercing nails
Oh to have forgiveness
Of god's begotten Son*

That He would give me glory
Even though I used my gun
To take the lives of others
For the struggle of mankind
Without a thought of who they were
Or who they left behind
As the blood flows from my wound
To stain the ground below
I will let my pen be still
And pray before I go
Remembering as I pass this life
My mother's tender story
Of the precious blood of Christ
And how we can rise to glory
Just then the soldier's failing hand
Fell limp to do no more
The pen slipped through his fingers
As he passed through heaven's door
It would do well for us to learn
The meaning of this story
To love our brother as ourselves
When reaching for God's glory

As I wrote the last eight lines of the poem I erupted in tears. I had no way of knowing whether or not this event truly happened in some young man's life all of those years ago during that terrible battle. But it felt real to me and brought to my mind, heart, and spirit an awareness that even now, thousands of years after the Savior died for us, we are still so captivated by the world and its agenda that we forget the price which was once paid for us and the responsibilities that are given when we take upon us His name. I reflected upon the meaning of glory, how the world perceives it and how God has presented it, realizing that we have so far to go. But I was blessed in having my mind open to God's mercy. He recognizes that as we are striving to walk the way He is guiding us, we will receive blessings that will help us on our way.

In the poem, the soldier has become lost and caught up in the world's agenda but in the moment he is tested by the pain of another, his compassion springs forth and he follows the prompting of the spirit even though it cost him his life. The poem was something that I sorely needed during what seemed like my own civil war and I would often reflect upon it whenever trials became too heavy for me to bear.

Archives

In the summer of 2001, I was asked to do a few firesides in Utah. When the first request came by email, I sat back in my chair, knowing that this would not be a one-time thing and that it would grow. I was aware that I would be speaking about my conversion and our story for many years to come. It seemed as if in some way I was being tutored in those private moments when I sat back and pondered on the meaning of events that were being processed in my life. I would ask Heavenly Father what I should do. What should I say? Then, as I would begin to outline my talks, I would be moved to cover certain parts of my life as well as Joseph's and Emma's and the family.

All the time that I spent trying to formulate a talk, there was that negative voice in my head saying things such as, "who do you think you are, you are nobody," and "you are not good enough or qualified to take on such tasks." Part of me didn't argue. I indeed did not feel as if I were anybody special, nor did I feel qualified to speak in front of hundreds of people at a time, but these doors were being opened up to me and I was being asked to speak. I have never been one to ask the Lord if He is sure about what He is doing. Many times, when a situation has been presented to me and I know I am to go that way, I do shake my head and wonder what in the heck is going on, but I go because I know to follow the spirit and it always makes sense later. The Lord always knows more than we do and that is why I go forward without knowing completely why I am being asked.

This particular trip to Utah coincided with the Joseph Smith Sr. reunion being held in Salt Lake City. I specifically spread the firesides out over a period of a few weeks because I wanted to spend some time in research. While there, I was asked by my cousin Gracia to bear my testimony at a fireside she was giving. The experience would magnify the desires to help heal the family.

There were still many blanks for me that needed to be filled in. By then, I knew the bulk of the history of the Church, but I did not know all of the events which had transpired to cause my branch of the family to become so divided and so bitter. I had pored through the journals of my grandfather and great-grandfather. I had sifted through all of my father's papers. I had the view from one side but it was very clear that side had become skewed in some areas. Now I wanted to see the history of events following Joseph's death from the perspective of the LDS Church and those who knew Joseph.

Shortly before my baptism in 1998, Merrill had asked if I would consider sending all of the family artifacts I had to one of the apostles, a friend of his, for this man loved church history. I was very hesitant. Not that I did not trust Merrill, but I was afraid these things would become lost in the mail. But something said it was okay and I agreed. After some time passed, I asked Merrill about the artifacts and he said he would check on them. To my horror there had been a misunderstanding and the recipient of the items thought they were being donated. Merrill straightened out the misunderstanding and I received my property which had been nicely catalogued.

On August 30, 2001, I walked into the church archives and approached the front desk. As I looked at the sign-in sheet a woman walked up to me and asked if she could help me. As I signed my name I said to her, "Yes, I would like to see some things about Joseph Smith." By then I had some idea of how significant Joseph and the Restoration had been to the world and I was somewhat aware of how revered he was amongst the Latter-day Saint people. The woman, whose name is Christy Best, broke into a smile of wonderment. Chuckling, she said, "What piece of that pie would you like to have?"iIndicating that I had requested somewhat of an extensive topic.

She directed me to a man and when I asked him the same question, he showed me where all of the rooms of research were and told me that if I had any questions, I could just ask. My problem was I did not know where to start. It

Hills & Valleys

wasn't just church history I was looking for, it was personal. Feeling somewhat disappointed, I returned to the desk. Christy, who had glanced at my name when I had signed in, was still at the desk and I told her I wasn't quite sure how to go about finding the information I needed. She took me to a table and we sat and began to talk. I told her that Joseph was my great-great-grandfather and I was trying to find information about the family, particularly insights from those who knew them personally.

Christy began to ask where I was from and when I told her Ava, Missouri, near Branson, a change came across her face and she bore a slight smile. I was then asked to tell her a little of my story which unfolded the connection with Merrill Osmond. Christy said to me that there was a descendant from that area who had sent a box of artifacts that had been given over to her to catalogue. I could have crawled under the table. Here was the very woman who had so nicely catalogued all of the pictures, letters and other various items. I told her how sorry I was but that I had never said that they were being donated; that some miscommunication had happened somewhere along the line.

It was actually Christy who saved all of my historical belongings from being processed, for she refused to do anything aside from cataloguing them until there was signed documentation by the donor. She was very gracious as I spoke of my desire to know more about events in Nauvoo with the family and she shared what knowledge she had. Then she asked if I would like to see some of the artifacts which were in the vault. These items consisted of Joseph's private journals, Hyrum's Book of Mormon, handwritten documents and other

Chapter Fifteen

various items. My heart leapt! Of course I wanted to see these things. I asked her if we could come back for I wanted to bring my children with me and she said it would be fine for it would give her time to get clearance.

On August 31, 2001 we were taken to a small room where there was laid on a table a history of Joseph's life in the form of books, documents, and the papyrus. It killed me that I could not touch them for I longed to run my hands along the words he had written. Seeing Joseph's belongings, which bore the scars of the times he lived in, brought the reality of his life to a more vivid state in my mind and heart. The trips to the archives would forge between Christy and me a very precious friendship and I knew that those visits would not be my last.

A Worthy Pen Never Rests

Back home in Missouri, I found myself once again immersed in a backlash resulting from my trip and the great experience I had just gone through, but I was determined that nothing would take away from the things I had seen, learned and felt. One day while the kids were at school, I sat at the computer studying for an exam for one of my classes at Drury University. I found my attention being pulled from 2001 Missouri and thrown into 1839 Liberty Jail. Why my thoughts were leaning in that direction at such a time I could not reason, but I would soon learn.

I pulled up a webpage and searched for information on Liberty Jail. I had never really read in depth the horrid and traumatic occurrences which had transpired while Joseph, Hyrum and some of the other brethren had suffered there. As I read, a feeling of gloom fell over me. I felt the sorrowful emotions that must have coursed through their hearts and the trauma of their families as they were being driven from Missouri and persecuted. The agony that these men felt as they were held in inhumane circumstances with no ability to aid their families must have been torrential. Being a descendant four generations down, I was feeling the pain of it to the point of uncontrollable tears. I could only imagine how Emma and her children must have felt.

As I reflected, I began to write upon my tablet. There was a door to that time opened to my heart and a vortex of emotion rushed forward. Within a few hours I had written Liberty, a four page narrative verse which came to me with inexorable force expressing feelings of turmoil, tears, pain, judgment, separation, humility, prayer and then light. The verse begins as if Joseph is telling what led to their imprisonment. Next, Joseph is kneeling in prayer. I stopped, realizing from that point on, I should use D&C 121 for reflection. So I looked up D&C 121 and began to process the writings into poetry form. It came very quickly.

"Oh God where art thou? Where is Thy grace?

And where is the pavilion that is Thy hiding place?"

I continued on, pouring out every word that came to me in rhyme, weaving it between the lines of 19th century scripture. After finishing, I read through the poem and broke into tears. Then, as I always do, I looked upward and I thanked my Heavenly Father for giving me such words to write. For if I have been blessed with any ability to write, it is through Him. I could never accomplish such a feat on my own.

Chapter Fifteen

The experience of writing this poem would take me days to overcome, for I had been left exhausted and depressed about those events which were experienced by my ancestors. I learned that if I was going to continue writing in such a manner, I would have to gain the ability to pull myself out of the darkness that I was sometimes exposed to. Prayer was always a given for obtaining relief, as well as scripture study. Then I always turned to humor to switch gears. Whether it was Loony Toons, Abbot and Costello, Andy Griffith or some other venue of wholesome, good clean fun, I would immerse myself and become lost in the folds of laughter, thus remedying the melancholy which often accompanied my lyrical excursions to the past.

A Voice of Warning

With all of the writing I was doing, it became evident that I was amassing quite a collection that could be put into a book. I knew that the Nauvoo Temple would be dedicated in 2002. So I gathered all of the poems I had and determined that if I could write a few more including one dedicated to the new temple in Nauvoo, I could possibly self-publish them as a commemoration of the Nauvoo Temple dedication. In May I made plans to travel with Judy, a friend of mine, to Nauvoo to meet with friends, one of whom was designing the cover of my book.

Two days before leaving, I had a dream that nearly caused me to cancel the trip altogether. I had learned from my mother that there are dreams, and then there are dreams that you pay attention to and record, especially dreams of warning. When I was young, I did not know what she meant. I had heard that the gift of dreams ran in the Smith family, and on my mother's side, particularly the women, there were many who had this gift. It could be that the Cherokee on my mother's side bears some influence for the passing of such a gift. But I had only had one experience in my childhood. After that, years would pass until just after my baptism, when I began to have many dreams that I knew I should record.

In this dream, I was getting ready to travel to Nauvoo. My friend Judy picked me up and we started down the road but on a curve she turned sharply and the van we were in rolled down a steep embankment. As we were rolling, I heard a voice tell me that if I asked Heavenly Father for help, He would answer. So I began to call out to Him, asking for His help. Suddenly the van stopped rolling and we were alright. As I jerked awake, I knew it was a dream of warning for it was so vivid and there was also a weight which fell upon me to be cautious. I considered calling Judy and telling her that I had decided not to go but it was early. I would wait until later in the morning to call. I did not have wait too long, for Judy called me and said that she would not be able go on this trip. I was overjoyed, not because she wasn't going, but this meant that the situation had changed. In the dream Judy was driving. Since she was not going, it meant I would be driving, so I felt safe in proceeding.

My time in Nauvoo was fun. I had met with four friends from Arizona and they decided to go to Branson, Missouri after leaving Nauvoo. They would follow me to Mansfield, where I could then direct them to the remaining fifty miles of their journey. Nauvoo to Mansfield is about a six hour drive and though we had tried to leave earlier in the day,

Chapter Fifteen

there had been delays which placed us one and a half hour away from home right as it was getting dark. All along this trip, I was not worried about any accident because I knew I would be driving the van. But I do not see very well after it gets completely dark outside.

We stopped in Camdenton, Missouri for a bite to eat and I thought about having one of my friends drive at least to Mansfield. I remembered the dream but it wasn't Judy who would be driving so I felt safe. It has to be mentioned here that I was asking someone who was not used to curvy and hilly roads that wind throughout wooded rural acreage to take over driving my van. But that did not even occur to me; I merely thought anyone who is a seasoned driver could take over. All of my friends had lived in the west most of their lives and were used to driving 10 to 15 miles over the speed limit. We were only ten miles out on the road when I became terrified. My friend was traveling nearly 65 MPH on a 55 MPH road which was riddled with sharp curves. I never like to criticize the driving of others so I did not say anything but my nails were digging into my legs every time we took a turn.

On one curve she edged off of the road just a bit and hit gravel. When she tried to correct herself she overcompensated, sending the van into a spin on a sharp curve. We are always told by those involved in accidents how everything changes into slow motion. It is true, for as we began to spin it seemed as if I were taken out of myself and things moved slowly. I could see a car's headlights coming from the opposite direction and I knew that since we had begun spinning on a curve, that we were going to collide. But we did not, and as we made one revolution, then another, I remembered the dream. Out loud I began to say, "Heavenly Father, please help us." It seemed as if I said it over and over again. Then, after the third revolution the van stopped spinning, glided over toward the ditch and began to travel backward along the ditch line until it came to a dirt road and slid backward onto it, coming to a halt as if we had just backed in and parked.

All was silent for a moment. I was in shock and all I could say was "I knew this was going to happen!" I was excited, not because of the wreck but because I had utilized what I had been told in the dream and my prayer was heard. I was amazed. Vans do not spin; they are top heavy. They roll, but our friends in the car behind us confirmed that it did indeed spin three times for they had watched as they approached from behind. The only damage that the van suffered was four blown tires.

My daughter Leah had been sitting in the back seat and received much of the trauma. Even though she wore her seat belt, her body was cast to and fro in a violent manner as the van was spinning. After we all got out, she came rushing to me. The first word out of her mouth was "Joseph." I leaned forward and asked her what she was trying to say and she answered, "I saw someone in the seat next to me and I thought it was Bryan but I remembered that he was at a football game with the band and that is when I knew it was Joseph." She told me he was there from the time the van began to spin until it came to a halt. I knew then that he had been a source of comfort for her that night. I had called out to my Father in heaven and He answered my plea for help. While I was thus engaged, the love of a grandfather was poured forth upon his

Chapter Fifteen

third great granddaughter in the form of visual comfort and support during a time of great fear.

A tow truck was called for and Leah and I rode in one of the other cars to Mansfield where my husband met us. I had very little to say to him for when I called to tell him about the accident, the first words out of his mouth were to ask what shape the van was in instead of inquiring about our welfare. The words dashed any desire I had to share with him about the miracle which had just passed. I began to talk somewhat about the wreck itself as we drove from Mansfield to Ava but when I mentioned the van turning three revolutions he chided me off as if I were exaggerating and I did not complete the story nor did I tell him about the dream. I remained silent for the remainder of the trip home, my mind still captivated by how richly we had been blessed. But I also admonished myself for not paying closer attention to the specifics of the warning, for I should not have let anyone drive but me.

As the date for the Nauvoo Temple dedication approached, I became more excited, but I was concerned about how to pay for the publication of the book. After speaking with a friend of mine in American Fork, Utah about self-publishing, she offered a two thousand dollar donation to get a supply of books published. I could not believe it. I was not used to such love from someone who would just give that much to someone they had not known for very long. But she said she believed in what I was doing. She had attended one of our firesides the previous year. I learned from this experience that if the Lord impresses a person to do a work, no matter how impossible it seems, if one walks forward and actively begins to pursue that work He will open the doors and make it possible.

When we arrived in Nauvoo for the dedication, I not only had the books with me, but I also had the Nauvoo Temple Poem printed on ivory silk paper in decorative font. It was my intention to hand out this poem to members of the Mormon Tabernacle Choir. I was sorely disappointed and hurt as I tried to do this because there were many who would not even speak to me. They walked right past as I tried to hand them the poem as a gift and explain what it was. I would not learn until later that the choir and other Latter-day)Saints had been bombarded often by anti-Mormon groups handing out malicious material disguised as something good, especially during celebratory events. I felt somewhat defeated. How could I get these words of love to these people? I eventually found one of the choir members and discussed it with her and she said if I would give her the whole stack of poems she would see that they were distributed to the choir members.

A New Temple

The day of the temple dedication arrived and Nauvoo was transformed into a media blitz. Gracia and Ivor Jones, Gracia's mother Lorena and many other descendants of the Smith family came to Nauvoo. Though there were many events going on around us, I could only focus on one thing. Years before when my son was three and we stood on the bare temple ground, looking out upon the Mississippi, my feelings were flooded with unidentified heaviness. I felt connected to this event in ways I could never adequately describe. There was silent communication between me and my ancestors. I

Chapter Fifteen

was sending them a love that knew no bounds with words such as "Grandfather, see here....it is finished, the Temple stands again." and "Here am I, and my children. We made it; we broke through that wall and waded through mire because I knew the light was here and here we stand."

Such verbiage meandered within me throughout the dedication on June 27, 2002 and I was answered with a showering of emotion filled with tenderness and love that can only come from family. With every step, it was as if they were there right beside us, and not just Joseph and Emma, but all of our family. It was the biggest family reunion I had ever experienced.

Later in the day we sat in the first row, with President Hinckley just a few feet away facing us, waiting for the wreath-laying ceremony at Joseph, Emma and Hyrum's grave. I wanted so to meet President Hinckley. I knew of his love for Joseph, but after the ceremony he was quickly swept away by body guards and I smiled, knowing that one day I would meet him, whether it was here or on the other side of the veil.

As the crowd dispersed, Bryan and I walked down to the fence line of the homestead and I asked him where he wanted to get his endowment when the time came. He looked at me and smiled, the light beaming in his clear blue eyes and said, "Mom, you should know. The Nauvoo Temple of course." I smiled back at him, tears brimming. My heart was filled that day knowing that my son would go through that temple for his endowment. With all of the media behind us packing their things and scurrying to the next place of interest,I enjoyed a quiet moment with my son and many others unseen who were still rejoicing.

Chapter Sixteen

A Knowledge of Faith and Trust

Not long after the Nauvoo Temple dedication, we traveled there once again to help my friend Sherry Saint cater an event. While working, we met some individuals who asked us to come to Utah and do a fireside. I contacted others who had been requesting firesides and assembled a four week tour throughout Utah. With each fireside, my mind was opened to better ways of phrasing things and more of an emphasis on the important role of the Savior in my life as I was growing up. I would find at times that while I was speaking, certain memories would come to mind out of the blue and I included them to better illustrate what I was saying. At each fireside many people would come to me and tell me that I said something they needed to hear. I could feel the hand of the Lord directing me in these matters.

I began to connect to the people and my heart opened up to them. I was also amazed at their stories. They had ancestors who had known and interacted on many levels with mine. It was often like one big family reunion and I loved every moment of it. The firesides were not about us at all, but about our Father in Heaven and how He interacts with His children if they will allow it; how He moves many of us to testify in order to help others and ourselves heal from our trials, enabling us to move forward as united family.

Chapter Sixteen

Upon our return from the 2002 series of firesides, I was met again with much darkness in our home. On one particular morning, there was an outburst of anger from my husband to the extent that it nearly destroyed me. Up until that point, there had been many activities I was involved with that kept my spirit strong. I read scriptures, talked to Father in Heaven daily, and had the missionaries over quite often to feed them and hear a message. I had music playing all of the time and I made sure that anything I watched was happy, funny or uplifting. But the recent violent outburst had stripped everything from me.

I remember holding back tears until I dropped the children off at school. When I got back into the car I broke down, asking Heavenly Father why I had to go through such turmoil when all I wanted was for everything to be at peace, for everyone to be happy. The bulk of the problem was that I was unwilling to give myself over to certain behaviors or lifestyles that could have made things at home more manageable and tolerant. In some ways I had, and it became the means of robbing me of my own identity. The more I resisted being someone that I knew was wrong, the more darkness pervaded our atmosphere.

Being a member of the Church helped immensely. I knew how to keep the spirit near and strong but there were a few times that I felt I would crumble. That day in the car was one. I poured out my heart unto the Lord and I asked why, saying aloud "You promised you would never give more than I could bear! Why do I have to go through this?" In that moment of tears as the morning sun peered through the window and the warmth of its rays bathed my face, I heard a voice. In my own hearing, three words fell before me: "Because you can."

I stopped crying instantly for I knew the source of the voice. I was in awe that He had enough trust in me to withstand what I was going through. He felt I was strong enough to get through it. I had never thought that the Lord would have that much faith in me. Faith was something I had always viewed as coming from us, His children. We were taught to have faith in order to believe, faith that He answers prayers. I had just been told that He had faith in me. *Me*! It opened a perspective about Heavenly Father and the Savior that I had never considered. The scripture "abide in me and I in you," took on a whole new meaning. I had poured out my heart to Him in tears that stemmed from my problems and frustrations. I turned to Him because I knew He would hear me and because I trusted Him that much. He was conveying to me that He trusted me as well. I placed my hands upon the wheel taking in a breath, then expelled the pain I had been feeling, replacing it with not just joy, but peace in His words.

Like a child who grins when her father says, "Go on, I know you can do it." I started the car, nodded with a smile and simply said, "Okay." I then drove home and faced things with more strength than I had ever known. But there would be another time of testing where I would need more than just a voice of encouragement.

I should express here that I in no way believe that my husband was to blame for every problem in our marriage. We were both to blame. When all was said and done, I realized that neither one of us had been ready for marriage. I loved him but I did not know at the time that he did not love me, not to the degree that a man should love a woman when taking vows. It is so important to take the time to truly know one another to see if compatibility is in place before deciding to knit souls together in such a sacred manner. I had never dealt with the effects of the molestation which had plagued my life. He had certain behaviors and attractions which worked against that part of me which had been violated. When I saw that side of him it caused me to recoil within myself.

The Lord had not been included as the foundation of our union. Because the right kind of love and compassion was not in place, it began on very unstable ground. Add to those ingredients a volatile disposition pitted against a passive one, and you have a very large pot of great suffering and misery. But I was taught once you are married, it is final. I was determined to make it work.

By the time I had the hysterectomy, I began to find my voice. But going through the physical change at such a young age was difficult. I had also stopped taking hormonal replacement therapy because the cancer risk was too high, especially given the high rate in Mom's family. But I found that I coped quite well without the hormones, except in the area of patience, and even in that case I managed well with everyone in keeping my temperament balanced as I always had. As time progressed, I began to feel like my old self in every way, but it was not so where my husband was concerned. Quite the opposite. I would hold my tongue with patience as often as I could, but if too much unfair criticism and unrighteous dominion began to pile up, I had no problem voicing my opinion. The pent up aggression from all of those years of verbal abuse and violent outburst would come rushing forth like a flaming sword. Then the passive side of me would feel guilty and I would do anything to make it right. It was quite a vicious circle and at times I felt the sacrifice was too great.

On one such morning, words passed which were not very kind. I was talking about the trip the kids and I would be taking to Utah the following summer. I noticed as I spoke, his countenance darkened. It was not as if I were taking away from time we could take as a family and go anywhere. He very seldom took time off for a family vacation. As long as I had saved the money to go, it wasn't robbing him of anything. In all fairness, I should mention that he never once tried to prohibit me from going. But he did not like it and anytime I talked of it, a darkness seemed to surround him.

He made comments which were not very kind, some of which were professed against my faith. I had been exhausted from a disagreement the night before and I turned to express my opinion in a mild but strident manner, conveying to him that if he did not appreciate the atmosphere there, he needed to move back in with his parents. I was shocked at the verbal assault I had hailed against him. It came out quite hateful and I could feel a surge of liberation as the words rolled off of my tongue. But the feeling was not a good one. Before I knew it, the glass he was holding was shattered against the floor and he let loose his temper, slamming the door as he left for work.

For one brief moment, I felt defiant and victorious. Finally, I had given him what-for instead of silently standing by and taking the angry outburst, crying afterwards and later doing whatever I could to appease him. But the victory was short-lived for it was not mine, but the adversary's. I had

Chapter Sixteen

allowed his methods to creep in and instead of calmly discussing things, I hurled a barrage of hateful words that did nothing but cause anger in return.

There was nothing of the spirit in what I had said. As I realized these things, I began to look at my whole married life: the emptiness, the lack of spirituality, no respect, no compassion. I had become so damaged by the lack of these needs that I was unable to be what he needed. I wanted out. I was finished. How could I go on in such an environment and preserve the sacredness of the spirit which had been brought into the midst of me and my children? How could I progress? It was as if one person had planted seeds then another walked over them as soon as they sprouted, over and over again.

As I thought about everything, tears began to fall uncontrollably until I was crying out loud in wails, releasing my hurt and sorrow. Then I stopped crying and walked down the hallway toward our bedroom. I was going to pack and leave. I reasoned that both of my children were old enough to tell a judge what they wanted so I was certain that I could have full custody with shared visits on the promise that Leah would not be forced to go, for she had a great fear of her father at the time.

As I made my way to the bedroom, my heart rate began to quicken. Was I truly, finally going to get out of what had felt like a prison for so many years? Part of me felt bad because I had promised myself I would try and make things work, but every time I attempted to bring a good spirit into our home it was dashed by opposition. No, it was time. As I opened our bedroom door a thought came into my mind as if a quiet voice had attended me. "You have not prayed for a confirmation on this."

I placed a palm upon my forehead in frustration. What? I didn't want to pray for a confirmation! I knew what I wanted to do! Why did I need to pray for a confirmation? I was living in an environment that was not welcoming to the spirit or the gospel at all. It was stifling me. It took all of the energy I had to be as active as I could for the kid's sake, but when they were in school I spent most of my time lying down. I didn't have the energy anymore. I then remembered the experience I had in the car a few months previous. I had been given to know that the Lord trusted and had faith in me, that I could bear all things. "But I do not think that He means for me to be destroyed by all of this!" I argued. "Pray for a confirmation on this decision." was the answer I got to the argument. I took in a long sigh of defeat. I knew when the Lord was speaking to me and I knew better than to act against it, for it would bring more problems upon my head than I already had.

Sulking back into the living room like a child who didn't get the plate of cookies she asked for and wanted so badly, I knelt in front of the couch to pray. Tears rushed forth instead of words. I just needed a really good cry to wring out all of the turmoil before I prayed. But as I processed the tears, I lost all energy, becoming so weak I had to lie down on the couch. In that moment I was given over to a kind of rest I had never experienced. It was not a sleep. I seemed to fade and completely relax and there before me was opened a vision.

In this vision, I was at the crucifixion, yet I was a ways off, behind the crosses. I could see the darkened sky and hear

Chapter Sixteen

the lamentation of the people. The wailing was so loud, not just from the people but from nature itself, as if the whole world and every living part of it was in mourning. It was so devastating to hear that I could not bear it any more. I turned to walk away and saw before me a glorious white room. The beauty and serenity of it called to me and as I walked in, my whole being was filled with a fullness of joy to the point that I could no longer stand. Falling to my knees I looked to the heavens and said, "Thank you Father, for this confirmation!"

    I slowly began to rouse from this experience and in my mind I was exuberant for I felt I had been given a confirmation to leave, but as I sat up and rubbed my eyes, an audible voice said to me in a softness that was so tender, "Stay a little." I knew what it meant and it was as if the world had crashed upon my shoulders. Once again the tears came and I cried harder than I ever had in my life. I went over everything in my mind, asking the Lord why I was shown the glorious white room and allowed to feel that pure joy if I could not leave to find it? For I knew it could not be found in the environment I was living in. Then the understanding of the vision was given to me. If the Savior could endure all that he did and sacrifice through great pain and suffering, even giving his life for us, then I could get through this trial. I would have to if I wanted to go into that white room and have that fullness of joy and peace. For one brief moment, I was allowed to feel the pure joy of being in the Lord's presence, which was what the white room represented. I believe I was given that so that I would have something to hold on to, a memory of what can be if I could just be strong and endure.

As the meaning of the vision was made clear to me, I knew what I had to do. It meant staying for at least five more years, maybe more and because I was shown that my suffering was minimal compared to that of the Savior, I knew I could find the strength to do it. I would try my best to turn things around and make them work. If that could be accomplished then there would be no need to leave at all.

The vision truly opened my heart and comprehension concerning forgiveness. Having a visual glimpse made the crucifixion more vivid to me. Instead of lashing out in anguish as He hung on the cross, blood running down in trails, Jesus forgave his oppressors. Seeing this so vividly was a key in understanding the concept of forgiveness:, that once we forgive sincerely no matter how heinous the crime, we are set free from the bonds of hatred. This type of freedom allows us to let go of the pain and move forward.

Just as I had in the car months before, I took in a deep breath and simply said, "Okay." With renewed strength I prepared to face my future. Conditions in some ways improved and in others grew steadily worse but I had been given the ability to process and handle it with greater ease, remembering the promise I had been given of blessings which come through endurance.

The years of 2003 and 2004 were filled with much growth and promise. We visited Utah twice as well as Nauvoo on several occasions. Both Mom and my sister Candy accompanied us to the west and they came to know the Latter-day Saint people more personally. They were both immediately aware that these people had the Holy Ghost and it impacted greatly upon their hearts.

Chapter Sixteen

Through the Lens

During the Joseph Smith Sr. reunion of 2003, I decided to have some pictures made of Bryan portraying Joseph in the Carthage Jail. My purpose in this was personal. I wanted images to go with some of the writings I had penned, for I am a very visual person. I happened to become acquainted with a man by the name of Grayson Hedrick, 2nd great-grandson of Granville Hedrick, the man who had organized The Church of Christ Temple Lot in 1862. Grayson was a photographer living in Nauvoo at the time. I asked if he would be willing to do the shots I wanted and he agreed. After I received clearance to do the pictures in the jail, we arranged to meet early one summer morning before the tours started. As I watched, I began to tell my son to look through the small opening in the dark room and think about how it might have felt to be imprisoned there, knowing he would not get out alive and never see his family again. Bryan has always been very deep, connected to emotion and feeling. When I saw the images I wept.

It occurred to me that since I had many ideas for images that I should take a course in photography during my time at Drury University so I signed up. It became immediately clear that I had a love and natural ability for the art. I would later learn that my father, grandfather, and great-grandfather all took an interest in photography but had never utilized their talent in it. I intended to take things a step further. In 2004, my final in photography was to tell astory in pictures. I chose to tell the story of my ancestors, Joseph and Emma. We traveled to Palmyra as a side trip to New York City, where Bryan was to sing with his high school choir at

Carnegie Hall. It would be my first experience in the Sacred Grove, as well as my children's.

I had previously attained permission to do the photo shoot. As we walked through the grove on a spring morning the sun's rays peered through trees mingling with shadows. I lagged behind Bryan taking shots of him as he walked and pondered about his own history. The experience was surreal, touching, emotional. The love I bore my great-great-grandfather was measured that day, not in knowledge of scholarly history recorded by man, but in the awareness gained by opening one's heart and soul to a memory, or spirit that transcends time, space, DNA and the veil. I understood none of these feelings. I only knew that they existed, an existence which was verified without explanation. The images would reflect all that I had been feeling concerning those precious moments in my ancestor's life which had opened the doors for the Restoration.

After getting the shots developed, I pored over each one, reliving history and bringing it to the present in a visual spectrum that penetrated my heart. As vivid as the images were to me, I knew that there should be more, so two weeks after returning home we took a weekend trip to Nauvoo where I had planned to do a series of black and white shots. We did a fireside and asked some of the site missionaries if they would mind being included in some of the photos, such as Joseph speaking at the pulpit in the Seventies Hall. It was arranged that we attended the prayer meeting of a district that met in the Seventies Hall at 8:15 in the morning. After their meeting, everyone remained seated for about fifteen minutes as Bryan bore his testimony of the gospel as Joseph. These pictures, with Bryan in costume turned out to be very precious.

Chapter Sixteen

I included Leah dressed as Emma in the Nauvoo shots. During those days she was not so welcoming to dressing up in period clothing and was adamant after having over fifteen bobby pins shoved into her head that she would have never worn the clothing women were restricted to in those days. She would rather have dressed as a boy. She's very lucky that I am not particular, as I could have been so meticulous as to have demanded a corset be included, but that would have sent the bobby pins flying.

Despite the issues of 19th century women's fashion, we took hundreds of shots that day and I finally had the makings of a photo essay for my final. Part of the final included that the photos be assembled as a book or portfolio and we had to present each page and tell the story behind it. Keep in mind that I was living in southern Missouri at the time, the middle of the Bible belt and headquarters to some of the most anti-Mormon religions in the United States. The only two members of the LDS Church in the whole class were me and the professor, Doug Himes, who I cherished as a teacher.

I chose my words carefully so that I would not sound too religious, which might offend some. At the end of my presentation I sat down, realizing that I had just given the first lesson of the discussions, mingled with the story of Joseph and Emma. I had organized the wording so that it came out just as a documentary would and many of the students were very touched by what the story and pictures expressed. I knew then that photography would continue to be a part of my life and work. I also learned the importance of gauging the audience one is speaking to when doing missionary work.

There are many ways to convey a single idea, thought, or principle and one must always get a feel for the people who are around them before they touch on topics which might be sensitive to some. I was glad to have had my mind opened up to a different way of teaching the gospel. I had for some time been hard on myself because some missionaries had tried to teach me to be bold, open my mouth, commit to giving out so many copies of the Book of Mormon in a week. There isn't anything wrong with that approach if it works for you; I have just never been bold and outspoken. Having been around my father's people, I witnessed how they closed up as soon as any other faith was mentioned and it caused me to be passive in the area of speaking to people about the Church. I never wanted to seem forceful. I thought something must be wrong with me and I should make myself change. But as I tried, I felt uncomfortable, fearing that people would see that discomfort and view it as indecision concerning my beliefs.

Instead, I did what came natural to me. I became friends first. Friendship out of a desire to bring people together always works wonders. When one has a sincere love for people and can share their humor, service, and gifts, eventually the people are touched in some way and then the Lord takes it from there. The spirit moves within them and if they allow those feelings to manifest they will begin to ask questions and search.

As I took all of these things into consideration, I began to realize what the Lord meant when he said that our gifts should be used to enrich the lives of others and lift them up. Everything I had been doing up to that point, the poetry and other writings, the photography, were falling into place as methods that could reach out and touch people in different ways by teaching the gospel, drawing forth hearts, and lifting the spirits of those who suffer.

So many times I had asked myself, "What can I do? Me, a nobody from a dinky little town?" I now had the answer before me and I began to use photography with writings as matted products. I wrote a poem called *Our Missionary Son* and put it in a mat that had a place for the picture of the missionary. I wrote several other poems that covered topics such as baptism, sealing eternal families and more. I took the models with me to Utah on our next trip and showed them to my friend Kerri Guthrie. She felt that something should be done with them so she invested the funds to buy mats, paper and other materials to mass produce product and I signed a contract with a distributor.

The next time I went to Nauvoo, my creations were in their stores. I began to put the money aside to help pay for our fireside travels because some stakes did not have funding to help with gas expenses. The wisdom of it all was that I was now using my talents to fund my personal mission and at the same time uplifting others through words and pictures.

Missionary In Training

As Bryan's high school graduation was approaching in 2004, several of the members of our ward began to question him about a mission. His response was," I will go when the Lord tells me it is time." His plan was indeed to go on a mission, but not from the pressure of others. If he went out of peer pressure, it would be for the wrong reason, which in turn would be out of sync spiritually. He wanted to go when he felt

Hills & Valleys

the Lord confirmed it was time. He continually prayed about it throughout the spring and became confused for he was feeling prompted to go to school. I responded that if that is what he felt led to do after praying about it, then that is what he should do. Follow the spirit in all things, I advised him, as my mother had me. He had my full support but it was not so from some of the members.

Some of our friends feared that Bryan would get caught up in the world and desires of career and dating. He asked me why they could not trust that he knew what he was doing. I told him that in many cases, kids do say they will go on a mission after a year or two of college and then it falls through because they meet someone and get involved, then do not want to wait to marry. It is one of the sacrifices all young men are met with and it is easier for them if they go on the mission first because the temptation to stay gets stronger with every new event in their life, especially girls and dating.

"But you know that no matter what, I will go when I receive a confirmation through prayer."

"Yes, I know that. But you have to understand they have seen this happen many times and many times it falls through. So try and see it from their perspective and don't let it upset you."

With that, Bryan applied to Drury University to major in music. He started concentrating on vocal but part of the requirement was a class in composition. It was something he had never considered but once he got into it he found a love for composing. By the end of the year he had perfected within himself the basics of arranging music. Because music is so inherent in both of my parents' heritage, it came very natural to him, opening a window to a world he embraced with fervor. By the end of spring 2005 as his first year was coming to a close, Bryan came to me and said, "I won't be applying for another year for I know I am supposed to go on my mission now." He then submitted all of the paperwork necessary.

While preparations for Bryan's mission commenced, we learned that my husband's grandmother had fallen ill. I had always been close to Grandma Loa Davis and she had told me on more than one occasion that if she ever became ill that I was to make sure she was not put in a nursing home. I promised her I would try my best. Grandma had some connection with the LDS Church in that her brother Royal had been a member years before. His wife was not a fan of the Church at all and had told numerous stories that had Grandma Loa convinced it was the devil's establishment. But she loved me and knew my heart and my children's as well.

As time progressed, so did her illness and she was placed in a nursing home just one mile away from her house. I knew it was destroying her to be out of her home. It was a nice three bedroom home with an added back room which had an eight foot harvest table. There were windows along each wall in this room and one could sit and view the Ozark Hills in their splendor. The house sits on twenty acres and it had always been a home that I found solace in. Throughout the years, the kids and I visited several times a week, sometimes every day in the summer, doing crafts, barbecuing, and making homemade ice cream. We always set off fireworks in her back field on the Fourth of July and I considered her to be a grandmother to me.

When I learned they had put her in a home, I was devastated. Once when I visited her in the nursing home, I found the room to be lively with a few cousins and my father-in-law, Dale. Grandma Loa just sat back in her chair and watched. Then she reached for my hand, pulled me to her and whispered, "Get me outta here!" I smiled and said, "You talk to Dale. If he agrees to it I will move in with you and take care of you." I meant every word. I am someone who feels as if the family should care for their elderly kin in the home if at all possible, just as they did in the old days. It would be a great sadness to have to spend one's final hours in a strange place full of sick people with few visitors.

For the next six weeks my world revolved around Grandma Loa. It was some of the most precious times I will ever recall, except for the last two weeks of her life when she had little memory recall and did not know me. Often times it resulted in some very singular situations, one of which included her beating me with an umbrella because she thought I was an intruder. I was not offended in the least and it did not hurt for she had little strength to contend with. I knew she could not help it and the image of her hitting me with an umbrella became the stock of humor, not because of her affliction, because it was so unexpected.

The last week of her life was spent in a sleep which takes one away from the world as they make that transition from this life through a door leading to welcoming arms of family which have passed before. On a bright summer day in 2005, Grandma Loa passed away. My life was about to change once again, setting a course which would magnify the possibilities of my hopes concerning missionary work in my immediate Smith relations.

Chapter Seventeen

A Home On a Hill

When Grandma Loa's will was disclosed it was bittersweet. The home that she had lived in for so many years was left to us. As much as I loved the dear house on the hill, it would not be the same without her. Her kindness was a gift to us for now we could fix our old house and put it on the market. Not having a house payment meant that things would financially improve which made things a little easier at home.

As the realization settled in that we would be moving into the home on the hill, I began to feel at least some sense of happiness. The beauty of nature inspired me to write more often and there were many times when I was alone in the house that I would play my favorite songs and pretend I was singing before an audience. It was a little childish but very therapeutic, for I felt deep inside that I should be doing something in that area but I knew I never would have the courage to do so.

Because change was involved, everybody was happy for a time. I spent my days arranging and making one of the rooms into a family history library. I printed out large maps and had color coordinating pins to mark the movement of my ancestors from the 1100's to present. It was my favorite room. My computer station was there and when I walked through those doors it was like passing from one time into another. There all modern worldly concern fell away and I basked in the histories of my family. This is where I truly began to delve into the intricacies of my ancestors' tangled webs and though I loved it dearly, there were times after poring through the mangled thoughts and judgment of a people now gone that I was glad to step through those doors back into the real world.

Furthering the Work

A good walk in the country did wonders for such spells of melancholy and I continually prayed to the Lord about how to remedy such a confused and chaotic canvas. For over a year, I researched the difficulties in the Smith posterity and had found confirmation for what I had already guessed. Each line of the descendants at some point had issues to contend with concerning what they had been told about their history, but when it came to my grandfather's line, I found them to be the most bitter, the most resolute about their conclusions of what happened after Joseph died. They had fixed their opinions decidedly against Brigham Young and other leaders of the Church who had gone west during the exodus of 1846. They were certain Joseph had become a fallen prophet, being persuaded by the minds of those around him instead of listening to the Lord's council.

I did not know what the answer was at that time. I only knew that every time I pored over their views and opinions I felt ill inside. It is a sickness hard to describe, something that grows like a canker. The sufferer is aware of that smothering growth, desiring with all strength to have it removed. I wondered how they could have tolerated that ill-feeling within them all of those years, and then I came to understand that they were not even aware of it. All of the things I had been exposed to through research had been their environment. They had grown up with it so it was accepted as how things were.

One fall afternoon, I sat at the harvest table in the back room watching the many colored leaves as they danced in the wind. My thoughts became lost in that dance. I began to wonder again what was different with me. How had I escaped the rigidness of the bitterness in the family? As I stared into the motions of those leaves in their meandering trails of downward spirals, I was reminded of the reason: the pure love of Christ. I had learned it from my mother long before I spent any of my impressionable years with Dad's family.

I recalled the many scriptures where the Savior had interacted with the people. He never tried to beat His words into them, but showed them love and friendship, speaking parables for those who understood and relating His words in meekness and kindness for those who did not. This drew the people to him out of love, not fear. He looked beyond the hardness of some, seeing their hearts in an attempt to bring to the surface the goodness He knew was there. These are the things which Mom gave me as a foundation. Every loving aspect of the Savior are qualities I had seen in my mother as I grew, so I tried to pattern myself after her, often times failing miserably, yet always striving.

As I rolled these thoughts over in my mind, it began to rain and the sounds that it made upon the roof roused my senses. Becoming aware of the hour, I went into the kitchen to start supper. Somehow the Lord would open a door that would allow me to soften the hearts of my family. I only knew that I must continue being myself, allowing them to feel the goodness that I felt. Any further direction would come as was needed. I would not wait for long.

That very evening I went to sleep with a parade of thoughts before me. What could I do to further this work? I thought of doing a family history notebook to give to my cousins there in Ava. It would be a pictorial book with writings and history but I would have to be careful not to mention anything to do with church for they became offended so easily. I fell asleep tossing ideas around in my head and in the process had a dream about Joseph.

In the dream, Bryan and I were in a small room. We were both sitting in front of a large cherry wood desk and behind the desk sat my great-great-grandfather, Joseph. He was dressed in 19th century clothing; a blue vest and cream colored blouse with full sleeves. His countenance was troubled and he looked at me and asked, "When is it do you think that the Savior will return?" To have been asked such a question was very profound. It was not as if I were with a bunch of friends and we were all talking it over to pass the time. This was Joseph, Prophet of the Restoration. But he was also my grandfather and I searched my heart for what to say. It had always been my feeling when thinking on such levels that the Savior would return within the next one hundred years or so, but that was just my feeling. I would never dare consider myself to have such gifts which would enable me to foretell such a thing. No one, not even the angels know the time.

As I expressed that I felt it would be in the next few generations, he was writing on a sheet of paper. When I finished talking, he turned the paper around and moved it over to where I was sitting. I looked at the writing and beheld the time of the Savior's return, but the information was immediately taken from my mind for as I said, no man knoweth. I only remember that it was sooner than I had thought. Joseph then sat back in his chair and began to talk of concern over his posterity and the Church in these modern times. The adversary would become even more ruthless against both and he was troubled by the many testimonies which had faltered in the face of even the smallest trial. As I listened, my mind had been opened to some of the things he was referring to, particularly those who had been strong in the Church but had wavered due to reasons ranging from offense from others, to reading what they deemed as contradiction in history.

The emotion of sadness which poured forth from him as he spoke was heart wrenching. Jerking awake, I grabbed my tablet and wrote everything down and when finished, I pondered over all I had seen. There was an awareness that I needed to redouble my efforts in doing the firesides. It dawned on me that these firesides that we were doing were not to just help our family by teaching the importance of healing and unity, but all families. I also became aware that I needed to try and do more in my own family, including my mother and sister, for they had felt the spirit when they were in Utah with me.

I lay back down but could not sleep, for a weight of responsibility in this church and in my lineage had fallen upon me in waves that could not be measured. I knew that riding those waves would be difficult but after seeing and feeling the impact of the sadness in my grandfather's countenance I was more than up to the task. I was ready.

Chapter Seventeen

The next day I called my sister who has always been very talented in woodworking. I asked her if she would be willing to come and stay with us and help remodel the old house. Having been out of work for some time, she was more than happy to oblige.

On the first evening of her stay, we were on the back porch. Candy began to talk of spiritual matters and asked me questions about the Church. The next morning the BYU channel was on while my sister was eating and they were discussing the very topics we had talked about the night before. I had to smile. Candy took her time getting ready to go work as she finished watching the program. For the next two days the same sequence of events occurred. In the evening we would spend hours talking about topics she had concerns with and the next morning those issues would be the topic of discussion on BYU. On the third morning, she stood and said, "Okay, something is going on here." Candy was very in-tune spiritually and knew when the Lord was trying to convey something to her. We began to talk again before she left to work and I finally said, "Look, why don't you just take the discussions. See it through, take them all and I bet you will get all of the answers you need if you will sincerely pray to know the truth." To my shock, she agreed.

The summer of 2005 had awarded us two amazing missionaries just perfect for Candy. Elder Paur was adept in the knowledge of not only modern scripture but ancient as well. His companion, Elder Ellis, was very soft spoken and when he testified the spirit burned within him, radiating throughout the room, two elements which made a perfect recipe for truth to be borne. Throughout July, the missionaries were at our home often and on Sundays I delighted in making huge meals and having the Elders as well as other church friends over, filling the harvest and dining room tables. It might be an inherited gift, but I have always loved having a house filled with happy people and providing them an abundance of food. I tried at least once a month to host such occasions because I loved my church friends. Every dinner would bring a refreshing spirit back into my home. By the first of August, Candy had taken all of the discussions and had a testimony of the Church.

Not long after Candy took the last discussion, we all traveled to Salt Lake City for the 2005 Joseph Smith Jr. family reunion. This was to be a big celebration for it was the two hundredth anniversary of Joseph's birth and many events were planned. The Joseph Smith Jr. and Emma Hale Smith Historical Society went to great lengths to accommodate those descendants who had financial difficulties making the trip. Descendants of Hyrum Smith and many other friends offered up their homes to avoid hotel costs so that their cousins could come and take part in the reunion.

To many nonmember descendants, the prospect of traveling to Utah was a harrowing thing indeed! After all there is a conspiracy there to eliminate all of Joseph's descendants, or so many have come to believe. One such gentleman was Bob Smith, and I include his story through his own words and with his permission.

"I was raised in the Reorganized LDS church, now known as the Community of Christ. All of my life I had been taught to distrust and fear the Mormon church which is headquartered in Utah. My journey to become a Mormon

Chapter Seventeen

started in the summer of 2005 when I ran across a web site: Joseph Smith Jr.com. I spent several hours reading what was there. I emailed the site and explained who I was. I was contacted the next day and was invited to visit Utah in August for a Joseph Smith Family Reunion. I was fearful to go. I left thinking I was like a sheep being led to the slaughter and I might be going out on a nice plane, but I was coming back in a pine box! But contrary to my beliefs, it actually was a delightful experience."

Bob had further experiences which testified to him of the authenticity of the fullness of the gospel in The Church of Jesus Christ of Latter-day Saints, yet he could not bring himself to join until he understood why Emma had been left behind in Nauvoo by Brigham Young, which was what he had come to believe from generations of tradition. But as he pondered upon those thoughts which troubled him, he was given an answer on a very personal level.

"In April of 2006, I was driving down the highway to work and singing along loudly to a Southern gospel radio station. I still remember the song I was listening to was titled: "Joy, Joy Wonderful Joy" by the gospel group Bill and Gloria Gaithers. Suddenly, to my dismay, the radio went completely silent. I was a bit irritated at this since the car I was driving was almost new. How could the radio break so soon? I hit the dash and fiddled with the radio dials, but finally gave up and just drove along the road alone and in complete silence.

In the quiet I started to ponder about my dilemma. Should I join the Mormon Church as I wanted and enjoy fellowship with the Saints? Would this upset my family and the many generations of Smiths who were angry that Emma had not been taken West along with the Saints? Suddenly, to my surprise, I clearly and distinctly heard a woman's voice speaking to me. It was as clear as if it had come through the radio. The voice said: 'Robert, Follow your heart. I stayed in Nauvoo because I was tired and could travel no further.' I knew instantly that the voice belonged to Emma Smith, my Great-Great-Grandmother. It was made clear to me at that moment that Emma had just given me her permission to be baptized into the Mormon Church! My ancestors would not be angry with my decision to join my new-found faith. My last remaining concern and stumbling block had just been miraculously removed. I was baptized on May 13th, 2006 by my cousin Michael Kennedy, the President of the Joseph Smith Family organization, and the first descendant of Joseph to receive the Melchizedek Priesthood."[1]

It still amazes me the lengths the adversary will go to keep us away from the truth. He uses fear so effectively and we seem always to buy into it. At the reunion, Bob came into contact with many members of the Church who exemplified the spirit that lay at the heart of our faith. Even though I was already a member, there were moments during the reunion which opened my eyes even more to the fullness of the spirit of the Latter-day Saints. Part of the reunion included a production which was put on by the youth of the Church. Several Stakes came together and the youth of those stakes combined their efforts in a production celebrating the life of Joseph Smith. Only youth and select guests were invited to attend and the posterity of Joseph Smith was among those invited. I panned the crowd incredulously as we sat in one of the mid sections of the Marriot Center. Upwards of twenty thousand youth and guests filled the auditorium and just before the production began, the announcer acknowledged the hundreds of Joseph and Emma Smith posterity, who sat among the thousands in anticipation of watching the production celebrating their ancestor's life. I had come to know in the years since my baptism of the deep and abiding love the Latter-day Saints had for Joseph, but that night I learned I had only a faint idea of the true depth of that love.

When the announcer recognized us and had us stand, there was a chorus of applause that rose in a crescendo that pierced my soul and brought me to tears. I looked to my right and my mother and sister were having the same emotions. Such an outpouring of love filled the auditorium and everyone stood as they applauded in devotion to our ancestor, bringing the deluge of precious and tender emotions to a point of awed wonder to some, and humble, gracious, appreciation to others.

Member and nonmember alike, we all left the Marriot Center changed. During our visit to Utah for the reunion, we were able to squeeze in a few firesides which would be the last until Bryan returned from his mission. At the last fireside, we arranged for Bryan's part to be video- recorded so that I could use it while he was gone. For my mom and sister, the reunion trip was one which defined within them a true image of the LDS Church and its members. For me it was a time which would forever be etched in my memory as another turning point in my spiritual life. No more would I allow fear and intimidation to hold me back in areas where I should be progressing. Speaking in public, though hard, was becoming easier for me because every moment in front of an audience there was an awareness of being attended by the spirit and my ancestors. I had reasoned that if the Lord trusted me and thought me good enough for such tasks, why should I allow anything or anyone, or even my own perceptions, to overpower all that is right and good.

To me, the rush of emotions in the Marriott Center that evening bore witness to the enormous responsibility that lay at hand and the importance of always walking forward, never backward. It was like having a view of what I was fighting for and just that momentary emotional glance was enough for me to know that I could never give up what I knew to be right and true. For I knew that there were bigger and greater things beyond that momentary glimpse and I wanted those things for me, my family, and all of the children of God.

Called To Serve

While in Utah during the summer of 2005, we also accomplished those tasks required for Bryan to turn in his mission papers. To that point none of us had said a word to his father about his desires to go on a mission. After all, he was an adult and it was his choice, but out of respect there would have to be a time to talk to his father. Bryan decided to wait until we returned home for none of us wanted the reign of terror about our heads before we went to the reunion.

One day in September, as we sat at home at the long harvest table, I started to talk to my husband about Bryan's desires to go on a mission. We were all bracing for what was to come and come it did, for he already knew and had known for some time. Somebody from our ward had seen him while we were on our trip and took the occasion to ask him if he was not proud of his son for making such a noble choice. The ward

Chapter Seventeen

member meant well. He could not have known how against the Church my husband was, nor could he have known we had chosen to remain silent for a time about Bryan's choice. The secrecy left my husband reasonably hurt but because of his violent temper in the past, we had accustomed ourselves to manipulating circumstances to prevent blow ups. It had become a learned behavior in order to bring peace into the home.

By the time we had been in the Church for several years, we had learned that secrecy was not the best way to handle anything and we did not intend to hide it or side step the issue, yet I did not want to bring it up until Bryan felt ready. The reaction would have been the same regardless, and it was. The eruption occurred and we side stepped him for days and days until things calmed down and we went on with our lives. One month later, Bryan received his mission call to the Canada, Vancouver Mission.

Finally the time arrived for Bryan to go through the temple for his endowment. We had discussed it years before and knew he would be going to the Nauvoo Temple. A couple of amazing things occurred previous to our trip. Candy had decided to get baptized but she wanted Bryan to do it. Time was running short for anything to be done and we all thought of how wonderful it would be for her to be baptized while we were all in Nauvoo. She agreed and after we got permission to do her baptism in Nauvoo, all was set for our trip. We also found out that Bryan would be the first descendant to personally go through the Nauvoo Temple for the Endowment, making his endowment one of great celebration to us all. Many of our friends in Utah came and we all stayed in the Bidamon Stables just beside the Nauvoo House where Emma had spent her remaining years. The Bidamon Stables were built by Emma's second husband Lewis Bidamon and I had stayed there many times because it was on the family property.

The day of Bryan's endowment was busy to say the least. We got up early in the morning and went to the Church where all of our friends from Utah had gathered for Candy's baptism. The spirit was amazing and I sat in awe that all of these events of hope were happening in the home town of my ancestors, a place when at one time all hope seemed lost. It was as if we were all witnessing the reconstruction of a bridge that had been altered ages ago. After the baptism, Bryan had to race over to the Joseph Smith Academy, grab a bite to eat and get to the temple. Since it was his first time through, he needed to be there much earlier than the rest of us did. Mom, Candy, and Leah stayed behind at the Bidamon Stables to rest.

Going through the temple that day was surreal to me. I absorbed every particle of emotion. There were moments where my mind recalled the journey which had brought me to where I was that day, the many twists and turns of murky roads where visibility at times was less than zero, compelling me to rely completely on faith and the spirit in deciding which route to take. Every time I trusted the Lord, it was as if the sun emerged and the way was made clear. Upon entering the Celestial Room, I spotted the beaming countenance of my son. I walked over to him and we embraced, acknowledging feelings and thoughts which the utterance of speech would diminish. As we separated, I caught a look in his blue eyes that was all too familiar.

Chapter Seventeen

The same gaze had caught my attention years before in a portrait at Grandma Smith's little log cabin. Suddenly I was aware that Bryan had more in common with his ancestor than looks and characteristics, both of which he bore quite humbly and sincerely. I was not sure what he would be doing in years to come, but I knew it held much significance, especially in our family. I was glad not to know the whole picture and only have glimpses. I like understanding and doing things one day at a time; it keeps me focused. I believe the Lord does things in such a way for that very reason. In the past it has been the mistake of man that when we are given the whole grand scheme of things, we seem to lose focus on the journey we must take to get there. There is an attempt to seize the glory immediately, instead of processing experiences which would make us humble and grateful to have any semblance of glory and bear it well.

As we left the temple, I could tell Bryan was exhausted and he told me later that the baptism and endowment in one day had taken a lot out of him. He said he had never felt so exhausted in his life! Nevertheless we all stayed up late and played games, enjoying the company of many friends and family. The next day would be spent sightseeing and enjoying some quiet time. There was one spot in particular I was determined to visit, an old "friend" which had called out to me many times.

About a block behind the Nauvoo House stands an old willow tree. I had passed by this tree on many occasions when visiting Nauvoo and it seemed to draw my attention in a sentimental way. I have been drawn to willow trees since I was little, but this one was different and I had intended to see this

Hills & Valleys

tree up close with every trip to Nauvoo but it seemed we always ran short on time. I had even written a poem about it a few years before which captured the tree as the narrator of all that had passed in Nauvoo as if it had actually been there in those days. But I knew that was impossible. Willows generally did not live beyond one hundred years.

One morning as I was getting ready for the day, my friend Christy Best came from outside and asked if I had ever seen the willow tree up close. I told that I had not had the chance but was planning to go see it. She replied that it was very unique for the newer branches had wrapped themselves around the older part of the tree as if they were supporting it. I told her I would be out in a minute.

As I walked toward the tree I looked down, my thoughts once again turned back to another time. How many times had my ancestors walked the same ground that I was walking? I looked back to my left and glimpsed The Mansion House and then looked down again. Did any of the trees and rocks which still remained carry the memory of sorrowful wails and cries of a widow and her fatherless children? And how many silent cries flew out upon the wind as she tried to move forward, her face solemn and tearless, as her heart was wrenched with silent longing. Emma would have been strong for her children, steadily moving forward as they tried to rebuild their lives. But the nature she was surrounded with would have heard every silent utterance which poured out of her mourning spirit.

As I grew closer to the willow tree, emotions poured over me, seeping into depths I did not know I had until I reached up to touch one of the willow branches that swayed in the breeze. Suddenly I broke down into tears which had welled up from someplace distant. These were not simple tears of remembrance. I was actually breaking down and as I did so there was a moment where I could feel that Emma had been by the tree in tears. It was just a glimpse and as Bryan came over to embrace me and ask what was wrong, the image faded.

"I don't know," I answered. "But something happened here."

Later in the day, I went to The Community of Christ Visitor's Center to ask about the old willow tree but no one knew anything about how old it was. So I strolled around the museum and found the paintings by Joseph and Emma's son David Hyrum Smith. One of them which he had painted in 1860 captured the unfinished Nauvoo House and behind it was the willow tree. I put my hand to my mouth in amazement. Emma died in 1879, so the tree was there during her life. That weekend in Nauvoo would be the foundation of many great things to come: my sister's new life in the Church, my son's mission and a memory of long ago which would inspire me to not only find my voice in music, but use it.

Chapter Eighteen

Departures

I had long prepared for my son's departure to Canada by stockpiling many projects, such as genealogy, and planning various other excursions so that my time would be filled to the brim while he was gone. My hope was that if I stayed busy, the time would fly by. One day, around four months after he left, I was doing dishes as I peered through the window glimpsing heavy snowfall. All of a sudden the words, "How many tears did she cry as the willow tree swayed," came to me. I knew I was going to write something, so I ran and grabbed a tablet. But as I wrote, a melody was coming so I went to get a recorder. The words were coming fast and I began to cry for there was raw emotion accompanying the lyrics. Within fifteen minutes I had the words and melody to a song called *Willow*.

I sat back in awe of what had just happened. I was used to writing poetry in such a manner but never had I written a song. Suddenly, I recalled my patriarchal blessing and what was said about music. I was dying to share what had just come to me with someone but there was no one there, so I filed it away and went about domestic responsibilities. My day, however, would be delightfully interrupted many more times. Before evening set in, seven other songs would come to me and I became aware that they were for a purpose, but I had no idea what. The following Monday I emailed my son all of the lyrics, exclaiming that I could not believe these things came to me while he was gone! He was the only one I knew who could help with arrangements. Now I would have to wait until he came home to progress further.

In the summer of 2006, Leah and I drove to Utah and I did several firesides. What I was most excited about was getting together with my friend Katherine Nelson, who played Emma in *Joseph Smith; Prophet of the Restoration*. She has the voice of an angel and I wanted her to help me with two of the songs I had written: *On His Knees* and *Don't Turn Away*. We spent several hours together and she was able to come up with a basic piano arrangement for the two songs. I wanted to get a head start on at least these two so that when Bryan came home we would have something to start with. Katherine would sing one of these songs at the concert following Women's Conference in Nauvoo, and it was met with favorable responses.

Coping

That first year of Bryan's mission did go exceedingly fast for I had taken a full schedule of writing classes which filled most of my hours with research and writing. I had noticed in my daughter, Leah, the same special spirit that Bryan had and she was mature beyond her years, but something had been bothering her for a long time. She still had a fear toward her father and when he was home she spent all of her time in her room drawing and working on art. It bothered me tremendously that she felt she had to seclude herself, but I understood it for I had done the same when I was young and though I was not sure what kind of traumatic experience had caused her to withdraw, I knew that she had suffered something when she was young. I had noticed a change in her behavior after age four and from that time, though I asked very general questions without pointing fingers at anyone, she was only able to tell me very little.

As the years went by, her memory was taken from her and she could not recall what had happened. I only knew that she exhibited the same behaviors I had when I was young. She needed counseling and I knew it. We tried a few individuals but it caused her to withdraw even more and she begged me not to take her anymore. I am someone who believes one should never force a child to come to terms with a traumatic event for the result could be disastrous. I told her that someday she would need to talk with someone who could help her reason it all out, especially before she gets married so that those locked memories do not jump out from somewhere straight into the middle of a happy union and wreak havoc. She agreed.

When Bryan left for his mission, Leah was fifteen. The Tourette's at that time had become increasingly worse instead of better because of the tension in the home and her ability to do home study had become near impossible. So I told her that she needed to concentrate on her art and before she turned 18 she would have to study and get her GED. Leah's goal was to attend college and study illustration and animation. She knew it was vital to get a GED and make plans for college, to have a goal set and work toward that goal. During what would have been her junior year in high school, I felt she needed to throw all of her emotions into art. It was therapy and it was what she needed at the time. But events would transpire soon after her 17th birthday which would thrust us both onto a path we did

Chapter Eighteen

not expect. That path would open a door to many things which had been touched upon in my patriarchal blessing and that of Bryan's as well.

In December of 2006, I graduated from Drury University with a BS in English and Writing. I felt uncertain about my future. For many years I wanted to be a teacher. But the public school systems of today are not the same as when I was in school. So many liberties have been taken away from the teachers and I found myself at odds with what our youth were being taught in certain areas. I turned my mind to a career in writing but had no idea where I would start.

A week before Christmas, I had a dream which would prepare me for a new journey. In this dream, I was a trusted helper to these elderly people who spoke English, but with what seemed like a Russian accent. Each part of the family lived in what looked like storage sheds. I needed to speak with the older man and woman, the head of the family, so I made my way up the hill passing their barn en route. There was a young man sitting by their barn in a lean-to, with shoulder length hair and rather poor looking. I was concerned because I did not know who he was so I was even more eager to see my friends. It was not proper to just walk into their home, so I knocked but there was no answer. I peeped in and called for someone and saw that the shed was sectioned off by curtains, or some thin material.

The man and woman of the house came to where I was and I told them my concern about the young man and they told me he was working for them. The old man then said that he needed some work done and one of his sons volunteered, but I said, "No, please let me," because I desired greatly to help them. So he said, "Very well, there are 200 pounds of hay that needs to be gathered in the field." He handed me a pitchfork and deep inside I wanted to back out because I knew how laborious the work would be, especially with a simple tool, but I said, "Okay," for the desire to help meant much to me.

It was nighttime and as I walked toward the field I was thinking about how hard the job was going to be with this simple tool. I said to myself, "How can such a huge task be accomplished with such a simple tool?" I passed the lean-to and there, where the young man had been there was a wooden sign that said, "For help call," I looked to the spot where he had been but he was gone. The lean-to was right by the field. The field was hidden by a curtain and on the ground nearby I saw pieces of hay. In alarm I pulled back the curtain and saw only stubble. I ran to tell the old man and woman about the hay and that the young man was missing, but as I walked in I saw the young man on a bed with wounds all over his body and he was bleeding badly. The old woman was dressing his wounds. I asked if he would be okay to which she replied, "He will be fine." Just then the phone rang and woke me up, ending the dream.

I could not answer the phone. My mind was focused on what I had seen in the dream. Grabbing my tablet I wrote the dream down. As I did so the meaning became very clear to me. So often in my life I had thought myself unworthy of anything good, or did not believe I had it in me to accomplish anything big or meaningful. I learned from this dream that no matter how small or simple I feel, or inadequate, I must always walk forward and do what I have promised to do, or

Chapter Eighteen

have been prompted to do, no matter how hard or impossible it seems.

As in the dream, if one walks forward with intention and genuineness, they will find that once they get to where they are going the Lord will lift their burden. In the case of me in the dream, I went there with the tools intending to do what I could even though I felt it impossible considering the simple tool I was given. But once I arrived I found that the Lord had already done the bulk of the work. I equated myself with that simple tool.

Christmas 2006 arrived with excitement. For me, Christmas was always exciting. I loved decorating and having a host of friends over for meals. This year the Davis family Christmas would be held in my home. Though I relished the opportunity and pulled out all of the stops to ensure a festive occasion, I felt somewhat removed. There was a shift I could not explain and I felt as if something was about to happen. As the time came for gift exchange, I surveyed the many elements that filled my living room. There were those who had judged me harshly mixed with those who had been fair and kind. It was the perfect example of two opposing forces which needed to be brought together as one in all sincerity, but I did not know how to do it, nor did I feel those attempts would be welcomed by some or appreciated. The healing in that family would have to fall to another for my direction had been fixed for some time on the Smith family.

As I watched the tradition of opening gifts unfold before me, my heart ached. Something deep inside knew of another time when such traditions were not mired and distorted by modern society's attempt to take Christ out of all things. I knew what spiritual elements should attend such a gathering. Was I old-fashioned? Of course! I believe in those Norman Rockwell illustrations. I believe in the family unit as it once was before modern minds began to redefine it and acclimate it to the standards set forth on soap operas, MTV, and reality shows. There was a time when family unity was strong material, binding all aspects of love, compassion, spirit, and service to others. When unity is strong it deflects the sting of unfair judgment, false conclusions and malicious gossip. Such unity only remains while Christ remains. It was the Savior I had thought of that evening as I pondered my situation, wondering why I was feeling as if a great change was coming.

Refuge Across a Frozen Mississippi

New Year's Day 2007 started out fun and lively with the missionaries coming over for a breakfast buffet. This is something that I often provided for my "boys." I loved to see them enjoy their food and the buffet was laid out like a restaurant with southern French toast, bacon, scrambled cheesy eggs, sausage gravy and biscuits, pancakes with strawberry sauce and orange juice. After their meal they left to go about their work.

Later in the day an incident occurred of such proportions that it removed any desire I had to keep trying to make my marriage work. As I eventually found myself alone, I walked through the house, numb and crying out to Heavenly Father that I truly could not bear any more. In the midst of pouring out my heart I heard something, almost soft as a

Chapter Eighteen

whisper, and the words "it is time to go," were spoken to my mind.

There was no need to pray for a confirmation for it was already there and in an instant I felt a weight lifted from me. There is no way to describe the excitement and joy I felt, yet at the same time I had no idea where I was going to go. I knew that the occasion of my departure would have to be done quietly while he was at work for I knew the alternative would bring disaster. I have never quite understood the greed that comes into play when divorce becomes necessary. I wanted nothing except my important papers and research, pictures, clothes, all of my personal things. I would be leaving the house, the car, and all the furnishings. The only thing I felt comfortable and justified in taking half of was what was in the bank. We had sold our home and I took out half of what was left, amounting to $5,000.00 which I felt was fair and only amounted to enough to live on for a couple of months while I got my footing and began to build a new life.

As I began to pack during the daytime hours, I felt as if I should extend one more gesture of attempt at communication. So I told myself I would give him three chances to talk about what had passed on New Year's Day. During the day, I would pack and hide items in the basement and when he got home, I chose a quiet hour to try and talk with him about what had happened, but he would not respond. For three days I repeated the same scenario, and on the third as I walked toward him I told myself that this was the moment which would decide all. Part of me was hoping he would not open up, the other felt that if he did and began to talk to me about things then I would stay and try to make things work, hopefully through counseling. But we had tried that route before to no avail. The third attempt turned out to be like the others, met with contempt and silence. I then said to him that the lack of communication and forgiveness has been the destroyer of many marriages and that it was very sad that he would not talk to me.

The next day I was pondering as to where I was going to go. It was time to call my sister, for she would have to come and help me put things into storage, then take Leah and me wherever we were going. After I finished talking with her, the phone rang and it was my friend in Nauvoo, Sherry, who we often helped with catering in the summers.

"I haven't talked to you in some time and was wondering how you were doing." It was true; it had been approximately four months since I had talked with her. Now she was calling me asking how I was doing? I was so dismayed that she had called at such a time and asked such a question. After a few seconds I told her what was happening and she grew very silent.

I had spoken to Sherry on several occasions about my situation and she always replied to my desire to leave with the response, "Are you sure that is what you should do?" My reply was yes, I just did not know when. I was expecting the same response as she had given before. Instead, she broke the silence with a calm voice. "Well, I have a job here and a place for you to stay while you save up for rent." I was stunned, and then I realized that the Lord had just opened a door which would place me in Nauvoo. All at once everything seemed to shift.

Chapter Eighteen

"When do you need me?" I asked, numbed by the whole conversation.

"Three days."

"I will be there." I hung up the phone and said in a whisper, "I am being prepared for something." I didn't know what exactly. I had learned by then that we do not always know the reasoning of everything. Many times we only are given a direction and we are to have faith and start walking that way, knowing somewhere along the road we will see the purpose. Before I could leave there were two things I needed to attend to: a son on a mission and a father-in-law.

I could not leave Ava without telling my son so I called the mission office and asked to speak to someone about the situation. I do not remember who called me back but when I explained what was happening I was given permission to call Bryan and apprise him of the situation. He was not surprised at all. He had been expecting it for some time. When he asked where we were moving to, I told him Nauvoo.

"What? Are you kidding?" I laughed at his response and then told him how it all came about. Then he grew quiet.

"Mom, are we being prepared for something?" He asked. I smiled excitedly.

"Yes," I answered, "But for the life of me I cannot tell you what it is. Once again we have to just walk that way."

"Well, that is what your life has always been, Mom." He said. I did not keep him for long because I knew he had his own work to do for that time. We said goodbye and I went to the car lot where I knew my father-in-law was. This particular day my husband had gone to Springfield on errands and I knew his dad was there alone. I walked in and he greeted me with a smile as he always did, jokingly calling me Kimberly Clark, a reference to the diaper company. I don't know why, but he had started it years before and it just stuck. I went into my husband's office to get some of my things I had left in a drawer and on my way out I stopped, turned to my father-in-law and said, "You know, life is too short not to say things that are in the heart that others should hear from time to time. I just want you to know that you have been like a father to me and I really appreciate it." He was not one who liked to show emotion but his eyes misted and he came over and gave me a hug.

I walked out that door knowing I would never go through it again and it broke my heart, for of all people, I did not want to hurt him. But I could not risk my husband finding out. On January 11, my son's birthday, my sister brought a van down from Springfield and we loaded most of my belongings into a storage unit in Ava. Then we loaded all we would be taking to Nauvoo and left.

It had started snowing and as we pulled out of the driveway and I glimpsed the home I had come to love so well, a calm release settled upon me. I smiled as I had never smiled before. Now, without a car, little money and few belongings, I was starting over.

All I could think of as we went down the road was that I had been set free. But even my departure had been riddled with stress. Though I dearly loved snow, I hated getting caught out in storms of any kind. Missouri often had heavy ice accumulation and the snow had turned into sleet three hours

Chapter Eighteen

into our trip. It soon became apparent that we would have to stay the night along the way so we pulled over in Osage Beach and found a hotel. My head hit the pillow, mind filled with what the future in Nauvoo held for me. For the first time in 24 years, I relaxed and slept peacefully.

The following morning we learned from the weather channel that we had a three hour window where the temperature was above freezing, but after that it would begin to sleet and snow again. It was just the amount of time we needed to get to Nauvoo and we would need to leave by ten o'clock. Candy went out at nine to start the van but it took her thirty minutes to get the door open because it was sealed by about a half inch of ice which covered the entire van. By ten we were able to get most of the ice off so that we could open doors and see out of the necessary windows and we headed toward Nauvoo. The entire ride was nerve wracking because we had to stay in the tracks that other vehicles had made. The wind was ferocious and it was still so slick that there was no way at all to go the speed limit. Every time a semi passed us my nails dug into my legs. It was another reminder that just because the Lord opens a door does not mean it would be smooth sailing!

As we drove into Keokuk, I began to relax a little. Soon we would be there, but we still had the river road with its curves, hills, and steep embankments to contend with. My thoughts were running wild as we drove over the bridge in Keokuk and I could see as I looked to the left that some of the water was frozen. I was suddenly put into remembrance of how Emma had crossed the frozen Mississippi. Although we had things much easier being in a car, safe and warm, still it was interesting that I was fleeing trauma in Missouri and crossing a frozen Mississippi to find refuge in Nauvoo. Then I measured all I had been through and compared it with what she had been through and found myself fortunate and grateful. I considered the pain and trial of my experiences to be very hard and debilitating but what the Saints went through was worse on many levels.

The river road was treacherous but we took it slow for there was not a lot of traffic. The Mississippi in its frozen state is quite an amazing sight. During such times, all life on the water ceases. The barges take their place of winter solace and the only movement is the leafless trees exposing the winter nesting home of the bald eagles. As we made our way into town and pulled into the Nauvoo Family Inn & Suites the reality of my situation fell in waves. Candy would be staying for a few days but after that she had to leave and I would be left with no car. But there was a small grocery store within walking distance and our apartment was located two blocks from the Inn where I would be working.

Our first home was in an apartment behind what is now home to Estel Neff's Old House Books on the corner of Mulholland and Warsaw streets. We went into the Inn & Suites and talked awhile with Sherry Saint and then she gave us the key to our apartment. It was very small but it was ours. I was just grateful to have something. After we unloaded the car, I went for a drive on the historic flats. As cold as it was, I had to go to the old home place. My emotions were raw and I needed to be alone in the spot I had been drawn to for so many years.

The temperature near the Mississippi river is colder than on the bluffs and when the wind blows it is unmerciful. I only had a sweater for I had always tolerated cold well but this kind of cold was different. It cut to the bone with every stinging assault of the wind. It was all I could do to stand there, but as I looked at the homes and down at the graves of my family, my mortal weaknesses were replaced by spiritual bliss. Feeling the arms of my ancestors around me, I fell into tears. "Grandfather, Grandmother, Uncle," I said, "I have come home." Crying all the harder, I realized that I was probably the first of Joseph and Emma's descendants to actually live in Nauvoo and call it home since their children and grandchildren left in the late 19th century. Four generations had elapsed since that noble woman, whose devotion to God was unyielding, passed from this life into the arms of the husband who cherished her so. But I was feeling more than emotions of sentimentality. My mind was brought to the time I stood atop Temple Hill with my three-year-old son, feeling a connection to that place and its history, yet not understanding what it meant. The weight of responsibility was now beginning to unfold before me but only in little pieces.

What came to me that day was a glimpse of my future direction. My biggest concern in making the choice to leave my husband was that I would not be able to do the firesides any more for I had no way to travel. But it came to me that I could indeed still do firesides! I would just offer to speak to the tour groups which came through Nauvoo. I became excited just thinking about it and I was in awe of how the Lord always allows His work to continue even when things look impossible. But there was more.

There was an awareness that I would be engaged in other things. I, like some of the other descendants who had come to the knowledge of the gospel and their heritage, would be telling Joseph and Emma's story, the human side of their lives. "But how could I do that?" I thought to myself. My cousin Gracia had done wonders expressing their lives in writing, my cousin Michael Kennedy and his family were making great strides with the Joseph Smith Jr. and Emma Hale Smith Historical Society, the Church had created a masterful movie of their lives in *Joseph Smith Prophet of the Restoration*. How could anyone, especially me, do anything more than what had been done.

As I would learn in my spiritual growth, the Lord does many things on many levels and in different varieties in order to reach all of his children. As I stood pondering in the freezing cold there was one simple word which fell into my mind: music. Then I remembered the songs I had written in 2006. I knew back then that they were for a reason and as that reason was beginning to emerge I was filled with a new hope that they would not be put away somewhere unrealized. I was renewed with excitement for I was reminded of my patriarchal blessing and how confused I was that music had been the focus of my talents with an emphasis on magnifying that gift for a purpose.

I still did not know how it was all going to fall together. I only knew that the Lord's timing is always different than ours, most often much longer. I had been brought to Nauvoo to live and my son would be home in less than a year and we could begin working on the music. Until then, I would work on starting my life over waiting for further doors and windows to open, always walking forward.

Chapter Eighteen

A Season of Time Perfects the Song

There were many days at work when time dragged slowly by, especially in the winter. When the snow measured in feet instead of inches, there were not many guests at the hotel. After I had attended to most of my duties, the only thing to do was research online while I folded sheets and bedding. Once again the impatience of not doing anything with the music started creeping in. I thought surely there was someone I could at least get advice from about directions to go in once Bryan came home. But who? I didn't know anyone in the music business except the Osmonds and their schedules were so insane it was hard to reach them at times.

Then I remembered a CD someone had given us before Bryan went on his mission. It was called *A Nashville Tribute to Joseph*. I simply loved it and I could tell that whoever wrote those songs knew the heart of my ancestors. I looked up the CD online and found the songwriter's name, Jason Deere.

I had no idea how I could reach out to him, or what I would say, but I typed his name in and found a site that had his email. That night I wrote a very detailed email about the songs and how they came to me, seeking some kind of direction. To my amazement, he wrote me the next day with the kindest response. I could tell he loved Joseph very much. His schedule was filled with many projects and he could not really help me in any way but for some reason I felt a kinship to this man and appreciated his email. I knew it was a stretch anyway and as I closed out my email I was reminded once again that I should just let things happen in God's time not mine, that I should wait for Bryan to return for this music should be developed and produced by the two of us. I shifted my focus to other tasks and bided my time.

Chapter Nineteen

"Everything You Can Imagine is Real."

—*Pablo Picasso*

Working at the Nauvoo Family Inn and Suites would become the therapy that I needed most. Physically, and at times emotionally, it was one of the hardest jobs I had ever taken on. The blessing of that employment came in the form of people. I love working with the public and in Nauvoo I was voluntarily doing more than I was required to because I wanted to make people feel welcome. My job description ranged from checking in guests to doing laundry and acting as hostess in the restaurant.

I spent a lot of time telling people about the sites and other places they could go which are not on the map, and then I would give them a brief overview of Nauvoo's early history, which included the Sauk and Fox Indians. I also touched upon the Latter-day Saints' time in Nauvoo and then later, the French Icarians. At times, I would be asked if I had grown up there and I answered, "No, but I had ancestors." Ninety percent of the time their reply would be that they had ancestors as well. I would generally steer the conversation to who their ancestors were and relax as they began to weave for me the stories of their past. I loved their stories and it wasn't that I did not want to share my history with them; I just never want anyone to think that I feel we are more special than they are.

Chapter Nineteen

Unless inspired, I rarely told people who my ancestors were but more often than not, people would end the stories of their ancestors with the question, "So who was your ancestor?" To which I would reply plainly, "Joseph and Emma Smith were my great-great-grandparents." Then there were always visitors who would see the last name on my tag and comment. I had begun to use my maiden name. Often people would see my name tag and say, "Smith, eh? You related?" To which I would reply with humor, "To whom?" or when behaving, simply, "yes," and then it would open the door to all sorts of discussions. I began to realize what a unique situation it was for me to be there. Not that I was anything remarkable, quite the contrary, but I was only four generations down and there I was in the place where so many dreams were born.

One of my favorite encounters was with an eighty-yearold man. It was during breakfast in the hotel restaurant. I had been called in for the morning shift. Normally I hated these slow days for it meant I was the only one out front. The only hostess, server, and cleanup and when it was slow, things were okay. But one never knew when a large group would come in. But this day indeed was very slow and there was only one man eating near to closing time. I walked up to his table and asked if everything was okay and did he need anything,

"No, ma'am!" He replied very chipper. "Tell me, have you always lived here?"

"No sir. I have only been here a few months."

The man straightened himself. He had a regal sort of bearing. "Do you know much of the history?" He asked. Oh boy, I thought, I get to share some history about Nauvoo. I loved doing it and it caused me to perk up from the boredom of the morning.

"A little. What would you like to know?"

"Well, I would like to tell *you* a few things!" he said excitedly. "For I had ancestors here, and can tell you everything." he said, arrogantly. I could not help but be entertained by his enthusiasm for what he was about to share. It took the edge of his prideful tone away.

"Really?" I said. "I had ancestors here too." I was not going to tell him who. I wouldn't dare, he was taking so much joy in wanting to tell his own history and I wanted him to keep that moment. Too many times, visitors would tell me the most wonderful things about their ancestors and then ask if I had any who were in the Restoration. When I would tell them, they would react as if their ancestry was not as important, saying things like, "Oh my goodness! Well, that IS special." It would make me feel bad because their ancestors were a pivotal part of everything that happened in early church history. None of it could have happened without them all. They worked hand in hand, side by side with my own ancestors.

The moment I told him I had ancestors as well, his eyes widened and he told me to sit down. Well we were not busy so I took a small break. The man leaned forward. He had a very weathered face, but kind. His thoughts seemed to be spinning as if he did not know where to start.

Chapter Nineteen

"You say you had ancestors here too?" I nodded hoping he would not ask. I wanted to hear what he had to say but then he erupted with a chuckle.

"Well," he said, "let me tell you. My ancestors were a big part of building up Nauvoo! Can you believe that? If it had not been for some of them it never would have happened!" The more he spoke the more arrogant he sounded, but I was finding humor in it for some reason and I thought I would have some fun with him.

"My ancestor was also a big part of building up Nauvoo!" I said.

"Well," he continued on taking a complete step backward into history covering the timeline of the Church. He proudly announced that his ancestors were at the forefront of this or that major event, to which I would follow up with a big smile, exclaiming, "So were mine!" We were having a ball enjoying the fact that our ancestors had been involved in so much together and it seemed to grow into one of those childish back and forth conversations of whose dad had the most impressive job, but it was all in fun for me because no matter what he said I would be able to say my ancestor was there too and names never came up, just events.

Then at one point he leaned forward earnestly and said, "Sister, let me tell you though, my ancestors were at the Whitmer farm when the Church was organized." and he sat back glowing with the achievement. There are times when I just cannot help myself and this was one of them. I leaned forward and said, "My ancestor organized the Church." The man's expression changed suddenly as he went over the words I had just said. Then, slamming his hand on the table with a chuckle he said, "Well sister, I can't top that one!"

Pageant

Making new friends became my favorite benefit of the job. It occurred to me that in many ways I was doing as Joseph and Emma once had when they would welcome people from the boats as they came into Nauvoo. In July, the tourist season was in full swing and the Nauvoo Pageant was about to commence. I had heard from many about the pageant and was told I should be involved in some capacity. I was introduced to Peggy Ricks and at length was allowed to take part in the final song, *The Spirit of God*. As the pageant crew and cast began to pour into Nauvoo, I was delighted beyond measure, for there amongst them were Nate and Amy Mitchell, two people who are very dear to me. Nate played Joseph in the Church produced film, *Joseph Smith: Prophet of the Restoration* and he and Bryan look so much alike they could be brothers. Amy is musically inclined and very loving and their children are a treasure. I enjoyed visiting with such dear friends

One day as I prepared to head down to the pageant field, I glimpsed the sky painted by the hues of pinks and blue cast by the setting sun. My eyes bored into the scene and I became lost in thought as I stood at the door with my pioneer costume and car keys in hand. It was one of those moments where you are there but not really. Physically you are there, but environmentally it seems as if time is standing still and there is a breath of knowledge, be it ever so small, which is opened up to you. Often times it is for you alone, a moment of clarity. I wonder at times such as these if the veil is not parted

Chapter Nineteen

for a moment in time so that we may be made aware of things or just receive a moment of protected peace which we need.

For me the moment was one of those instances when I was reminded of sections of my patriarchal blessing which spoke of future works. I had only been standing a few seconds when the softest voice poured into my mind saying, "Are you ready?" Three words which could mean many things. Are you ready to go? Are you ready to meet some people? Are you ready to rest? Are you ready to have fun? But this time I knew in an instant what it meant even though the meaning wasn't given in words. There was just a knowing that it meant are you ready to move forward and step up in the work you are doing? In realizing instantly what was being said to me, there was also a knowledge that I stood to lose everything I had, meaning material things. With that knowledge spinning in my mind, I hesitated only for a moment as I remembered those who had passed before me and all they had lost. In tears I said, "Yes I am." The hues of the sky had grown more intense during those moments and I felt a warm breeze across my cheeks as I opened the door and walked with a fullness of joy to my car.

Pageant is the most amazing experience anyone could ever have. No matter what your mood is before seeing it, you leave filled with the spirit of hope. One of the General Authorities told Bryan and me that the Nauvoo Pageant was the jewel of pageants. For me it was a door which led me into the lives of some of the most amazing people I would ever know. It was through some of these individuals that firesides were arranged in Utah in late August.

Our visit to Utah happened at the same time the filming of *Emma Smith: My story*. Through my friendship with

Katherine Nelson, who played Emma, I was invited along with Leah to be extras and we were included in several scenes. It was such an amazing experience for me as I have always been interested in the media of film in the form of storytelling. The history of my family was brought alive within me in a whole new dimension. I would email Bryan while he was on his mission, telling him all of the experiences and the process of making the film. It was killing him. His love of film was as great as mine.

After two weeks, we went back to Nauvoo and the film crew followed shortly after. During the filming I was allowed to tag along and do photography. These moments were very precious to me as I captured images from long distances using my zoom so that the actors were not aware I was taking pictures. Because of this, I was able to capture true and undisturbed emotion. The evening before the cast and crew left for Utah, I asked Katherine to sing one of my songs while we were at Emma's Nauvoo House. Katherine had put some arrangements to two of the songs, one of which I sang months before with my friend Sharalyn Howcroft at Women's Conference. I was gifted with a glimpse of how these songs would sound once Bryan returned and could begin arranging. As the film crew left, I fell back into a normal routine, though I felt as if I would never truly know what normal was again. Nauvoo became quiet and I settled in for the winter as I prepared to welcome my son home.

Mission Accomplished

In late November, I drove to the Saint Louis airport. Finally, after two years, I would be picking up my son. Of

Chapter Nineteen

course I couldn't be composed at such a moment. The mischievous side of me surfaced as we approached the area he would be coming through. I pulled Leah aside, telling her we should hide in a book store close by until we saw him pass and then we would follow him, seeing how long it would take before he turned around and noticed us.

We both hunkered down behind some display shelves, positioned so that we could peer through an opening between the shelving. After about ten minutes, we saw him pass and I could see from there the anxiousness in his face. He was excited to see his family, but where were they? After he had walked far enough ahead we rushed out and quietly filed in behind him. I saw him turn his head slightly to the left and right looking for any familiar faces. It was all Leah and I could do to keep from laughing out loud but we held ourselves well until we all turned a corner and headed toward the luggage area. Then I started to giggle uncontrollably and it was a sound he knew well. In a fraction of a second he turned, dropped everything he was carrying and bowled into us with an embrace that nearly knocked us over. Who was this man? I saw my son but there was more. Even in those seconds, I could see how much he had grown spiritually.

There was a light in his countenance that beamed, brighter than I had ever seen in him. It was already six o'clock when I picked him up and we had a two-hour drive to Kirksville, Missouri so that he could be released by the Stake President and another hour and half after that to Nauvoo. The ride to Kirksville was filled with stories he had to tell, and adventures I had to share.

Hills & Valleys

We arrived in Kirksville and Bryan was absorbing what was about to happen. Being released was something he welcomed yet dreaded at the same time. It is a heavy weight to want so badly to be with family again and proceed with your life, mixed with wanting to remain a missionary. When he walked out of the Stake President's office I could tell that he was very emotional. The tears came in measure as we walked to the car and as he climbed in, he broke down. He told me he did not realize it would be so hard, that truly he did indeed feel that mantle being lifted from him and it was a great sadness. As we pulled out of the parking lot, it began to snow lightly.

"Don't worry," I said. "Your work is not finished. It never will be." And then I proceeded to tell him of the many firesides which were scheduled and the wonderful things I had experienced while in Nauvoo

The next day was Sunday. Finally, we got to go to church as a family! That evening we attended a Sunday sociable, as it is called in Nauvoo, at the visitor's center where many missionaries would be who had been desirous to meet Bryan. From the time he was on his mission to that point, I had used a DVD to play his part of the fireside, and now they would get to meet him. It was the best medicine for Bryan. Being surrounded by all of the missionaries lifted his spirits. Soon he began working at the hotel as well. Before long, there were many opportunities to be of service to people in many ways. It was the best means of adjustment he could have hoped for.

Throughout the following year we worked hard to get by, doing firesides along the way for tour groups. It was an

Chapter Nineteen

easier way for us because it did not require travel. For so many years we had struggled to find the means to do firesides, for we do not get paid to do them. By the time Bryan had come home, we were doing three or four a month during the busy season and a few on the off season. These firesides were given to individuals from all over the United States and they would leave me their contact information in case I ever came near their area. I felt that would be impossible given our impoverished situation, but I kept all of the names in a file labeled *contacts*.

As July 2008 approached and pageant was in full swing, our lives began to shift in ways I never expected. A week before pageant started, I was just getting off from work and as I walked to my car there was a moment where I became completely lost in thought. I was amazed at the many ways the Lord had provided for us. Sure, we were very poor, but we had a roof over our head, food and clothes and someone had given us a car! As I was musing over the wonderment of how our lives had been blessed with employment and temporal needs, something impressed upon my mind that I was to quit my job. I sat down in the driver's seat dumbfounded. I had experienced this before, utterly aware of what promptings were and where they came from. It was the most frightening thing because human reasoning stepped in. Quit my job? We were barely making it as it was! I got back out of the car and walked back to the lobby where Bryan had just started his shift.

It was the afternoon and no one was around, a good time to broach what I felt would be a controversial subject. He saw the look on my face right away and asked what was wrong. I didn't know how to say it. I started a few times and then stopped, then finally looked at him in wonderment and said, "I know this sound's crazy, but I have been given to know that I am to quit my job and I don't know why." The reaction he gave was the last thing I expected. He chuckled with a wide grin and said, "I have been prompted to do the same." I knew what his laugh was about. Many times we had received the same experiences and it was no surprise to him that it had happened again.

"Why, do you think?" I asked. He shrugged his shoulders and I left with a smile on my face. It was a smile of reassurance, for I had always known before that promptings do not always make sense and not to worry. I walked back to the car and drove home, in wonder of what was coming.

Time to Sing

Bryan had worked on the arrangements for my songs on his off time and we were both aware that we needed to be in a studio, or have some kind of software to help with some of the arrangements. My heart was aching and I was feeling the urgency to get the songs recorded and perform them, but how? I did not want to be the one to sing them but I had to in order to see how they would be received. The thought terrified me. At length we were able to get *Willow* to the point that I could sing it at the firesides and the impact was amazing. Many expressed how they were touched by it and that our music needed to be out there but as we tried to reach out for help or advice it was to no avail. We were at a loss as to how to achieve such a feat with no funding. This was all new territory for us and we were not sure which way to turn so we did what we knew best; we kept moving forward until an answer came.

Chapter Nineteen

I began to pray for a way to be opened so that we could make a demo of our songs. Virtually penniless and barely surviving it seemed an impossible goal. At times one feels as if they should toss it all aside and work a nine-to-five job, focusing on property, home, and longevity. But when the Lord gives you a work and you are aware of it, there is a burning, almost ache to see it done. Many times I wept because I felt weak and useless because I could not figure out how to make things work. Opposition would attack us to the point that we wondered if we had targets on our backsides. Then a window would open and all would work out.

We were continually learning that the trial is always greatest before a miracle. Now when things get crazy and we are at a loss, it dawns on us and we say, "Oh, something good is coming," then we toss off the darkness that has gathered. One day a thought came to me. I needed to start inviting friends to the firesides we did for tour groups. I knew that I could say all I wanted to people about the songs but nothing would take root unless they actually came to the fireside and heard them.

One of our friends asked us over for lunch one day. She had heard our fireside and wanted to know more about what we were doing. I told her that I knew the songs were for something special and she said that she could feel the spirit in them. I then explained that what we needed to do is cut a demo but the cheapest way to do that was on a home system. When she asked what was required for the system Bryan told her, "A Mac laptop, the software, and a couple of good mikes would result in a low end but decent demo." She did not even ask about how much it cost. She simply said to order it for she

Hills & Valleys

wanted to see these songs out there. I could not believe it. There was not a selfish agenda whatsoever in the offer. She wanted nothing in return but to see us get the songs out there. Within a week, we had all we needed to get started.

As Bryan began to arrange the music with the new tools he had received, everything seemed to fall into place. We were able to put more songs together and use his laptop to do the musical tracks for the firesides and I sang two songs. I was still petrified to sing in front of people and I told Bryan that we should just get someone in the areas we would be speaking and have them sing the songs instead of me.

"Mom!" He said incredulously, "Do you know how crazy that is? It would be insane to try and arrange that considering the many firesides we will be doing!" I knew what he meant. We would have to send the music ahead to each stake and there were times in the past when we were in several stakes in one week.

"Look," he continued, "you have an amazing voice; you just do not realize it. You need confidence. You need to sing these songs yourself because they came to you and the only way the people will feel the spirit as you did is if you sing them. Besides, I am going to push play when it comes time for the songs and you can either sing or stand there and look silly." I knew he would do it too. Like it or not, I was going to have to sing these songs and learn to overcome my fear of being ridiculed.

As I agreed with him, my mind was taken back again to my patriarchal blessing where it referred to artistic talents and gifts in music. The words passed through my mind and fell upon my heart in great waves of wonder. I was amazed because the blessing had also revealed that I was to cultivate and magnify these gifts for the lifting of heart and spirits. It suddenly dawned on me that what we were doing with these songs was indeed healing to those who heard them. I knew by the feedback we were getting from those who attended our firesides. I began to realize the fullness of what had been entrusted to me and the responsibility of using my talents to heal and lift others began to outweigh the fear of ridicule in my mind. Even though I still felt ill- qualified, I was determined to move forward and do the best I could.

Chapter Twenty

Following Promptings

Nearly two weeks had passed since Bryan and I had talked about the new direction we were headed. As pageant continued, we approached our last day of work. I was just getting ready to leave my final shift when a lady asked at the front for Kim Smith. I turned to her and said, "That's me." She apologized for not noticing me and said she had been at our fireside a couple of nights before and wanted one of my poetry books. The gift shop was out of them, but I told her I could meet her the next day and get one to her. After all, I wouldn't be working so I didn't mind. She conveyed to me they would be leaving around 9:00 a.m. and I smiled gingerly and said that was fine, groaning on the inside, for it had been a long time since I had slept in. But I never refused visitors, for I was drawn always to be there for them in any capacity. We had agreed to meet at the homestead where they would be taking pictures before leaving.

I sighed as I walked to the car, considering how life is never boring and always filled with challenges and surprises. Quitting my job, however, was a curve ball I never expected. I drove home aware of the leap of faith I was taking. It was like being blindfolded and stepping off of a cliff, trusting there was a safety net below because someone said so. I would take that step, trusting as always that voice which had brought me thus far.

Chapter Twenty

About the time I had received the prompting to quit my job, Jason Deere and the Nashville Tribute Band were performing in Sarasota, Florida. While there, Jason befriended Darren Dixon, a man on fire for the gospel with eagerness and abilities to spread it in many various capacities. Jason and Darren talked at great length about the mission behind the Nashville Tribute Band. While discussing their journey, Jason mentioned that the band had been invited to Australia to take part in a mission project concerning gathering the 1/3 of the posterity of Joseph and Emma Smith who lived there. Jason also wanted to organize some stake firesides so they could perform during their stay there, but he was having a problem getting clearance with stake presidents in Australia and funding was an issue as well.

Darren showed immediate interest when Jason asked him if he would manage the project for him. Taking the reins, Darren swore he would see this project happen even if he had to pay for it himself, which is exactly what happened. With funding in place, there was still the issue of clearance to do firesides. Talks and frustration with how to make these ends meet bounced back and forth until one day Jason voiced his desire to just drop it and go on faith that all would work out. They just needed to start walking that way and the Lord would open a door.

The Nashville Tribute Band, which was comprised of Jason Deere, Dan Truman, Matt Lopez, Tim Gates and Brad Hull, traveled to Nauvoo, arriving on the same day I finished my final shift. Darren Dixon and his family, along with Sean and Stephanie Green and their family came as well. It was an entourage with a mission; a small group of individuals walking forward in hope, searching for open doors as they spread the spirit of their music along the way. I had no idea they were in town.

The crowd which had attended pageant that evening was amazing. I spoke with many individuals afterward who had traveled great distances to be there. It was a spiritual feast which fed many, nonmembers and members alike. As I was leaving, I bumped into a sister missionary from Australia who I had come to know very well. She told me that some people had been in the visitor's center that day asking about a Smith gathering which was going to be taking place in October in Australia. I told her I was aware of the gathering, but that there was no way we could go. She went on to say that these people were a group or band and they were trying to find information about the events which were being planned. Something inside me stirred. As she spoke I felt impressed to ask about how to get in touch with these people. She told me that I could get it from Sister Wisenet, one of the Public Relations missionaries.

That night was incredibly restless. My mind would not shut down, barely seeping into the edge of deep sleep, only to be awakened again by curiosity, fears and excitement. What were we going to do if we quit our jobs? What did the Lord have planned for us, and who were these people asking about the Smith gathering? When 8 o'clock rolled around, I did not want to get up. I was supposed to meet the woman and give her the poetry book but I was exhausted. I had her phone number and I thought to just call her cell and ask for her address so I could send the book to her. But something nudged me, a strong feeling that I must fulfill the promise I had made.

Chapter Twenty

I argued with myself like a little kid as I stumbled to the bathroom. I had very little energy for I had not eaten much the day before and had not slept well. Looking in the mirror I erupted in laughter for the tossing and turning of the night before had wrought before me the apparition of a banshee.

Exhaustion had pushed me to the point of rebellion and I refused to shower. I reasoned I would just be coming straight back. "Well," I argued with myself, "You can't go looking like that." So I combed through my hair and fixed it as best as I could, changed into some sweats and a T-shirt and accomplished the goal of looking like a polished bum. The lady, after all, had seen me the day before and I had looked well dressed. Maybe she would assume I was out jogging. I would simply drive down, give her the book, drive back home and crawl back into bed. I should have remembered that when I come to such well laid plans with bad foundations that it usually winds up culminating in an embarrassing situation.

As I pulled into the Homestead parking area, the woman and her family were walking from the monuments to their car. I didn't even have to get out, for the woman spotted me and walked over to where I was parked. Then came the moment that taught me never to leave in jogging apparel unless I was truly going to walk or jog. She explained to me that they had been running late all morning and did not have time to go through the Smith homes tour.

"Would you mind terribly giving us a brief overview?" I immediately said I would be glad to, for it was a part of my love for the area and my ancestry to tell of the history. But in my mind, I reprimanded myself severely. As she walked back to her family, telling them to gather by the monument, I mumbled to myself, "Okay hobo Kim, this is where you learn to quit throwing caution to the wind." Deep inside, I knew I probably didn't look that bad, but I felt that I did and that always takes away from my ability to communicate positively with people because I am too concerned about not looking appropriate. But as I spoke to them about the history and they asked questions about my conversion, all went well and my focus fell upon the subject at hand.

The morning was very pleasant and the aroma of spring flowers reminded me that what mattered more than anything was the spirit of the people who sacrificed their lives and built this beautiful city. I was glad, even in my sweats and t-shirt, to be an instrument which could bring such a feeling to these people.

We said our goodbyes and as I pulled out to head home I stopped, deep in thought. What had just been experienced was so uplifting as I bore testimony of my ancestors and their lives. I could not just go home. Since it was so beautiful out, I rolled down the window and turned around to head past the Red Brick Store. Slowly I drove along the road which bordered the river and curved toward Parley Street where the Saints had departed Nauvoo in 1846. No one was there. It was very quiet except for the geese and other wildlife communicating within their societies. I mused momentarily over the magnitude of emotions which still resided in Nauvoo as a whole.

If one is familiar with events which occurred between 1839 and 1846 in Nauvoo, it is hard to visit and not feel the imprint of the lives of those who experienced them. The very energy of trial, sacrifice, love and joy still wafted throughout every building, road, and wooded land. Even the river seemed

Chapter Twenty

to carry whispered accounts of every soul which had bonded with that land. These were stalwart missionaries surrounded by adversaries which sought their demise while they carved out an existence which testified of the Savior.

As my car crawled along the trail of hope I still did not feel like going home. As I glimpsed the temple on the hill I stopped, gazing as I become lost in thought once again. I had so much to do at home. As I pressed the gas pedal again, something impressed upon my mind that I should go to the visitor's center. Oh, how I did not want to do that! I mean there I was dressed so tacky and I was being led to walk into the visitor's center where there were nicely dressed missionaries and visitors. Well, I reasoned, the fault was mine not the Lord's that I was in such disrepair. I shouldn't have argued with the little voice that said "you never know who you might bump into." The human side of me had said, "But I am going straight down and back. I won't see anyone else." This human side of me had a bad habit of forgetting that sometimes the Lord sends us on an errand when we are out and about!

I knew I had to go because the prompting was strong and would not go away, so I turned left and headed toward the visitor's center. Unsure at first of the little side venture, my mind was distracted as I passed the pageant field. The core and family casts were practicing on stage, the music blaring from the speakers. If you have ever been to pageant you would understand that when the music starts playing it just puts you right there as if it were yesterday. Yesterday, I thought. Then I remembered the conversation with the sister missionary and it fell to me then why I was led to go to the visitor's center. I needed to see Sister Wisenet. Still feeling inadequately dressed, I slipped in the door closest to the elevator and went straight to Sister Wisenet's office. She was just leaving and smiled brightly as I met her at the door.

"Pardon my bumminess," I said chuckling. "I had an early errand to run. I didn't expect to stop here but I remembered I was supposed to ask you about some people who were inquiring about the Smith gathering this fall in Australia."

"Oh, yes! They were just here yesterday watching the Joseph movie." She went back into her office and found the phone number of Darren Dixon. We said our goodbyes quickly for she was on her way to a meeting and I slipped back to the car and grabbed my cell phone.

"Something is going on." I said aloud, for a feeling of excitement coursed through me as I dialed the number. There were several rings before someone picked up and said hello.

"Yes, uhm, this is Kimberly Jo Smith and someone gave me your number. You wanted information about the Smith gathering in Australia?" The voice on the line asked me to hang on. When Darren came back on he introduced himself and said that he was in town with Jason Deere and the Nashville Tribute Band. As soon as he said Jason's name I smiled. So we were supposed to meet after all. I still did not understand the purpose behind everything, for I knew it was not about our music. Darren went on to ask if we could get together with them that evening for supper. I agreed and then went home. By then I was too excited to go back to bed so I went about doing the usual domestic chores one usually gets behind on when working.

The day crawled by. I could not shake the feeling that there was something more than just dinner and meeting new friends in the offing. I was so keyed up that I could not accordingly do any constructive housework, so I watched *Pride & Prejudice*, the six hour version! What better way to get your mind somewhere else than to go back in time with Jane Austen? As the ending credits rolled, I raced to the bathroom to don my pioneer costume, preparing for dinner then pageant.

Leah and I greeted Darren and his family outside of the Hotel Nauvoo. This particular hotel has a buffet that has been running strong ever since I first started coming to Nauvoo. We were seated at a long table and little by little other members of the party arrived. Here, on this most special evening, I became friends with some of the most wonderful people! The Dixons, with their adorable sun-kissed children, hailed from Florida, as did the Greenes,—Sean, Stephanie and their children. Then there were the members of the Tribute band: Jason Deere, Dan Truman, Tim Gates, Brad Hull, and Matt Lopez. As I met each one, I was aware of genuine friendship and realized that another door had opened. I didn't know where it would lead, but that evening I basked in the loveliness of the camaraderie which comes with those who are like-minded.

There I was at a table filled with individuals who spent all of their time spreading the message of the gospel through music and I could tell it burned within them. It was a passion which only those who feel it can describe. There is an aching to take that passion and cast it like a mist upon thousands so that they may feel the same burning.

We talked about my conversion, their music, their mission, and then their desire to do firesides in Australia. As they talked of the roadblocks they had been encountering while attempting to organize firesides, my mind went over the events of the past couple of days and how we had met. I felt this was leading to something amazing for these new friends and I wanted to be of help in any way I could, so I gave them the contact information of my cousin Mike Kennedy, who is president of the family organization in charge of the reunions. It was Mike who was heading the events in Australia. It wasn't much, but it was something and I hoped that it would be of use to them.

The next few days were a blend of work and excitement. I was able to arrange for the Dixons, Greens, and the band to view the *Emma Smith: My Story* movie at the Adventure Zone. I can't describe in words the stirrings that went through me that day. There I was in a room filled with people who yearned to tell the story of my ancestors and the Restoration in song. As every scene in the movie unfolded, I wondered if they experienced the same emotions as I did, for such scenes had penetrated into my heart and soul for many years. I longed for them all to know the gravity of the situation with the descendants, the longing to have them healed and at peace.

As we left the theater, someone asked me if we had made our travel arrangements for Australia and I chuckled exclaiming there was no way we could afford to go. "Well, ya never know," he said as we all walked to our cars. No, I thought to myself. You don't understand. We have no savings and are living check to check; soon we would not even have that income. The next day we all went to Carthage and as we were walking into the small theater to view the movie before entering the jail, Darren asked if we had passports. I replied

Chapter Twenty

no. He then said, "You need to get one, all three of you, for we are taking you to Australia with us." Then he walked in the room and sat down. I followed in shock.

For most of the movie I sat in a daze. I was afraid to think it real. So many times people had promised to help with our work and more often than not those plans would fall through. Then my thoughts shifted to travel. I loved to fly, but was terrified of it. For many years I had endured nightmares about flying that were so terrible in nature that I had not flown since Bryan was a baby.

Unbelievable, I thought to myself. I have this chance to be a part of helping the family and I am going to say no because of my fear of flying? My focus was then drawn to the screen for it was the scene where Joseph is hugging Emma and his children goodbye before leaving for Carthage. Tears fell down my cheeks and a question was put to me. Would you really say no if you knew the Lord wanted you to go? As I watched the scene unfold I silently answered, "No, I will always go where the Lord tells me. If I know I am to go, I will go." The trip to Australia would allow me to get to know the large population of Joseph and Emma's posterity that lived there.

A wave of thick July heat rushed upon me as we walked out of the small, cool theater toward the jail and I felt as if I were in another world. As the missionary spoke about the jail, a slow realization of why I was prompted to quit our jobs opened up to me. The words at the end of the film echoed in my mind, "Has the time for miracles ceased..." No, indeed they have not. For if one walks in the path the Lord has set for them, even though it looks impossible, He will provide the means. I was not sure exactly why we were to go to Australia beyond helping with the family gathering; I only knew we were to go. The next few months were filled with securing passports and getting my mom to Nauvoo so she could watch the house while we were gone.

As October approached, I became more nervous about flying, yet was determined to go. My brother, Tim, told me not to worry. Thousands of flights occur every day without incident. It was safer to fly than to drive. Either way I was preparing to go on my first international flight.

Chapter Twenty-One

Leaving On a Jet Plane

On September 15, 2008, we departed the house around 6:00 a.m. for the three-hour drive to St. Louis. Mom drove us and the whole way I was gearing up to do this flight. I finally told myself, "I know I am supposed to do this and if the plane goes down, it goes down." I chose instead to focus on a certain manuscript which was in my carry-on bag.

Two days before we left, I remembered that there was a type-written manuscript on foolscap. It was titled *Our Wallamba Childhood* and was written by Glory Wright, my grandfather's niece. Glory's mother was Grandpa's sister Ina, who had married an RLDS missionary named Sidney Wright from Australia. Ina and Sid raised their large family in Australia, culminating in establishing approximately one third of Joseph and Emma's posterity there. This manuscript told of their history and was among Grandpa's papers. I wondered if any of our Australia cousins had a copy, or even knew about it. I was intrigued to find out why I had been prompted to grab it just before we left.

As we boarded the plane and prepared for take-off, I calmed my nerves as best as I could. The first stop on our trip would be Florida. We were scheduled to do a fireside and stay for about a week with the Dixons. By the time our flight cruised over the everglades, I had come to the conclusion that my brother was right. The chances of incidents in the air were

Chapter Twenty-One

rare and I should just relax and go with it. It had been a pleasant flight on a calm and sunny day. As we landed, I became more confident that all would be well. While in Florida, the Dixon family afforded us the most wonderful visit. We filled our days with beautiful sights, awesome beaches, a fireside and new friendships. By the time September 20th approached, we were all anticipating the trip ahead and what it held for us.

We boarded at the Tampa international airport and enjoyed yet again a wonderful flight. I was really getting the hang of flying the friendly skies as we arrived at the Washington Dulles airport late in the afternoon! But in D.C the skies were not so friendly! We boarded our connecting flight to L.A. and our seats were toward the tail section. As I fastened my seat belt I could hear squeaks and vibrations. I leaned over and jokingly said to Leah, "This sure is a rickety old plane." Rickety has since become a word that she cannot stand to hear.

The plane began to glide down the runway as we all leaned back, ear buds secured to our individual entertainment. All of a sudden, as the plane thrust forward with full power to lift off, there was a loud bang, like a gunshot. I had flown many times in my life and I knew that sound was not ordinary. As the plane climbed upward I turned and looked at Bryan and said, "What was that?" He shrugged his shoulders as he pulled out his ear buds. "That was not normal." I said. Leaning forward I got Darren's attention and he assured me that all was well. But just then the passengers in front of us began to yell and wave their

Hills & Valleys

hands. I heard five words that caused me to freeze, "THE WINDOW HAS BLOWN OUT!"

The flight attendant, who was sitting at the very rear of the plane, could not hear the commotion so my daughter rose from her seat, waved and yelled, then pointed to the scene in front of us, which had now been intensified by insulation flying through the air.

The captain was immediately notified and the plane leveled out. I noticed that it was taking a slight turn toward the direction from which we had come. We were turning around. It felt like hours before the captain addressed us through the intercom. Throughout that time I sat silent. I am not a person who becomes hysterical at such times. Instead, I clamp my mouth shut and clench my legs with my hands until the situation has passed. It was evident however to Darren that I was afraid. In his best cool, beach-dude attempt, he waved a hand and said, "Hey, I have flown hundreds of times. Trust me, the only time you need to worry is when they lose an engine." Part of me felt a little better but the other part of me didn't know if they had not lost an engine. It felt like forever before the captain addressed us through the intercom.

After assessing the situation, they concluded that the casing around the hydraulics had blown and in the process blasted the vent panel away from the floor. The force of the incident caused insulation to be sucked through the now fractured vent opening. There was a powdery substance in the air as a result and some had to get oxygen masks to avoid breathing it. The windows were all secure, but I knew the role hydraulics play in the operation of a plane and depending on the damage, this could be a serious problem.

Chapter Twenty-One

We were instructed to remain calm and a very gracious captain explained exactly what was at hand. The plane was loaded with thousands of pounds of fuel so it was too dangerous to land. They had the choice of dumping it or burning it down to a safe level. They chose to burn off the fuel. This meant we were to fly in a holding pattern for about an hour and at the time he made the announcement he was not sure whether or not it would be an emergency landing.

For about forty five minutes we sat in silence. My feelings ranged from fear and anger to wanting to talk to my family. But amidst those range of emotions came to me the reminder that there was much for us to do. Our time had not yet come. Those thoughts helped immensely but more than anything I wanted to get my feet back on the ground. Then the captain addressed us once again. We were told that this would not be an emergency landing, but we were to stay in our seats once the plane landed until we were instructed to leave.

As the plane descended I prayed like never before. The wheels jolted as they made contact with the runway and I breathed a sigh of relief. But we were not going over to the airport for some reason. Instead we had paused on the runway while emergency vehicles and fire engines raced over to us. It was like something out of the movies. It turned out to be a precautionary measure to ensure that the plane was safe to proceed to the terminal. As we finally emerged into the airport, Darren said he would find out what was going on as far as rescheduling. I looked at him, me, the one who usually stays quiet because I do not want to cause problems, and said, "I do not care what they do to fix that plane. I am not getting back on it!"

It turned out that they grounded that plane and we were given complimentary rooms at the Hyatt Regency and a new flight was arranged for the next day. Needless to say, I did not sleep well that night. Had this happened on our return it would not be so bad, but there was still at least eighteen hours of flight time left. Before we left Nauvoo, some friends told me to take medicine for motion sickness so I would be less focused on the trip. I tried that once when I was working for Headstart when we had to drive for an hour and a half on a windy, curvy road. The results were less than positive. Oh, I didn't think at all about the ride because I had become so hyper and giddy that I was laughing at everything, telling wild stories, and seeing the world in a whole new way. If I were to take that in the air they would toss me out!

Our flight to L.A. went fine and we had an eleven hour layover before our connection to Australia left that evening. So Darren got us a taxi and we went to eat and then to see the L.A. Temple. It was a much-needed day after our experience, but still my nerves were on edge. I kept reassuring myself that all would be well. By the time evening came, I was exhausted and didn't care anymore, until it came.

I was sitting in my seat, looking out into the night sky and slowly the big, white monster pulled up to the terminal. This was our plane, an airbus. I had never seen a plane so big. Part of me liked the fact that it was so big for I hate small planes. Still, it was terrifying at the same time. It loomed high above the terminal like a monster waiting to devour anything in its path. Of course I have an animated imagination so the windows appeared to be slanted angry eyes, the nose arrogant and snobbish and I visualized a sly and demeaning grin. "Stop it Kim," I said to myself. I decided to turn the negative into a positive and envision a smile, slanted happy eyes and a Jimmy Durante nose. As I walked forward to show my ticket and board, I was determined to leave all fear behind and focus on the reasons we were going to Australia, even though I did not know them all yet! I would soon find that was easier said than done!

There are all sorts of entertainment on a long flight to keep one busy: movies, visiting, magazines, and music. You would think I could have employed one of those options to pass the time but I could not. I did not want to put on earphones because I was afraid if something happened I would not hear it. I didn't want to sleep for the same reason. At some point I heard a thud and grabbed Bryan's arm saying, "what was that!?" Bryan said, "Mom, I dropped my iPod." Needless to say, the kids got a good laugh at me on that flight. I sat in my seat for the whole twelve hour flight just staring ahead. The upside was that I didn't suffer from jet lag like everyone else. The next night, as soon as my head hit the pillow I was gone and slept hard.

The Wonder of the Land Down Under

Australia was amazing. It was a trip filled with wondrous beauties and new friendships. We traveled with the Nashville Tribute Band to their firesides and each one was a spiritual feast which brought the people closer to the Savior, telling the story of Joseph, Emma, and the Restoration in new and lasting ways.

One day, we met with our cousin Robyn Mah and her husband Steven. This visit was a jewel to me for I have always

Hills & Valleys

believed that all of the cousins could be friends no matter what their beliefs. We found in the Mahs a genuine regard for free agency and they knew after some time that we were not there on any specific agenda except to meet cousins and become friends. Talk of religion seldom surfaced. Instead, we spoke of their culture, and the natural environment of Australia. Toward the end of the day, her husband, who excelled in the culinary arts, created an amazing meal for us.

It was during this visit that I spoke to Robyn about the manuscript. I had brought it with me to show her and she had never heard that such a work existed. I was instantly excited and decided to leave the manuscript with her. By the time we left her home, I knew that I would not be taking it back with me. I left it so that she could make me copies and then before we went back to the states, I officially donated it to the family during a small ceremony celebrating the Wright's heritage at the Tuncurry museum.

By the end of the day, I would learn the reason why I had felt prompted to grab the manuscript before we left Nauvoo. Glory's daughter Joan actually had the first draft of the manuscript, where I had the finished draft, or a more updated one, which contained a lot of information which answered many questions that Robyn had concerning the history of the family. It felt good to be able to give them something that helped fill in the blanks on part of their history!

Through Robyn and the manuscript, I learned all about Ina Smith Wright's life in Australia. Ina and Sid were strong members of the Reorganized Church of Jesus Christ, which was one of two strongholds for Ina that kept her from being homesick, for she was so far away from the green hills of Missouri and a loving family with whom she was deeply bonded. The other element that brought her comfort was the environment she lived in, especially their little farm which was called Silverfern. The rolling green hills adorned by trees were a sweet reminiscence of the places she had dwelled with her family in Iowa and Missouri. But outside influence would penetrate the comforts which reminded Ina of home, and in time it would render her terribly homesick, longing for the cultural and spiritual aspects which had formed the very core of who she was.

In the midst of raising their family in the wilds of Australia, Sid Wright began to turn his interest to the philosophies of Robert Ingersoll, an American who was well known for his agnostic views and one of the foremost critics of the Holy Bible in the mid nineteenth century.[1] As time progressed, Sid embraced agnosticism, finding that it appealed more to his way of thinking. The result would be devastating for Ina, whose heart and soul was wrapped around the teachings of her grandfather Joseph Smith, Jr. She also adored her father, Alexander, and abided by the precepts of the Reorganized church of which he was Patriarch. As each of their children grew and began to think for themselves, there was a split in what had been unity of belief in the Reorganized Church. One of the descendents of the Australian branch of the family said:

"The children were raised to question the then-established religious dogma and look more to nature and community spirit for their beliefs and under-pinning values, The Australian bush was rich in trees, flowers and grasses, always a symphony of bird calls and glorious blue skies. They were living within the cycles of nature, barefoot and free. The minds of Sidney's children grew from a practical life of love, freedom and a dual view of god and nature. To this day the majority of the extended family holds a great reverence and respect for the overwhelming power and beauty of nature and a more conservative, slightly cynical, but respectful view of religion per se."[2]

As a result of their more conservative influences, some of the family would emerge with more agnostic views, while others remained in the Reorganized Church of Jesus Christ of Latter Day Saints, or embraced other religious affiliations. Ina, who loved her family dearly, had found the core of who she was ripped away from her. She was isolated, the only one in her environment who carried a memory of what her faith meant. She had firsthand accounts and memories of the price which had been paid for eternal truths. She could recall the bonding of history and her childhood in Nauvoo, Illinos; Lamoni, Iowa;, and Independence, Missouri. It was in her blood and had become a cycle of life that carried over into her marriage and now that cycle was broken. In the midst of heartache, Ina reached out to the one thing that would bring her solace; home.

In 1915 Ina sailed to America and visited her extended family for several months. By then, her father Alexander had passed, but her mother was still living.[3] By the end of her visit, she had reconciled herself to the choices of her own family and settled back into life in Australia to raise a family with strong bonds of kinship and love. Today hundreds of her descendants live in Tuncurry, Foster, Sidney, and various locations of the

Chapter Twenty-One

glorious land down under. I found them to be a gracious and loving people who strive to live life with zest.

At one point during our trip, Robyn took us to a place called The Green Cathedral, a beautiful outdoor place of worship carved out of the lush green rainforest palm trees which border Wallis Lake. The cathedral of nature was the idea of Sid Wright's father as a gift to Ina in 1922 and it culminated in the first church reunion in Australia with over 200 members in attendance. I was enthralled as I walked the trail that led to the Green Cathedral. It was a narrow walkway bordered by a blanket of palm trees on both sides. They seemed ancient and the farther I walked, the more it felt as if I was being swallowed up by an enchanted jungle forest. Then I came to a clearing that opened up to an aisle of dirt which divided church pews made of the native trees. The aisle led to a large altar and podium, also made from native trees, and behind the altar the sandy surface edged down into Lake Wallis. It was a very special visit to a serene and sacred place. One could truly forget the hindrances of this world in such a place.

Toward the end of our trip, there was a special gathering of Smith descendants where the Nashville Tribute Band played and a viewing of the movie *Emma Smith; My Story* was arranged where, for the first time, many descendants were able to glimpse a history of their heritage. I was thrilled by the connection I felt to so many people, the camaraderie that was instantly felt. Soon we would have to leave and I felt sad that we did not have more time, but I somehow knew that there would be another visit. It was time to move on.

We would be arriving in Nauvoo with no money, no job, and a mission to prepare for. I only knew we were to go and do. The details were not clear to me as we boarded the plane to head back to the states. It felt as if I were getting on yet another roller coaster, aware that it could get wild and scary, yet knowing it would stop at one point so I could get off, recuperate....and then climb on again.

Chapter Twenty-Two

"Every tomorrow has two handles. We can take hold of it with the handle of anxiety or the handle of faith."

—Henry Ward Beecher

After being home for a few days, Bryan and I took a drive down to the flats in Nauvoo. As we coasted along the street that borders the pageant field, I felt a pang of loneliness. Every time the pageant folks took their "exodus" back to the west there was a deep hole of emptiness. I often thought what I was sensing was just a tiny semblance of what those who stayed behind in 1846 may have felt. As we took a right turn and drove up past the temple, I felt I should drop in on our friend Sherry Saint who was now managing Zion's Mercantile, a quaint gift shop with a restaurant. Business had started to ebb into the slow fall season and she had ample time to visit.

I found her in the office and in my usual prankster mode found an opportunity to sneak up behind and scare the living daylights out of her! After a good laugh, we sat down and she asked how my visit to Australia went. After I regaled her with the amazing sights and sounds we had experienced, she asked what my plans were. I answered, "I have no idea. But something needs to be decided soon."

"Well," she said, "Since all of the students who were helping have gone back to class I have been in dire need of a

Chapter Twenty-Two

couple of new employees and every time I pray about whom to consider your name always comes to mind."

I started to cycle mixed feelings. I loved working for Sherry but I knew I was supposed to quit my job for a reason. As days went by, I began to consider that the reason may have been simply so that I would be free to go to Australia. When I saw Sherry again about a week later, we had the same conversation and I told her I felt as if she was right. So Bryan and I started working in November. For the rest of winter and spring we were blessed to have an income.

We were fully immersed in the 2009 summer season when once again the prompting came and I knew that we were to quit our jobs, but this time there was a component of finality to it. We were to go on the road and do the firesides full time. It wasn't the thought of doing them on such a large scale that worried me, it was how. But I had been through enough leap-of-faith situations to know that if I just walk that way, all would work out. So I set up a route and started emailing people who had asked me to contact them whenever we were coming their way. Within a few weeks I had a six month schedule confirmed. For all three of us there was a confirmation that Nauvoo would not be our home for much longer.

In the fall of 2009, we covered three western states and did twenty four firesides in a twelve week period. The schedule was planned for only twelve firesides, but visitors from other stakes who attended wanted to organize one in their stake and it just mushroomed. I would never refuse because it was why we were there, and it did not matter how tired we were. As soon as we stepped into those church doors we were filled with energy! I was completely amazed and humbled at the same time. The only help we had was with gas expense and sometimes that was not always available. But when funds ran short, more became available and it was never more or less than we needed. That first trip proved to me that if we are truly willing to do what the Lord asks of us He will provide the way.

Many times we were worried about how we were going to get from one place to the next, or how we could afford maintenance for the car. Such times caused me to reflect about those early pioneers who set out on foot never knowing what lay before them. It taught me not to complain but I have to admit that there were many times I worried that we were not going to be able to meet our needs. My concerns were not about finances as much as the desire to be able to get to each place and share our message, but the Lord opened every door to make it possible.

The year of 2010 was even more amazing. We were asked by Mike Kennedy to be ambassadors for the Joseph Smith Jr. and Emma Hale Smith Historical Society and helped as often as we could to reach out to our cousins, inviting them to the reunions. We drove approximately 60,000 miles and did over 155 firesides, at times doing five days in a row. The travel routes spanned from the west coast to the east coast, including historical sites such as Martin's Cove, Adam-ondi-Ahman, Palmyra, and Nauvoo. As anyone who has been to such marvelous places will express, they were some of the most moving experiences in our lives. I took many long walks through the Sacred Grove in deep reflection and study.

One day while in the grove, I found a special spot and sang the song On His Knees, which I had written in 2005. It was such experiences which brought an awareness of familiarity, a memory not my own, a time I was not a part of, yet it was a part of me. I had felt such emotions before, especially in my childhood, when that presence was near, the one I thought to be a guardian angel. It was the same presence I felt when I saw the portraits. As I walked through the grove the realization that it had been my great-great-grandfather who watched over me so many times became very clear to me. It was he that expressed his heart and love to me as I wrote and made those long visits to Nauvoo.

Of course, along with the great moments during our travels came the opposition. As things seemed to progress and our music was becoming well received, we ran into those who approached in friendship yet attempted to defraud us. There were encounters which promised hope only to lead to devastation due to the foul and selfish intentions of others. I learned during those times the ways in which I needed to be cautious and to never expect what is being offered to come to fruition until I actually witnessed it.

It was during these times we found that our home in Nauvoo had mold issues that we were unaware of when we had moved in. The impact was lessened by the knowledge that we would be on the road for a few months but it still left me unsettled. I had many precious belongings which were strewn throughout a few states in the care of friends and family, for I could not leave them in the house in Nauvoo. We had lost our home because of the hazardous conditions there and my mind reflected on the time I stood in the door before going to pageant in 2008 and I heard the words, "Are you ready?" knowing I stood to lose everything. The reminder brought upon me an odd sense of comfort for I knew those losses came as we sacrificed to do what we knew to be right.

In the last couple of years there have been situations which were so overpowering and confusing that they threatened to tempt me away from the Church and the work I have been engaged in for so long. But because of what I have gained from my heritage and this Gospel I know that even though a day may be eerily shrouded by dark clouds, or white ones that seem cheerful, the sun is still on the other side. The clouds will come and go in various shades and shapes, blown by careless winds until they dissipate. But the sun will always be in its place and in its fullness. That is how I see this gospel: it is always there in its fullness, regardless of those who wish to manipulate or distort, meandering and creating all manner of different versions. I will never be moved from where the Holy Ghost has led me: through all of those clouds to a bright sun. Amidst the opposition came those who were instrumental in helping. Without the help of such stalwart individuals, we would not be able to do these firesides and our music would not be available to the public.

Spring and summer of 2011 found us in California, Missouri, and several other states with bookings keeping us on the road for almost six months. Throughout all of this time, we had no home but stayed with friends along the way. In the fall, we moved to Utah for Bryan was accepted into BYU. The move brought many challenges because it meant finding a place to stay with no money. It is during such times that one finds those who know what sharing the burdens of others truly means. I was surprised by those who had capability and room to temporarily help yet felt it an inconvenience, then amazed and touched by those who came out of left field to help even though they had very little. Before long, we found ourselves temporarily settled for the semester, renting a place which was available until May of 2012. Until that time, we kept busy with concerts and firesides throughout the Salt Lake valley and beyond.

> *"Music can name the unnamable*
> *and communicate the unknowable."*
>
> —Leonard Bernstein

By the time we started doing concerts in January 2012, we had our full CD completed and available for purchase. It was a moment I had been awaiting for nearly seven years. The long wait taught me the value of patience and the Lord's timing. The accomplishment was something that lifted a weight from my heart and I never had a moment where I felt deserving of any credit at all for getting the music to that stage. I only know that when I held the CD in my hand I gazed upward to the heavens and thanked the Lord for allowing me to have the privilege of receiving such inspiration and even more so for giving me the courage to actually sing.

I had come to a point in my life where I had nearly overcome the struggle of inadequacy. Looking back, I could see that it was true that the adversary knows of our missions in life, that he does all he can to thwart those missions. I know this because every area he hit me with then are the same areas I excel in now. This awareness was brought to completion by an email my cousin Gracia Jones sent me not long after we had recorded our CD. I was working on an article for Meridian

Magazine and I had expressed to her my discomfort of writing or even feeling any form of self-praise for fear of people thinking I valued myself too dear in arrogance.

"Don't be afraid to toot your horn Kim," she wrote to me. "The little girl who could not lift her head to meet anyone in the eye, or speak in public has been healed through the power and Spirit of the gospel of Jesus Christ, and is now fearlessly doing the things that she was robbed of doing as a young girl. This miracle is incredible. What you and Bryan are doing is a gift to us all. If the title had not already been taken by a big movie, I would want to title this 'Incredible Journey."

I couldn't believe she said those words about me. Me? As I read the email, thoughts poured into my mind as tears fell down my cheeks. "Yes, Kimberly, you have worth. You are a child of God, now go and sing the hearts of those who once walked this earthly plain. Tell their stories. Sing to the world what nature can only say in its own tongue so that all may know what the mountain river and forest breeze truly mean."

I sat back in my chair and peered through the window. The trees were moving gracefully as the wind stirred their branches, the sun's rays dancing to and fro with the movement as if both were partners in a graceful waltz from long ago. Looking back, I marveled at just how hard the adversary tried to stop me from progression and how cruel his efforts had been. I was almost ashamed that I had let him have that much power over me for so long but then a thought halted that perspective. It would only be a shame had I not picked myself up and moved forward despite my fears. There are many who do not reach that point and knowing that compels me even more to tell my story because there is a way to be made whole from any sorrow.

We have seen many miracles happen within families in our journeys. I have received emails from those who express their gratitude because they feel we have helped them to overcome pain in many variations, and at one fireside we saw two families in tears as a brother and sister who had not spoken in years embraced and forgave one another. Though they send us these heartfelt emails of gratitude, I do not take credit at all. Any healing that happens as a result of what we or anyone else do when testifying of the healing power of Christ, comes from the Savior, not us. But oh, what a blessing to be a witness to it, and how precious to be able to sing the songs we have been inspired to write, knowing that the music itself promotes its own healing.

I have come to think of music as a fine mist that settles into the crevices of our spirit and souls where nothing else can reach. Because it has that much power, it is so important to be mindful of what we are listening too. Just as spiritual and uplifting music has the power to heal, dark and negative music has the power to destroy and it is lethal in its subtlety to the point that the listener does not know or understand that he or she is being transformed.

Progression

We are all human and many times will come face to face with trauma and sorrow. All of the trauma and pain I endured made me who I am today only because of the choices I made following incidents. How I processed those dark periods of, not just my life, but the lives of those who passed before me, determined who I am today. The saying, "That which does not destroy us makes us stronger," is true. If we process dark and negative occurrences using positive solutions then we indeed do become stronger for it. The tools my mother gave me at a young age enabled me to have a door to walk through to receive strength.

We are now in the midst of our 2012 spring and summer tour, telling our story, teaching of the importance of healing and family unity, singing our songs, and relaying the importance of knowing the Savior and implementing His teachings in our lives. Without Him being central in our lives, we cannot overcome anything. It is important that we all learn how to love one another and ourselves, forgive one another and ourselves, and let go of any issues of the past or present, for we cannot hold on to those issues and the Savior at the same time. We need Him to overcome all things.

As we do this we begin to feel lighter, even when times are hard. We are happy even in the face of difficulties. We are at peace even in times of sorrow. That is what the Atonement does for us. That is what we receive when we abide in Him. He abides in us and makes it possible to process all manner of hardship with an understanding of peace, and more importantly, a knowledge that there is hope in all things through Christ. In essence, if we embrace the Atonement, we are given the same abilities to withstand trial as the Savior had when he was tried and tested. It allows us to pass through trials with peace in our heart, mind, and spirit.

Is your family divided? There is hope in the Savior and His Atonement. If our family can go through the events we have experienced all of these generations and come full circle to find healing, uniting as a family, then any family can. Have you been abused? There is hope in the Savior and his compassionate love for you. People who have known me for years would never have guessed I had been molested as a child. Truly, the Lord can remove the pain of such traumatic events in our lives to the point that it feels as if it never occurred. But we have to allow Him to do it. He is always willing; it is we who have those moments of self-doubt. But there is a Father in Heaven who trusts that we can become strong and endure. He wants His children to know their value and self-worth.

In order for the afflicted to define their self-worth, they must remove the negative effects that past traumas have poured upon them. These effects place a weight of self-doubt upon the wounded, robbing them of energy, confidence and spirit. It is necessary to clean our inner home of all negativity, even the smallest amount, for the adversary loves the residue and left-over doubts. What we leave behind, he will use against us. This kind of healing can be accomplished through prayer, the Atonement, service, scripture study, uplifting music, and anything that is positive which adds to spiritual growth. Had I not walked in the direction laid before me I would still be in my room, isolated.

We live in a time and day where many voices pour forth claiming to be prophets or leaders who know the better way. They rail against The Church of Jesus Christ of Latter-day Saints in a language filled with hatefulness and disrespect, a language crafted by the adversary. There are those who have attempted to sway me with elaborate and fanciful tales of visions and experiences. I have seen it all. I have read it all. The anti-material has passed to and fro before my eyes and I stand today and proclaim that I will never be moved from my place. This is Christ's church. It has been given to us to maintain, build, and carry forward until He returns. How can we do that when we continually abandon our posts?

For those who have become inactive or left the Church due to offence or other issues, I can only emphasize the importance of staying where the Holy Ghost has led you, no matter what. We have to follow the example of the Lord. Where would we be today if He had retreated into isolation, abandoning His earthly ministry, at the onset of offence and maltreatment? What hope would we have if He had thought the task too hard, giving in to the adversary's temptations? We must likewise remain steadfast in the pure love of Christ, carrying this work forth with love, faith, patience and endurance.

The Church of Jesus Christ of Latter-day Saints contains the fullness of the gospel of Jesus Christ. Through this church one can come to a greater knowledge of the Savior and the Plan of Salvation. I have witnessed the beautiful workings of the pure love of Christ in my own life. History is filled with examples of others who testify of that love, including my own ancestors Joseph and Emma Smith.

I bear witness to all that the Savior lives and loves all of us. I am grateful for His noble sacrifice, that He would die for me that I might have eternal life. That through His death, He paved the way to our Father in heaven, laying the plan of salvation before us. I am grateful that He loved me when I hated myself, walked with me when I felt alone, and lifted me when I was on my knees immersed in tears of hopelessness.

I bear witness that as a prophet of God, my great-great-grandfather Joseph Smith Jr., brought forth the fullness of the Gospel of Jesus Christ. The Book of Mormon was translated by him so that we might have a second witness of Christ. Joseph's wife, Emma, stood behind her husband and upon her deathbed bore witness to the authenticity of his calling of God as a prophet. I also acknowledge the important role of all of those stalwart pioneers who walked side by side with my ancestors in the great work of the Restoration. I love them as much as my own. They were all engaged in this work as a team and each family has a story of sacrifice, joys, sorrows, love and pain. They purchased what we have today at great costs. Because of this I will never stray from what I know to be true.

I have seen many things on my journey, broached many swollen rivers with rapids seeming too furious to cross. But I knew that if the Lord trusted that I had the capability then surely I could tread that water and get to the other side. Some crossings left me bruised and battered, but never once did the Savior fail to fulfill His promises as long as I was willing. Faith is the vessel that will carry us over any rapid and protect us from sinking beneath the surface as we sail forward in some of the most treacherous of waterways. It is such faith that has carried me to where I am today.

As I come to the end of this account of my life so far, I cannot help but reflect on one so close to my heart, the man whose clear blue eyes reached out to my wounded heart and spirit from a portrait: Grandfather Joseph. He gave his all to the building of the Kingdom of God so that man would have a full knowledge of Heavenly Father's plan for His children. Knowing of such a sacrifice I can only reflect upon D&C 128, reiterating Joseph's plea from the heart, "Shall we not go on in so great a cause?"

Epilogue

"Life can only be understood backwards;
But it must be lived forwards."

—Søren Kierkegaard

As I look back at some of the issues in our family which caused problems, the lack of empathy, compassion and binding love lay at the heart of the divisions and contentions. There was some love there but it was held back. We should never allow ourselves to become divided simply because we believe differently. There can be great differences in different Christian religions. The important thing to remember is that, as Christians, we all share a common, vital thread: we believe in the Savior, Jesus Christ. As such, we should love one another, being accepting and giving in friendship and kindness because one day our Father will call us together and will want an accounting of our treatment of each other.

We are not charged to judge others, but to follow the guidance given to us individually. I have found it so much more peaceful to move in the direction I have been given and to love my fellow brothers and sister, Christian and non-Christian alike.

So my story goes on. In the previous chapters, I took readers through rising hills and sinking valleys to where I am today, in a beautiful clearing where there are still rough roads

Epilogue

ahead. But I will happily pass through them with a peaceful heart and mind.

Today I can say that my whole family has learned from the heartbreaks of the past, making both good and bad choices and learning along the way. I have shared the many trials we went through, but must say here that even though times were hard and harder still to understand, we shared a great love and camaraderie. Our sense of humor got us through most of those times so there was a lot of laughter to combat the darker periods.

My experience is an example of what happens when one truly believes in Father in Heaven, accepts the Savior, follows His example, and listens to the guidance of the Holy Ghost in all things. Having faith, believing in oneself, and having a compassionate and forgiving heart reinforces those attributes, molding a nigh unbreakable suit of armor that can withstand much affliction. There will always be wounds, but having the pure love of Christ is the best healing balm. Such knowledge has kept our family strong.

My father is now a man who travels and speaks to Restoration groups and individuals about the importance of building Zion and unity. He is and always has been a genuinely good man who, like all of us, made mistakes along the way as he tried to build his life. But what counts is who he is today; a wonderful man who has learned the value of the roles of husband, father, and grandfather. He absolutely loves and adores my mom. I love him dearly.

My mother remains the center of the family. She is a woman who has remained faithful to the Lord, her husband

and children throughout all manner of trial and affliction. To know that one can find light in any situation and keep that light strong within is an invaluable lesson she has taught me. I have loved her since ages past. My mother and father live in Missouri, as does my sister. When she isn't working, Candy's focus is on humanitarian work in Africa. She is continually searching for avenues that will link her with organizations that can use her knowledge and experience.

My brother, Tim, lives with his wife, Suzy, and daughter Scarlett, in New York City. Tim is an amazing artist and manages an art gallery. He is one of the wisest individuals I have ever known. He has another daughter, Amber, who lives with her husband Chris in Kansas.

My son Bryan is currently attending BYU in hopes of getting into their Media Music program. When he isn't in school, we are on the road doing firesides and concerts. We will be recording our next CD in the summer of 2013. I keep teasing him, reminding him that I am ready for grandchildren. He has assured me that he is looking, "for Mrs. Right, hopefully a soprano so we can have a trio." Singing with him has been one of the privileges of my life. It is a precious experience.

Leah has been a talented artist for most of her life. She could draw Disney in the second grade at a high school level. She will soon be applying for BYU and eventually hopes to get into their animation program. She has often traveled with Bryan and me when we tour, fitting somewhere in a crevice of our little Elantra. Our road trips have always been a blast. Leah is very unique. She has special talents and has always been an old soul.

Epilogue

As for me, we already have our six month schedule set. Firesides and concerts are what we do and will do until the Lord says we are finished. Aside from this work, I am currently working on a historical romance novel, a photo essay/poetry book, photography projects and putting together plans to do seminars about the role music plays in healing. My life is full and I thank my Heavenly Father for all that I have. I am very blessed.

Mom and Dad 1956

Hills & Valleys

*Kimberly Jo in
Tennessee*

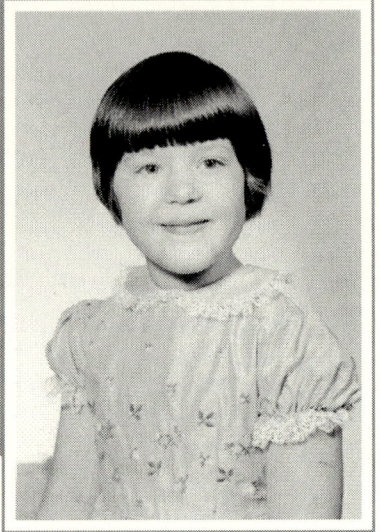

*Kimberly Jo
at age 9*

Candy and Tim in Oregon

Epilogue

Mom, Tim, Candy and Kimberly Jo

The Smith family (2000)
From left: Kimberly Smith, Bryan Davis, Sue Smith, Tim Smith, Joseph Smith, Amber Smith Mounts, Leah Davis & Candy Smith

NOTES

Introduction

1. Evans, Richard L., "The Power and Privilege of Repentance." *Conference Report*, April 1950, pp. 102-106

2. Christofferson, D. Todd, "That They May Be One in Us." General Conference. October 2002 <https://www.lds.org/general-conference/2002/10/that-they-may-be-one-in-us?lang=eng>

3. Letter From Emma Smith. The Joseph Smith Papers. Web. 2012 <http://josephsmithpapers.org/paperSummary/letter-from-emma-smith-7-march-1839>

Chapter One

1. Jones, Gracia N., *Emma's Glory and Sacrifice* (St. George: The Art Press, 1987) p. 3.

2. "LDS Women of the Past: Personal Impressions, "Woman's Exponent 36 (February 1909): 1.

3. Patriarchal blessing given to Emma Hale Smith, 9 December 1834, Kirtland, Ohio, Patriarchal Blessing Book No. 1, Archives of The Church of Jesus Christ of Latter-day Saints.

4. Jones, Gracia N., "My Great Great Grandmother Emma Hale Smith", Ensign, August 1992

5. Avery, Valeen T., and Linda K. Newell. Ensign, September 1979

Notes

6. "A History of the Church of Jesus Christ of Latter-day Saints." Church History in the Fullness of Times. Salt Lake City, UT: The Church of Jesus Christ of Latter-day Saints, 2003. (p. 172)

7. Doctrine & Covenants 38:39

8. "A History of the Church of Jesus Christ of Latter-day Saints." Church History in the Fullness of Times. Salt Lake City, UT: The Church of Jesus Christ of Latter-day Saints, 2003. (p. 174)

9. "A History of the Church of Jesus Christ of Latter-day Saints." Church History in the Fullness of Times. Salt Lake City, UT: The Church of Jesus Christ of Latter-day Saints, 2003. (p. 173)

10. "A History of the Church of Jesus Christ of Latter-day Saints." Church History in the Fullness of Times. Salt Lake City, UT: The Church of Jesus Christ of Latter-day Saints, 2003. (p. 280)

11. Jones, Gracia N., Emma and Joseph, Their Divine Mission. American Fork: Covenant Communications, 1999. (p. 292)

12. Jones, Gracia N., Emma and Joseph, Their Divine Mission. American Fork: Covenant Communications, 1999. (p. 304)

13. Jones, Gracia N., Emma and Joseph, Their Divine Mission American Fork: Covenant Communications, 1999. (p. 299)

14. Oaks, Dallin H., and Joseph I. Bentley, "Joseph Smith and Legal Process: In the Wake of the Steamboat Nauvoo." BYU Studies 1979: pp. 1, 2.

15. Oaks, Dallin H., and Joseph I. Bentley, "Joseph Smith and Legal Process: In the Wake of the Steamboat Nauvoo." BYU Studies 1979, pp. 15, 16.

16. Newell, Linda K., and Valeen T. Avery. *Mormon Enigma: Emma Hale Smith*. Champaign: University Of Illinois Press, 1994. 2nd Edition. 200

17. Youngreen, Buddy,. *Reflections of Emma*. Orem: Grandin Book Company. 1982: pp. 61, 118

18. Ehat, Andrew F., *Joseph Smith's Introduction of Temple Ordinances and The 1844 Mormon Succession Question*, Master's Thesis, Brigham Young University, Provo (December 1982) p. 55

19. Youngreen, Buddy, *Children of Joseph and Emma, the Unknown Story*, DVD. The Joseph Smith Jr. and Emma hale Smith Historical Society, 2009

20. Shields, Stephen L., Divergent Paths of the Restoration. Bountiful, Utah: Restoration Research, June 1982 (p. 65)

21. Anderson, Mary Audentia Smith, ed., Memoirs of Joseph Smith III *1832-1914*. Independence: Price Publishing, 2001. (p. 72)

22. Smith, Alexander Hale. *My Heritage Sermon* KauKura, Tahiti. November 10, 1901

23. Anderson, Mary Audentia Smith, ed., Memoirs of Joseph Smith III 1832-1914. Independence: Price Publishing, 2001 (p. 27)

24. Newell, Linda K., and Valeen T. Avery. Mormon Enigma: Emma Hale Smith. Champaign: University Of Illinois Press, 1994. 2nd Edition. 203-204.

25. Anderson, Mary Audentia Smith, ed., Memoirs of Joseph Smith III 1832-1914. Independence: Price Publishing, 2001. (p. 38)

26. Ibid

27. Smith, William. "Mormonism, A Letter From William Smith, Brother of Joseph the Prophet." *Illinois State Chronicle.* (Decatur) 11, June 1857. Vol III, No. 52

28. Letter from Joseph Smith III to Samuel B. Smith. 28, November 1898. Author's Note: Gracia N. Jones provided photo copies of this and other letters: Jones was given these photo copies by Virginia Smith Musser, St. George, Utah. Musser, now deceased, was a niece of Jay Winters Smith, a son of Samuel H. B. Smith. Jay Winters Smith had the original letters in his possession until his death; Jay Winters Smith had no posterity. The present location of the originals is unknown, however, photo copies are held by several members of the Samuel H. B. Smith family.

29. Young, Brigham, *Journal of Discourses.* July 1857: vol. 5, p.77

30. *The Revised and Enhanced History of Joseph Smith By His Mother.* Scot F. Proctor and Maurine J. Proctor, Ed. (Salt Lake City: Bookcraft, 1996) p. 459

31. Avery, Valeen T. and Linda K. Newel, *New Light on the Sun: Emma Smith and the New York Sun Letter.* Journal of Mormon History Vol. 6, 1979: pp. 24, 25

32. Ibid

33. Taylor, John, *Another Mormon Expose.* Times and Seasons 15, Jan. 1845: Vol. 6

34. Ibid

35. Anderson, Mary Audentia Smith, ed., Memoirs of Joseph Smith III 1832-1914. Independence: Price Publishing, 2001.

Chapter Two

1. Smith, Vida E. Story of Alexander Hale Smith, *Journal of History Vol 4*. (January 1911): p. 5

Author's note: *This source came from a transcription which was taken from an accounting of Alexander's life through his memoirs, edited by his daughter Vida. The same content can be found in The Community of Christ Journal of History. The transcriptions were of volumes 4 through 8. Several copies were made and preserved by the family sometime in the early 20th century. One copy belonged to my Grandfather Arthur and is now in my possession. This information can also be found in The Biography of Alexander Hale Smith by Ron Romig.*

2. Ludlow, Daniel H., ed., *Encyclopedia of Mormonism*, New York: Macmillan Publishing Company, 1992

3. *Letter from Joseph Smith to Emma April 4, 1839*. Liberty, Liberty, Missouri. Church Archives, used with permission.

4. Black, Susan Easton "How Large Was the Population of Nauvoo?" *BYU Studies 35*, 2 1995: 91

5. Smith, Vida E. Story of Alexander Hale Smith , *Journal of History Vol 4* (January 1911): p.5

6. Ibid

7. Ibid

8. Jones, Gracia N. "Elizabeth Agnes Kendall: One Saint Who Remained After the Mormon Exodus from Illinois, Her Story, Her Legacy" The Joseph Smith Jr., and Emma Hale Smith Historical Society. Michael Kennedy, Ed. 15 Jan 2011. 7 May 2012. <http://www.josephsmithjr.org/tng/w/index.php/KENDALL,_Elizabeth_Agnes_-_I17>

9. Ibid

10. Smith, Vida E. Story of Alexander Hale Smith, *Journal of History* Vol 4. (January 1911): p. 5

11. Jones, Gracia N., *Priceless Gifts*. Murray: Roylance, 1989: 6

12. Smith, Vida E., *Story of Alexander Hale Smith*. Journal of History Vol. 4 (January 1911): p.5

13. Ibid

14. Ibid

15. Ibid

16. Ibid

17. Smith, Alexander H. "My Heritage" Sermon. KauKura , Tahiti 10 Nov 1901. Vision no. 53 (July 2006) 21-22

18. Smith, Vida E., *Story of Alexander Hale Smith*. Journal of History Vol. 4 (January 1911)

19. Ibid

20. Ibid

21. Ibid

22. Ibid

23. Ibid

24. Ibid

25. Ibid

26. Quinn, Michael. "The Practice of Rebaptism at Nauvoo." *BYU Studies 1978 Vol.* 18:2

27. United States Circuit Court of Appeals. *The Church of Christ of Independence, Missouri vs. The Reorganized Church of Jesus Christ of Latter-Day* Independence: December Term 1894. No. 516.

Author's Note: *This source was taken from a book that was not actually published, but compiled by my grandfather, Arthur Smith. Being an established book binder, he compiled copies of court transcripts and bound them into a hardback book which is in my father's possession. This particular law suit was to determine which of the two churches had the legal right to the temple lot, where Joseph had designated the New Jerusalem Temple would be built. As such, early leaders of the church, who were at the time of 1857 living in Salt lake City, were either called back to testify, or gave depositions in Utah.*

28. Smith, Vida E. Story of Alexander Hale Smith, *Journal of History* Vol. 4 (January 1911)

29. Ibid

30. Ibid

31. Smith, Alexander H. "My Heritage" Sermon. KauKura, Tahiti 10 Nov 1901. Vision no. 53 (July 2006) 21-22

32. Ibid

33. Jones, Gracia. Email interview. 26 Jul 2011.

34. Jones, Gracia N. "Alexander Hale Smith." *Joseph Smith Jr., and Emma Hale Smith Historical Society.* 10 Dec 2009. 25 May 2012. <http://www.josephsmithjr.org/history/children/67-alexander>

35. Smith, Vida E. Story of Alexander Hale Smith, *Journal of History* Vol 8. (1915): p. 4

36. Ibid

Chapter Three

1. Smith, Arthur M., Personal Memoirs. 1960: pp. 1-5

Author's note: *My grandfather's memoirs are not available to the public and are limited to one copy which is in the possession of my father. Someday in the future I hope to make available a more concentrated history of his life, including his memoirs.*

2. Ibid

3. Ibid

4. Ibid

5. Ibid

6. Ibid

7. Ibid

8. Ibid

9. Ibid

10. Ibid

11. Compton, Todd, In Sacred Loneliness : The Plural Wives of Joseph Smith, Signature Books 1998: p. 208

12. Bennett, Sherri, "Arthur Smith: A Wise and Gentle Soul." *The Joseph Smith Jr. and Emma Hale Smith Historical Society.* 5 March, 2010

13. Smith, Kenneth J., "A Tribute to The Wise and Gentle Spirit of Apostle Arthur M. Smith."

14. Ibid

Hills & Valleys

15. Ibid

16. Ibid

17. Ibid

18. Ibid

19. Ibid

20. Ibid

21. Ibid

22. Ibid

23. Smith, Arthur M, Personal Memoirs. 1960: pp.1-5

24. Bennett, Sherri., "Arthur Smith: A Wise and Gentle Soul." The Joseph Smith Jr. and Emma Hale Smith Historical Society 5 March, 2010

25. Smith, Kenneth J., "A Tribute to The Wise and Gentle Spirit of Apostle Arthur M. Smith."

26. Smith, Arthur M., Personal Memoirs. 1960: pp.1-5

Chapter Four

1. *Sevier County, Tennessee Deaths 1850 Mortality Schedule* <http://files.usgwarchives.net/tn/sevier/census/1850/1850mort.txt>

2. Proctor, Victoria, *Marion's Brigade: The Men Who Served With Marion.* 25 Aug 2006 <http://sciway3.net/proctor/revwar/swampfox_NCO_M.html>

3. Roberts Methodist Church Cemetery. John Roberts Tombstone inscription 1826-1908: 2007

Notes

4. Smith, Mary S. Personal interview. 27 May 2012.

5. Ibid

6. Noland, Lynn J., Esq. Milesian Mountaineers Mountaineer Graphics: 1986

7. Rogers, John W., Hugh Rogers History, *Chronicles of Haywood County, North Carolina* <http://www.findagrave.com/cgi-bin/fg.cgi?page=gr&GRid=20493615>

8. Noland, Lynn J., Esq. *Milesian Mountaineers* Mountaineer Graphics: 1986

9. "State of North Carolina v Peter Noland." 85 N.C. 504 (Supreme Court Reports, N.C.) Haywood County Courthouse.

10. Noland, Lynn J., Esq. Milesian Mountaineers Mountaineer Graphics: 1986

11. Smith, Mary S. Personal interview. 27 May 2012

12. Ibid

Chapter Five

1. Smith, Joseph. Reply to author by letter. 20 April 2012

2. Ibid

3. Smith, Tim. Re: "Our Home Life" Message to the author. 10 April 20120. Email.

4. Smith, Mary S. Personal interview 20 April 2012

Chapter Six

1. Smith, Tim. Re: "Our Home Life" Message to the author. 10

April 2012. E-mail.

2. Ibid

Chapter Eight

1. The Bee Gees. *When Do I*. Trafalgar IBC, 1971. LP

2. The Moody Blues. *Candle of Life*, To Our Children's Children's Children. Threshold Records, 1969. LP

Chapter Nine

1. Smith, Joseph, Times and Seasons Vol. 3 Nauvoo: 1842

Chapter Seventeen

1. Smith, Bob, "Emma: I was Too Tired to go West." Meridian Magazine. 25 Jan 2011. Web. 28 May 2012

2. Ingersoll, Robert. Ideas and Ideals Lecture by Robert Stovold, Brighton and Hove Humanist Society, 10 January 2006. <http://homepage.ntlworld.com/robert.stovold/humanist/files/robert_ingersoll_talk.pdf>

3. Mah, Robyn, Personal interview 26 July 2012

4. Jones, Gracia, Personal interview. 27 May 2012.